Docker Orchestration

A concise, fast-paced guide to orchestrating and deploying scalable services with Docker

Randall Smith

BIRMINGHAM - MUMBAI

Docker Orchestration

First published: January 2017

Production reference: 1190117

Published by Packt Publishing Ltd.
Livery Place
35 Livery Street
Birmingham
B3 2PB, UK.
ISBN 978-1-78712-212-3

www.packtpub.com

Credits

Author

Randall Smith

Reviewer

Vincent De Smet

Commissioning Editor

Pratik Shah

Acquisition Editor

Rahul Nair

Content Development Editors

Radhika Atitkar
Sanjeet Rao

Technical Editor

Bhagyashree Rai

Copy Editor

Tom Jacob

Project Coordinator

Kinjal Bari

Proofreader

Safis Editing

Indexer

Tejal Daruwale Soni

Graphics

Kirk D'Penha

Production Coordinator

Melwyn Dsa

About the Author

Randall Smith is a senior systems administrator at Adams State University. He has been administering Windows, Linux, and BSD systems since 1999.

He has been active in helping other sysadmins solve problems online and off. He has presented at the Colorado Higher Ed Computing Organization and Educause conferences on topics including Linux KVM and Ceph.

In his spare time, Randall streams Let's Play gaming videos at Music Free Gaming on YouTube and Twitch.

I would like to thank my family for their support and understanding as I disappeared into my bedroom for hours at a time to write this book. I would like to thank Adams State University for providing servers used for testing and the opportunity to play with really cool software such as Docker. Finally, I would like to thank the reviewers and everyone at Packt who helped make this book possible.

I want to give a special shout-out to all of the developers and companies who have open-sourced the tools described in this book. You all make it so much much easier for the rest of us to get the job done. Thank you all so much.

About the Reviewer

Vincent De Smet is a Docker Captain with experience as an IT consultant and a DevOps engineer in Vietnam and Singapore, respectively. He's also a co-organizer of the Docker Saigon and Cloud Native Singapore meetups. Vincent loves to deep dive into container internals, is an active speaker, and publishes articles to the `docker-saigon.github.io` blog.

www.PacktPub.com

For support files and downloads related to your book, please visit www.PacktPub.com.

Did you know that Packt offers eBook versions of every book published, with PDF and ePub files available? You can upgrade to the eBook version at www.PacktPub.com and as a print book customer, you are entitled to a discount on the eBook copy. Get in touch with us at service@packtpub.com for more details.

At www.PacktPub.com, you can also read a collection of free technical articles, sign up for a range of free newsletters and receive exclusive discounts and offers on Packt books and eBooks.

https://www.packtpub.com/mapt

Get the most in-demand software skills with Mapt. Mapt gives you full access to all Packt books and video courses, as well as industry-leading tools to help you plan your personal development and advance your career.

Why subscribe?

- Fully searchable across every book published by Packt
- Copy and paste, print, and bookmark content
- On demand and accessible via a web browser

Customer Feedback

Thank you for purchasing this Packt book. We take our commitment to improving our content and products to meet your needs seriously—that's why your feedback is so valuable. Whatever your feelings about your purchase, please consider leaving a review on this book's Amazon page. Not only will this help us, more importantly it will also help others in the community to make an informed decision about the resources that they invest in to learn.

You can also review for us on a regular basis by joining our reviewers' club. **If you're interested in joining, or would like to learn more about the benefits we offer, please contact us**: customerreviews@packtpub.com.

Table of Contents

Preface

Docker containers are a powerful tool for building and deploying services consistently and reliably. As the number of containers increases, they also become a problem to manage. The problem is only exasperated when the containers are run on multiple hosts. This book shows you how to get started bringing order to the chaos through orchestration.

This book starts by showing you how to get started with Docker then delves into the building blocks that are needed for a Docker cluster. It shows you how to use the "Big Three" orchestration tools—Docker Swarm, Kubernetes, and Mesosphere. It will also introduce two additional tools, Fleet and Cattle, which can be simpler to use and install, but very powerful.

Finally, you will be introduced to tools that make life simpler for people managing clusters and developers creating images that will be run. You will explore tools to monitor clusters and see where the performance bottlenecks are. You will see how to use continuous integration to consistently and reliably build, test, and deploy Docker images. Finally, this book will show you how to apply the same principles to the hosts that Docker is running on.

What this book covers

Chapter 1, *Getting Started with Docker Orchestration*, gets you started with using Docker. It shows you how to install Docker locally and on popular cloud services such as Amazon Web Services, Google Compute Engine, and Microsoft Azure.

Chapter 2, *Building Multi-Container Applications with Docker Compose*, provides an introduction to building multi-container applications with Docker Compose. It also shows how to use named networks for data isolation and data volumes to share data.

Chapter 3, *Cluster Building Blocks – Registry, Overlay Networks, and Shared Storage*, describes the building blocks that are needed for a Docker cluster. You will explore the registry, overlay networks, and shared storage and learn why they are needed.

Chapter 4, *Orchestration with Docker Swarm*, shows you how to create and manage a cluster with Docker Swarm. You will learn how to manage services, run them with multiple replicas, and perform "zero downtime" upgrades.

Chapter 5, *Deploying and Managing Services with Kubernetes*, explores the basics of using Kubernetes to orchestrate a Docker cluster. You will see how to create services provided by multiple containers, how to provide load balancing for those services, and how to seamlessly upgrade them. Finally, you will see how to create persistent volumes to share data between containers.

Chapter 6, *Working with Mesosphere*, delves into using Mesosphere and DC/OS for orchestration. You will learn how to create and manage containers, load-balance them, and provide persistent storage. You will also see how to create health checks to ensure that services are running properly and how to perform "zero downtime" upgrades.

Chapter 7, *Using Simpler Orchestration Tools – Fleet and Cattle*, takes a look Fleet and Cattle. Fleet is a low-level tool that can be used to base custom management tools on. Cattle is a powerful, but easy to use, orchestration tool from Rancher. You will see how to use each to manage containers and services.

Chapter 8, *Monitoring Your Cluster*, explores the important task of ensuring that clusters, and containers running in them, are behaving properly. You will learn how to aggregate logs from all your containers in Elasticsearch and view them in Kibana. You will also learn how to use collectd, InfluxDB, and Grafana to collect performance data.

Chapter 9, *Using Continuous Integration to Build, Test, and Deploy Containers*, explains how to use continuous integration in GitLab to build, test, and even deploy containers. This helps to ensure that images are built consistently and reliably.

Chapter 10, *Why Stop at Containers? Automating Your Infrastructure*, looks beyond containers to show how the same principles that go into building and orchestrating Docker containers can also be used with the hosts those containers run on. You will see how configuration management can be used to configure hosts and ensure that they stay configured. The chapter also shows you how to use Packer to build host images that can be deployed locally or to cloud services. Finally, it will introduce Terraform, which can be used to create an entire Docker cluster from scratch.

What you need for this book

You will need a place to run Docker hosts. This can be in a local cluster such as OpenStack or a cloud hosting provider such as Amazon EC2, Google Compute Engine, or Microsoft Azure. The first chapter shows you how to install Docker on Linux and the rest of the book assumes that the tools are run from Linux. Ubuntu, CentOS, and Red Hat Enterprise Linux are, currently, the best supported.

A text editor, such as Emacs, will be needed as most orchestration tools store their configurations in text files. Many of the tools and examples described within this book require a web browser to access.

Who this book is for

This book is for developers and system administrators who have a basic knowledge of Docker and now want to deploy and manage containers across multiple hosts.

Conventions

In this book, you will find a number of text styles that distinguish between different kinds of information. Here are some examples of these styles and an explanation of their meaning.

Code words in text, database table names, folder names, filenames, file extensions, pathnames, dummy URLs, user input, and Twitter handles are shown as follows: "Containers are started using `docker run` command."

A block of code is set as follows:

```
#cloud-config
users:
  - name: "demo"
    passwd: "$6$HpqJOCs8XahT$mSgRYAn..."
    groups:
    - "sudo"
    - "docker"
```

When we wish to draw your attention to a particular part of a code block, the relevant lines or items are set in bold:

```
#cloud-config
users:
  - name: "demo"
    passwd: "$6$HpqJOCs8XahT$mSgRYAn..."
    groups:
    - "sudo"
    - "docker"
```

Any command-line input or output is written as follows:

```
$ wget -qO - https://get.docker.com/ | sh
```

New terms and **important words** are shown in bold. Words that you see on the screen, for example, in menus or dialog boxes, appear in the text like this: "Select your account then click **Allow** on the next page."

 Warnings or important notes appear in a box like this.

 Tips and tricks appear like this.

Reader feedback

Feedback from our readers is always welcome. Let us know what you think about this book-what you liked or disliked. Reader feedback is important for us as it helps us develop titles that you will really get the most out of. To send us general feedback, simply e-mail feedback@packtpub.com, and mention the book's title in the subject of your message. If there is a topic that you have expertise in and you are interested in either writing or contributing to a book, see our author guide at www.packtpub.com/authors.

Customer support

Now that you are the proud owner of a Packt book, we have a number of things to help you to get the most from your purchase.

Downloading the example code

You can download the example code files for this book from your account at http://www.packtpub.com. If you purchased this book elsewhere, you can visit http://www.packtpub.com/support and register to have the files e-mailed directly to you.

You can download the code files by following these steps:

1. Log in or register to our website using your e-mail address and password.
2. Hover the mouse pointer on the **SUPPORT** tab at the top.
3. Click on **Code Downloads & Errata**.
4. Enter the name of the book in the **Search** box.

5. Select the book for which you're looking to download the code files.
6. Choose from the drop-down menu where you purchased this book from.
7. Click on **Code Download**.

Once the file is downloaded, please make sure that you unzip or extract the folder using the latest version of:

- WinRAR / 7-Zip for Windows
- Zipeg / iZip / UnRarX for Mac
- 7-Zip / PeaZip for Linux

The code bundle for the book is also hosted on GitHub at `https://github.com/PacktPubl ishing/Docker-Orchestration`. We also have other code bundles from our rich catalog of books and videos available at `https://github.com/PacktPublishing/`. Check them out!

Downloading the color images of this book

We also provide you with a PDF file that has color images of the screenshots/diagrams used in this book. The color images will help you better understand the changes in the output. You can download this file from `https://www.packtpub.com/sites/default/files/down loads/DockerOrchestration_ColorImages.pdf`.

Errata

Although we have taken every care to ensure the accuracy of our content, mistakes do happen. If you find a mistake in one of our books-maybe a mistake in the text or the code-we would be grateful if you could report this to us. By doing so, you can save other readers from frustration and help us improve subsequent versions of this book. If you find any errata, please report them by visiting `http://www.packtpub.com/submit-errata`, selecting your book, clicking on the **Errata Submission Form** link, and entering the details of your errata. Once your errata are verified, your submission will be accepted and the errata will be uploaded to our website or added to any list of existing errata under the Errata section of that title.

To view the previously submitted errata, go to `https://www.packtpub.com/books/conten t/support`and enter the name of the book in the search field. The required information will appear under the **Errata** section.

Piracy

Piracy of copyrighted material on the Internet is an ongoing problem across all media. At Packt, we take the protection of our copyright and licenses very seriously. If you come across any illegal copies of our works in any form on the Internet, please provide us with the location address or website name immediately so that we can pursue a remedy.

Please contact us at copyright@packtpub.com with a link to the suspected pirated material.

We appreciate your help in protecting our authors and our ability to bring you valuable content.

Questions

If you have a problem with any aspect of this book, you can contact us at questions@packtpub.com, and we will do our best to address the problem.

1
Getting Started with Docker Orchestration

Initially, Internet services ran on hardware and life was okay. To scale services to handle peak capacity, one needed to buy enough hardware to handle the load. When the load was no longer needed, the hardware sat unused or underused but ready to serve. Unused hardware is a waste of resources. Also, there was always the threat of configuration drift because of the subtle changes we made with each new install.

Then came VMs and life was good. VMs could be scaled to the size that was needed and no more. Multiple VMs could be run on the same hardware. If there was an increase in demand, new VMs could be started on any physical server that had room. More work could be done on less hardware. Even better, new VMs could be started in minutes when needed, and destroyed when the load slackened. It was even possible to outsource the hardware to companies such as Amazon, Google, and Microsoft. Thus elastic computing was born.

VMs, too, had their problems. Each VM required that additional memory and storage space be allocated to support the operating system. In addition, each virtualization platform had its own way of doing things. Automation that worked with one system had to be completely retooled to work with another. Vendor lock-in became a problem.

Then came Docker. What VMs did for hardware, Docker does for the VM. Services can be started across multiple servers and even multiple providers. Once deployed, containers can be started in seconds without the resource overhead of a full VM. Even better, applications developed in Docker can be deployed exactly as they were built, minimizing the problems of configuration drift and package maintenance.

The question is: how does one do it? That process is called **orchestration**, and like an orchestra, there are a number of pieces needed to build a working cluster. In the following chapters, I will show a few ways of putting those pieces together to build scalable, reliable services with faster, more consistent deployments.

Let's go through a quick review of the basics so that we are all on the same page. The following topics will be covered:

- How to install Docker Engine on **Amazon Web Services** (**AWS**), **Google Compute Engine** (**GCE**), Microsoft Azure, and a generic Linux host with `docker-machine`
- An introduction to Docker-specific distributions including CoreOS, RancherOS, and Project Atomic
- Starting, stopping, and inspecting containers with Docker
- Managing Docker images

Installing Docker Engine

Docker Engine is the process that actually runs and controls containers on each Docker host. It is the engine that makes your cluster work. It provides the daemon that runs and manages the containers, an API that the various tools use to interact with Docker, and a command-line interface.

Docker Engine is easy to install with a script provided by Docker. The Docker project recommends that you pipe the download through `sh`:

```
$ wget -qO - https://get.docker.com/ | sh
```

I cannot state strongly enough how dangerous that practice is. If `https://www.docker.com/` is compromised, the script that you download could compromise your systems. Instead, download the file locally and review it to ensure that you are comfortable with what the script is doing. After you have reviewed it, you could load it to a local web server for easy access or push it out with a configuration management tool such as Puppet, Chef, or Ansible:

```
$ wget -qO install-docker.sh https://get.docker.com/
```

After you have reviewed the script, run it:

```
$ sh install-docker.sh
```

 The user that runs the install script needs to be root or have the ability to use su or sudo.

If you are running a supported Linux distribution, the script will prepare your system and install Docker. Once installed, Docker will be updated by the local package system, such as apt on Debian and Ubuntu or yum on CentOS and **Red Hat Enterprise Linux** (**RHEL**). The install command starts Docker and configures it to start on system boot.

 A list of supported operating systems, distributions, and cloud providers is located at https://docs.docker.com/engine/installation/.

By default, anyone using Docker locally will need root privileges. You can change that by adding them to the docker group which is created by the install packages. They will be able to use Docker without root, starting with their next login.

Installing with Docker Machine

Docker provides a very nice tool to facilitate deployment and management of Docker hosts on various cloud services and Linux hosts called **Docker Machine**. Docker Machine is installed as part of the Docker Toolbox but can be installed separately. Full instructions can be found at https://github.com/docker/machine/releases/.

Docker Machine supports many different cloud services including AWS, Microsoft Azure, and GCE. It can also be configured to connect to any existing supported Linux server. The driver docker-machine uses is defined by the --driver flag. Each driver has its own specific flags that control how docker-machine works with the service.

Starting a host on AWS

AWS is a great way to run Docker hosts and docker-machine makes it easy to start and manage them. You can use the **Elastic Load Balancer** (**ELB**) to send traffic to containers running on a specific host or load balance among multiple hosts.

First of all, you will need to get your access credentials from AWS. You can use them in a couple of ways. First, you can include them on the command line when you run `docker-machine`:

```
$ docker-machine create --driver amazonec2 --amazonec2-access-key AK*** --amazonec2-secret-key DM*** ...
```

Second, you can add them to `~/.aws/credentials`. Putting your credentials in a credential file means that you will not have to include them on the command line every time you use `docker-machine` to work with AWS. It also keeps your credentials off of the command line and out of the process list. The following examples will assume that you have created a credentials file to keep from cluttering the command line:

```
[default]
aws_access_key_id = AK***
aws_secret_access_key = DM***
```

A new Docker host is created with the `create` subcommand. You can specify the region using the `--amazonec2-region` flag. By default, the host will be started in the `us-east-1` region. The last item on the command line is the name of the instance, in this case `dm-aws-test`:

```
$ docker-machine create --driver amazonec2 --amazonec2-region
us-west-2 dm-aws-test
Creating CA: /home/user/.docker/machine/certs/ca.pem
Creating client certificate:
/home/user/.docker/machine/certs/cert.pem
Running pre-create checks...
Creating machine...
(dm-aws-test) Launching instance...
Waiting for machine to be running, this may take a few minutes...
Detecting operating system of created instance...
Waiting for SSH to be available...
Detecting the provisioner...
Provisioning with ubuntu(systemd)...
Installing Docker...
Copying certs to the local machine directory...
Copying certs to the remote machine...
Setting Docker configuration on the remote daemon...
Checking connection to Docker...
Docker is up and running!
To see how to connect your Docker Client to the Docker Engine running on
this virtual machine, run: docker-machine env dm-aws-test
```

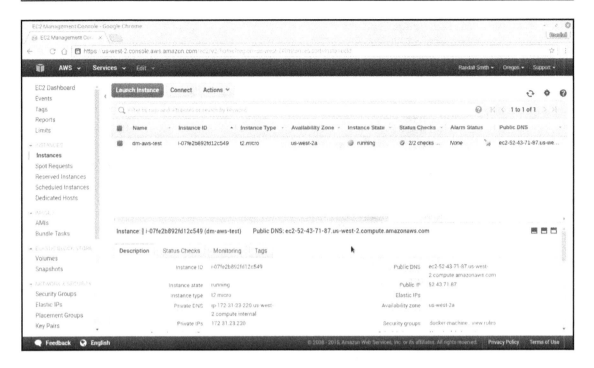

The command takes a couple of minutes to run but when it's complete, you have a fully-functional Docker host ready to run containers. The `ls` subcommand will show you all the machines that `docker-machine` knows about:

```
$ docker-machine ls
NAME          ACTIVE      DRIVER        STATE       URL                       SWARM
DOCKER        ERRORS
dm-aws-test   -           amazonec2     Running     tcp://52.43.71.87:2376
v1.12.1
```

The machine's IP address is listed in the output of `docker-machine ls`, but you can also get it by running `docker-machine ip`. To start working with your new machine, set up your environment by running `eval $(docker-machine env dm-aws-test)`. Now when you run Docker, it will talk to the instance running up on AWS. It is even possible to `ssh` into the server using `docker-machine`:

```
$ docker-machine ssh dm-aws-test
Welcome to Ubuntu 15.10 (GNU/Linux 4.2.0-18-generic x86_64)
* Documentation:   https://help.ubuntu.com/
Get cloud support with Ubuntu Advantage Cloud Guest:
http://www.ubuntu.com/business/services/cloud
New release '16.04.1 LTS' available.
Run 'do-release-upgrade' to upgrade to it.
```

```
*** System restart required ***
ubuntu@dm-aws-test:~$
```

Once you are done with the instance, you can stop it with `docker-machine stop` and remove it with `docker-machine rm`:

```
$ docker-machine stop dm-aws-test
Stopping "dm-aws-test"...
Machine "dm-aws-test" was stopped.

$ docker-machine rm dm-aws-test
About to remove dm-aws-test
Are you sure? (y/n): y
Successfully removed dm-aws-test
```

 There are a number of options that can be passed to `docker-machine` `create` including options to use a custom AMI, instance type, or volume size. Complete documentation is available at `https://docs.docker.com/machine/drivers/aws/`.

Starting a host on GCE

GCE is another big player in cloud computing. Their APIs make it very easy to start up new hosts running on Google's high power infrastructure. Google is an excellent choice to host your Docker hosts, especially if you are already using other Google Cloud services.

You will need to create a project in GCE for your containers. Authentication happens through Google **Application Default Credentials** (**ADC**). This means that authentication will happen automatically if you run `docker-machine` from a host on GCE. If you are running `docker-machine` from your own computer, you will need to authenticate using the `gcloud` tool. The `gcloud` tool requires Python 2.7 and can be downloaded from the following site: `https://cloud.google.com/sdk/`.

```
$ gcloud auth login
```

The `gcloud` tool will open a web browser to authenticate using OAuth 2. Select your account then click **Allow** on the next page. You will be redirected to a page that shows that you have been authenticated. Now, on to the fun stuff:

```
$ docker-machine create --driver google \
--google-project docker-test-141618 \
--google-machine-type f1-micro \
dm-gce-test
```

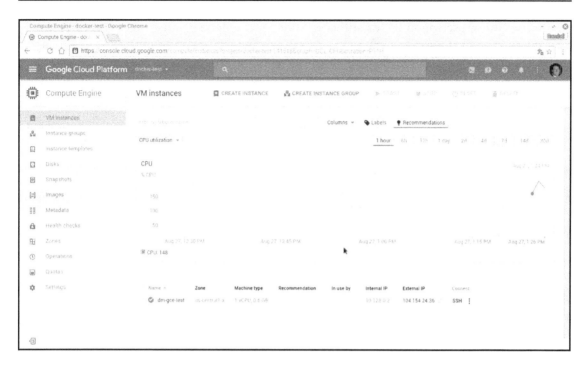

It will take a few minutes to complete depending on the size of image you choose. When it is done, you will have a Docker host running on GCE. You can now use the `ls`, `ssh`, and `ip` subcommands just like the preceding AWS. When you are done, run `docker-machine stop` and `docker-machine rm` to stop and remove the image.

 There are a number of options that can be passed to `docker-machine` including options to set the zone, image, and machine time. Complete documentation is available at
`https://docs.docker.com/machine/drivers/gce/`.

Starting a host on Microsoft Azure

Microsoft is a relative newcomer to the cloud services game but they have built an impressive service. Azure underpins several large systems including Xbox Live.

Azure uses the subscription ID for authentication. You will be given an access code and directed to enter it at `https://aka.ms/devicelogin`. Select **Continue**, choose your account, then click on **Accept**. You can close the browser window when you are done:

```
$ docker-machine create --driver azure --azure-subscription-id 30*** dm-
azure-test
```

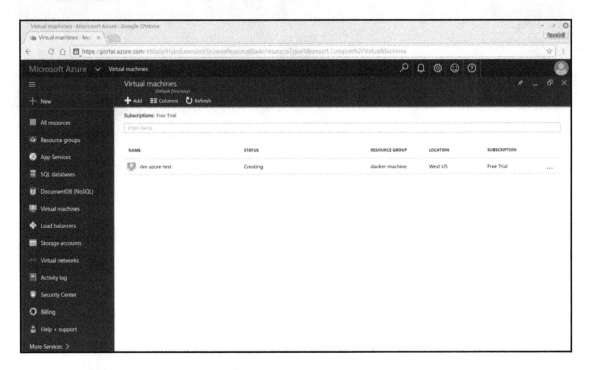

Again, it will take some time to finish. Once done, you will be able to run containers on your new host. As always, you can manage your new host with `docker-machine`. There is an important notice in the output when you remove a machine on Azure. It is worth making sure that everything does get cleaned up:

```
$ docker-machine rm dm-azure-test
About to remove dm-azure-test
Are you sure? (y/n): y
(dm-azure-test) NOTICE: Please check Azure portal/CLI to make sure you have
no
leftover resources to avoid unexpected charges.
(dm-azure-test) Removing Virtual Machine resource.  name="dm-azure-test"
(dm-azure-test) Removing Network Interface resource.  name="dm-azure-test-
nic"
(dm-azure-test) Removing Public IP resource.  name="dm-azure-test-ip"
(dm-azure-test) Removing Network Security Group resource.
```

```
name="dm-azure-test-firewall"
(dm-azure-test) Attempting to clean up Availability Set resource...
name="docker-machine"
(dm-azure-test) Removing Availability Set resource...  name="docker-
machine"
(dm-azure-test) Attempting to clean up Subnet resource...  name="docker-
machine"
(dm-azure-test) Removing Subnet resource...  name="docker-machine"
(dm-azure-test) Attempting to clean up Virtual Network resource...
name="docker-machine-vnet"
(dm-azure-test) Removing Virtual Network resource...  name="docker-machine-
vnet"
Successfully removed dm-azure-test
```

 There are many options for the Azure driver including options to choose the image, VM size, location, and even which ports need to be open on the host. For full documentation refer to
https://docs.docker.com/machine/drivers/azure/.

Installing on a running Linux host

You can also use a generic driver of `docker-machine` to install and manage Docker on an existing host running a supported Linux distribution. There are a couple of things to keep in mind. First, the host must already be running. Docker can be pre-installed. This can be useful if you are installing Docker as part of your host build process. Second, if Docker is running, it will be restarted. This means that any running containers will be stopped. Third, you need to have an existing SSH key pair.

The following command will use SSH to connect to the server specified by the `--generic-ip-address` flag using the key identified by `--generic-ssh-key` and the user set with `--generic-ssh-user`. There are two important things to keep in mind for the SSH user. First, the user must be able to use `sudo` without a password prompt. Second, the public key must be in the `authorized_keys` file in the user's `$HOME/.ssh/` directory:

```
$ docker-machine create --driver generic --generic-ip-address 52.40.113.7 -
-generic-ssh-key ~/.ssh/id_rsa --generic-ssh-user ubuntu dm-ubuntu-test
```

This process will take a couple of minutes. It will be faster than the *creates* on cloud services that also have to provision the VM. Once it is complete, you can manage the host with `docker-machine` and start running containers.

The only difference between the generic driver and the other cloud drivers is that the stop subcommand does not work. This means that stopping a generic Docker host has to be done from the host.

 Full documentation can be found at
https://docs.docker.com/machine/drivers/generic/.

Introducing Docker-specific distributions

One of the benefits of running services with Docker is that the server distribution no longer matters. If your application needs CentOS tools, it can run in a container based on CentOS. The same is true for Ubuntu. In fact, services running in containers based on different distributions can run side-by-side without issue. This has led to a push for very thin, Docker-specific distributions.

These distributions have one purpose: to run Docker containers. As such, they are very small and very limited in what comes out of the box. This a huge benefit to cloud wranglers everywhere. Fewer tools mean fewer updates and more uptime. It also means that the host OS has a much smaller attack surface, giving you greater security.

Their focus on Docker is a great strength, but it can also be a weakness. You may find yourself up against a wall if you need something specific on your host that is not available. On the positive side, many tools that might not be available in the default install can be run from a container.

CoreOS

CoreOS (https://coreos.com) was one of the first Docker-specific distributions. They have since started their own container project called **rkt**, but still include Docker. It is supported on all major cloud providers including Amazon EC2, Microsoft Azure, and GCE and can be installed locally in bare-metal or in a local cloud environment.

CoreOS uses the same system that Google uses on their Chromebooks to manage updates. If the updates cause a problem, they can be easily rolled back to the previous version. This can help you maintain stable and reliable services.

CoreOS is designed to update the system automatically which is very unique. The idea is that automatically updating the OS is the best way to maintain the security of the infrastructure. This process can be configured, by default, to ensure that only one host in a CoreOS cluster is rebooting at a time. It can also be configured to only update during maintenance windows or turned off completely. Before you decide to turn it off manually, remember that a properly configured orchestration system will keep services up and running even when the hosts they are running is on reboot.

CoreOS includes Docker but does not enable it. The following example from the CoreOS documentation shows how to enable Docker on boot. This is done by creating a new `systemd` unit file through `cloud-init`. On AWS, this is placed in the user data instance configuration:

```
#cloud-config

coreos:
  units:
    - name: docker-tcp.socket
      command: start
      enable: true
      content: |
        [Unit]
        Description=Docker Socket for the API

        [Socket]
        ListenStream=2375
        BindIPv6Only=both
        Service=docker.service

        [Install]
        WantedBy=sockets.target
```

CoreOS uses a default `core` user. Users can be added through the `cloud-config` file:

```
#cloud-config
users:
  - name: "demo"
    passwd: "$6$HpqJOCs8XahT$mSgRYAn..."
    groups:
      - "sudo"
      - "docker"
```

As SSH key can also be added with the `ssh-authorized-keys` option in the `users` block. You can add any number of keys to each user:

```
#cloud-config
users:
  - default
  - name: "demo"
    ssh-authorized-keys:
    - "ssh-rsa AAAAB3Nz..."
```

CoreOS also supports `sssd` for authentication against LDAP and **Active Directory** (**AD**). Like Docker, it is enabled through `cloud-config`:

```
#cloud-config
coreos:
  units:
  - name "sssd.service"
    command: "start"
    enable: true
```

The `sssd` configuration is in `/etc/sssd/sssd.conf`. Like the rest of CoreOS, the configuration can be added to `cloud-config`:

```
#cloud-config
write_files:
  - path: "/etc/sssd/sssd.conf"
    permissions: "0644"
    owner: "root"
    content: |
      config_file_version = 2
      ...
```

> Full configuration of `sssd` is beyond the scope of this book. Full documentation is at the following website:
> https://jhrozek.fedorapeople.org/sssd/1.13.1/man/sssd.conf.5.html

RancherOS

Rancher (`http://rancher.com`) was designed from the ground up to run Docker containers. It supports multiple orchestration tools including Kubernetes, Mesos, and Docker Swarm. There are ISOs available for installation to hardware and images for Amazon EC2, GCE, or OpenStack. You can even install RancherOS on Raspberry Pi!

RancherOS is so unique; even the system tools run in Docker. Because of this, the admin can choose a console that fits what they're comfortable with. Supported consoles are CentOS, Debian, Fedora, Ubuntu, or the default BusyBox-based console.

Rancher provides a very nice web interface for managing containers and clusters. It also makes it easy to run multiple environments including multiple orchestration suites. Rancher will be covered in more detail in Chapter 7, *Using Simpler Orchestration Tools – Fleet and Cattle*.

The `cloud-init` package is used to configure RancherOS. You can configure it to start containers on boot, format persistent disks, or do all sorts of other cool things. One thing it cannot do is add additional users. The idea is that there is very little reason to log in to the host once Docker is installed and configured. However, you can add SSH keys to the default `rancher` user to allow unique logins for different users:

```
#cloud-config
ssh_authorized_keys:
  - ssh-rsa AAAAB3Nz...
```

If you need to add options to Docker, set them with `cloud-init`:

```
#cloud-config
rancher:
  docker:
    args: [daemon, ...]
```

Project Atomic / RHEL Atomic

Project Atomic (`http://projectatomic.io`) grew out of the Fedora Project but now supports CentOS, Fedora, and RHEL. Images are available for Linux KVM and Xen-based virtualization platforms as well as Amazon EC2 and bare-metal installation.

It uses OSTree and `rpm-OSTree` to provide atomic updates. In other words, every package is updated at the same time, in one chunk. You do not have to worry that one package might have failed updates and left the system with an older package. It also provides for easy rollback in case the updates cause problems.

Project Atomic comes pre-installed with Docker and Kubernetes. (Kubernetes is covered in detail in Chapter 5, *Deploying and Managing Services with Kubernetes*.) This makes it an ideal base for Kubernetes-based clusters. The addition of SELinux adds an extra level of security in case one of the running containers is compromised.

Deployment on almost any local cloud system or EC2 is made easier by the use of `cloud-init`. The `cloud-init` package lets you configure your Atomic hosts automatically on boot, instantly growing your Kubernetes cluster.

You can use `cloud-init` to set the `password` and enable SSH logins for the default user:

```
#cloud-config
password: c001-pa$$word
ssh_pwauth: True
```

You can also add SSH keys to the default user's `authorized_keys` file:

```
#cloud-config
ssh_authorized_keys:
  - ssh-rsa AAAAB3Nz...
  - ssh-rsa AAAAB3Nz...
```

 The name of the default user depends on which version of Atomic you use. For Fedora, the username is `fedora`, for CentOS it is `centos`, and for RHEL it is `cloud-user`.

Running single container applications

Before we get into the nuts and bolts of Docker orchestration, let's run through the basics of running single applications in Docker. Seeing as this is a tech book, the first example is always some variant of `Hello World` and this is no different.

 By default, `docker` must be run as the root user or with `sudo`. Instead, you could add your user to the `docker` group and run containers without root.

```
$ docker run --rm ubuntu echo "Hello World"
```

This example is really simple. It downloads the `ubuntu` Docker image and uses that image to run the `echo "Hello World"` command. Simple, right? There is actually a lot going on here that you need to understand before you get into orchestration.

First of all, notice the word `ubuntu` in that command. That tells Docker that you want to use the `ubuntu` image. By default, Docker will download images from the Docker Hub. There are a large number of images, most uploaded by the community, but there are also a number of official images of various projects of which `ubuntu` is one. These form a great base for almost any application.

Second, take special note of the `--rm` flag. When `docker` runs, it creates an image for the container that contains any changes to the base image. Those changes persist as long as the container exists even if the container is stopped. The `--rm` flag tells `docker` to remove the container and its image as soon as it stops running. When you start automating containers with orchestration tools, you will often want to remove containers when they stop. I'll explain more in the next section.

Lastly, take a look at the `echo` command. Yes, it is an `echo` alright, and it outputs `Hello World` just like one would expect. There are two important points here. First, the command can be anything in the image, and second, it must be in the image. For example, if you tried to run `nginx` in that command, Docker will throw an error similar to the following:

```
$ sudo docker run --rm ubuntu nginx
exec: "nginx": executable file not found in $PATH
Error response from daemon: Cannot start container
821fcd4e8ae76668d8c508190b338e166247dc46cb6bc2582731566e7f2c705a: [8]
System error: exec: "nginx": executable file not found in $PATH
```

The "`Hello World`" examples are all good but what if you want to do something actually useful? To quote old iPhone ads; *There's an app for that*. There are many official applications available on the Docker Hub. Let's continue with `nginx` and start a container running `nginx` to serve a simple website:

```
$ docker run --rm -p 80:80 --name nginx nginx
```

This command starts a new container based on the `nginx` image, downloading it if needed, and telling `docker` to forward TCP port 80 to port 80 in the image. Now you can go to `http://localhost` and see a most welcoming website:

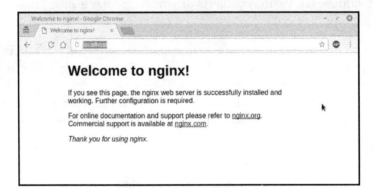

Welcoming people to Nginx is all well and good, but obviously, you will want to do more than that. That will be covered in more detail in `Chapter 2`, *Building Multi-Container Applications with Docker Compose*. For now, the default will be sufficient.

If you run the preceding example, you will notice that the console appears to hang. That's because `docker` starts processes in the foreground. What you are seeing there is `nginx` waiting for a request. If you go to `http://localhost`, then you should see messages from the `nginx` access log printed to the console. Another option is to add `-d` to your `run` command. That will detach the process from the console:

```
$ docker run -d -p 80:80 --name nginx nginx
```

   The `-d` and `--rm` options are mutually exclusive.

There are multiple ways to stop a container. The first way is to end the process running in the container. This will happen automatically for short running processes. When starting a container like `nginx` in the preceding example, pressing *Ctrl + C* in the session will stop `nginx` and the container. The other way is to use `docker stop`. It takes the image ID or name of the container. For example, to stop the container that was started earlier you would run `docker stop nginx`.

Let's take a moment and look at how Docker deals with remote images. Remember, when you first ran `docker run` with the `ubuntu` or `nginx` images, `docker` had to first download the images from the Docker Hub. When you run them again, Docker will use the downloaded image. You can see the images Docker knows about with the `docker images` command:

```
$ docker images
REPOSITORY              TAG                    IMAGE ID              CREATED
VIRTUAL SIZE
ubuntu                  latest                 ae81bbda2b6c          5 hours ago
126.6 MB
nginx                   latest                 bfdd4ced794e          3 days ago
183.4 MB
```

Unwanted images can be deleted with the `docker rmi` command:

```
$ docker rmi ubuntu
```

Ack! What do you do if you deleted an image but you still need it? You have two options. First, you can run a container that uses the image. It works, but can be cumbersome if running a container changes data or conflicts with something that is already running. Fortunately, there is the `docker pull` command:

```
$ docker pull ubuntu
```

This command will pull the default version of the `ubuntu` image from the repository on Docker Hub. Specific versions can be pulled by specifying them in the command:

```
$ docker pull ubuntu:trusty
```

Docker pull is also used to update a previously downloaded image. For example, the `ubuntu` image is regularly updated with security fixes and other patches. If you do not pull the updates, `docker` on your host will continue to use the old image. Simply run the `docker pull` command again and any updates to the image will be downloaded.

Let's take a quick diversion and consider what this means for your hosts when you begin to orchestrate Docker. Unless you or your tools update the images on your hosts, you will find that some hosts are running old images while others are running the new, shiny image. This can open your systems up to intermittent failures or security holes. Most modern tools will take care of that for you or, at least, have an option to force a pull before deployment. Others may not, keep that in mind as you look at orchestration tools and strategies.

What is running?

At some point, you will want to see what containers are running on a specific host. Your orchestration tools will help with that, but there will be times that you will need to go straight to the source to troubleshoot a problem. For that, there is the docker ps command. To demonstrate, start up a few containers:

```
$ for i in {1..4}; do docker run -d --name nginx$i nginx ; done
```

Now run docker ps:

```
$ sudo docker ps
CONTAINER ID            IMAGE               COMMAND                     CREATED
STATUS                  PORTS               NAMES
e5b302217aeb            nginx               "nginx -g 'daemon off"      About a
minute ago     Up About a minute    80/tcp, 443/tcp       nginx4
dc9d9e1e1228            nginx               "nginx -g 'daemon off"      About a
minute ago     Up About a minute    80/tcp, 443/tcp       nginx3
6009967479fc            nginx               "nginx -g 'daemon off"      About a
minute ago     Up About a minute    80/tcp, 443/tcp       nginx2
67ac8125983c            nginx               "nginx -g 'daemon off"      About a
minute ago     Up About a minute    80/tcp, 443/tcp       nginx1
```

You should see the containers that were just started as well as any others that you may have running. If you stop the containers, they will disappear from docker ps:

```
$ for i in {1..4}; do docker stop nginx$i ; done
nginx1
nginx2
nginx3
nginx4
```

As you can see if you run docker ps, the containers are gone:

```
$ docker ps
CONTAINER ID            IMAGE               COMMAND                     CREATED
STATUS                  PORTS               NAMES
```

However, since the --rm flag was not used, docker still knows about them and could restart them:

```
$ docker ps -a
CONTAINER ID            IMAGE                       COMMAND                     CREATED
STATUS                          PORTS               NAMES
e5b302217aeb            nginx                       "nginx -g 'daemon off"      3 minutes
ago        Exited (0) About a minute ago                          nginx4
    dc9d9e1e1228            nginx                   "nginx -g 'daemon off"      3
```

```
minutes ago          Exited (0) About a minute ago
nginx3
    6009967479fc          nginx                  "nginx -g 'daemon off"   3
minutes ago          Exited (0) About a minute ago
nginx2
    67ac8125983c          nginx                  "nginx -g 'daemon off"   3
minutes ago          Exited (0) About a minute ago
nginx1
```

These are all the stopped `nginx` containers. The `docker rm` command will remove the containers:

```
$ for i in {1..4}; do docker rm nginx$i ; done
nginx1
nginx2
nginx3
nginx4
```

Until a container is removed, all the data is still available. You can restart the container and it will chug along quite happily with whatever data existed when the container was stopped. Once the container is removed, all the data within that container is removed right along with it. In many cases, you might not care but, in others, that data might be important. How you deal with that data will be an important part of planning out your orchestration system. In `Chapter 3`, *Cluster Building Blocks – Registry, Overlay Networks, and Shared Storage*, I will show you how you can move your data into shared storage to keep it safe.

Inspecting your container

There comes a time in the life of anyone working with containers when you will need to jump into a running container and see what is going on. Fortunately, Docker has just the tool for you in the form of `docker exec`. The `exec` subcommand takes two arguments, the name of the container, and the command to run:

```
$ docker exec -it nginx bash
```

I slipped an option in there that is important if you are starting an interactive process. The `-it` option tells Docker that you have an interactive process and that you want a new TTY. This is essential if you want to start a shell:

```
$ sudo docker exec -it nginx bash
root@fd8533fa2eda:/# ps ax
PID TTY      STAT   TIME COMMAND
  1 ?        Ss     0:00 nginx: master process nginx -g daemon off;
```

```
 6 ?         S        0:00 nginx: worker process
13 ?         Ss       0:00 bash
18 ?         R+       0:00 ps ax
root@fd8533fa2eda:/# exit
```

In the preceding example, I connected to the container and ran `ps ax` to see every process that the container knew about. Getting a shell in the container can be invaluable when debugging. You can verify that files were added correctly or that internal scripts are properly handling environment variables passed in through `docker`.

It's also possible to run non-interactive programs. Let's use the same `ps` example as earlier:

```
$ sudo docker exec nginx ps ax
PID TTY        STAT    TIME COMMAND
1 ?          Ss      0:00 nginx: master process nginx -g daemon off;
6 ?          S       0:00 nginx: worker process
19 ?         Rs      0:00 ps ax
```

As you might expect, there's not much to see here, but it should give you an idea of what is possible. I often use them when debugging and I do not need a full shell.

Summary

In this chapter you have learned the basics of using Docker. You saw how to quickly install Docker on AWS, GCE, Azure, and a generic Linux host. You were introduced to a few Docker-specific distributions and saw a little bit of how to configure them. Finally, we reviewed the basics of using the `docker` command. In the next chapter, I will walk you through using Docker Compose to build new single and multi-container applications.

2
Building Multi-Container Applications with Docker Compose

Modern applications have a lot of moving parts. A web application almost always uses a database such as MySQL or MongoDB to store data. There may be a load balancer or SSL proxy. Often there are tasks scheduled to run regularly that perform routine maintenance or backups. On a traditional server, these tasks might all be installed on a single server or spread across numerous hosts. The challenge faced by system administrators is how are all these parts deployed consistently and reliably?

Rather than having a single container that does everything, you can split your application into smaller chunks. Each container has a specific task and does only that task. For example, you might have one image that is a Perl-based web application; a second that runs MySQL; a third that runs HAProxy to load balance and provide SSL termination for the Perl application. Each separate container can be run, upgraded, and tested independent of each other. Your developers can work on the web code all they want, and you do not have to worry about what they might do to your database install.

This chapter will show you how that is done. The process starts with a single image, defined by a `Dockerfile`. It then proceeds to build a small multi-container application using both custom images and images from the Docker Hub. Along the way, you will see how to use Docker Compose to define your application; how networks can be used to isolate your data; and how volumes can keep your data safe.

The following topics will be covered in this chapter:

- Building an image from a `Dockerfile` with Docker Engine
- Installing Docker Compose
- Using Docker Compose to build single and multi-container applications
- Using environment files to change how your application runs
- Extending Docker Compose files
- Controlling the container start order
- Using named networks for data isolation
- Using volumes for data persistence

Building an image with Docker Engine

They say the longest journey begins with a single step. In this case, an application begins with a single image. More often than not, existing images will not be perfect fits. This will certainly be the case if you are deploying your own services.

It all starts with a `Dockerfile`. This file provides detailed instructions to Docker for building an image. There are a lot of things that can be done in a `Dockerfile`. Specific operating system packages or language libraries can be installed; configuration files can be put into place; and a default command can be set. It is best to base a new image for an application off an official image, when possible. For example, an application written in Ruby should be based off of the official `ruby` image. A full reference of the `Dockerfile` directives can be found at `https://docs.docker.com/engine/reference/builder/`.

Building from a Dockerfile

Back in `Chapter 1`, *Getting Started with Docker Orchestration*, we started with a container that ran Nginx and displayed the default welcome page. This time, let us add a custom website to the container. Start by creating an empty directory somewhere. In that directory, download the examples from the GitLab repository for this book:

```
$ git clone https://gitlab.com/perlstalker/docker-orchestration-examples
$ cd docker-orchestration-examples/ch02
```

Then, create a file named `Dockerfile` with the following content:

```
FROM nginx:1.10
COPY sample-website /usr/share/nginx/html
```

This is a simple file but there are two important pieces here. First is the FROM command, which tells Docker that your container extends the nginx image that was used before. Basing your custom images on the existing images can save a lot of time and hassle. They may not be perfect out of the box but often it only takes a few changes to get what you need.

Second, there is the ADD command. The nginx container uses /usr/share/nginx/html within the container as the document root. The ADD command places the content of the website directory in /usr/share/nginx/html when the container is built.

The ADD command can add single files, directories, or tarballs. The TAR files will be unpacked in the directory that you specify. The TAR file can be compressed with gzip, bzip2, or xz. The ADD command can also take a URL. The file pointed to by ADD will be downloaded and placed in the given directory in your image. A tarball added via URL will not be unpacked.

In addition to the ADD command, there is a command called COPY. It simply adds the given files or directories with any of the automated unpacking that ADD does. The COPY command is preferred when adding simple files or directories to an image.

Now, it is time to build the container. Change to the directory with your Dockerfile and website directory and run docker build. When the build completes, you will have an image named website ready to use with docker run:

```
$ docker build -t website .
```

Tagging the image

The -t flag allows you to give your image a name. The name may include a : followed by a tag. The most common way of using this is as a version number. It might also be a date, Git tag, or something else that makes sense in your environment. For example, the official ubuntu image has tags for releases such as ubuntu:trusty or ubuntu:xenial, which refer to the appropriate Ubuntu release:

```
$ docker build -t website:0.1 .
```

Image versioning will be important going forward. At some point, you will be deploying an updated version of your service. It is possible to reuse a name and version, which may be fine while you develop the application, but different versions will make it easy to roll back to a previous, known good image in the event of a failure. It also allows you or your QA team to test an image without overwriting the image your production services are started from.

Additional tags can be added to an image after it has been built. You can think of this as an alias. Image tags are a good way to identify images that are in a certain state. For example, after you have built the website, you could tag it to show that it is ready for testing with `docker tag website:testing website:0.1`. After testing, the image can be tagged as `website:latest` or `website:production` to show that the image is ready for production. Repeat the process as each new image moves through the development process. Having a consistent image name will make it easier for developers to know which image to download. Using version numbers will make it easier to see which version of an image is being used. It also allows for easy rollbacks of an application in case the new version is broken.

Skipping the build cache

Another useful flag is `--no-cache`. Normally, Docker will try to reuse existing images as much as possible. This will speed up the build process but might cause problems with your build. A common example is when adding packages to an image. Take this small `Dockerfile`, for example. It is based on the latest Ubuntu image. It simply updates `apt` and installs `nginx`:

```
FROM ubuntu:16.04
RUN apt-get update
RUN apt-get -y install nginx && apt-get clean
```

Because Docker caches each step, `apt-get update` will not be run on subsequent builds. APT will then attempt to install `nginx` based on what is in the cache. It is possible that the version the image wants to install no longer exists on the mirror and the install will fail. This happens most often if you are changing the list of packages to install. The `apt-get install` command is rerun but `apt-get update` is not. When that happens, adding `--no-cache` will force Docker to rerun every step rather than use the cache.

There is one more flag that I want to point out – the `--pull` flag. It tells Docker to download a newer image of any images that are used. This is important if you want to be sure that you have the latest version with all security patches applied. However, that might mean updated libraries which could cause problems for your application. The good news is that with versioned builds, you will not break anything running in production:

```
$ docker build --no-cache --pull -t website:0.1 .
```

Running the image

Once your image is built, you may run a container using the image with the following command:

```
$ docker run --rm -p 80:80 website:0.1
```

That should look very familiar. This time, instead of running the `nginx` image, Docker will run your newly built image complete with the sample website. Once started, you can then open the site in a web browser. If the container is running on your desktop, go to `http://localhost/` and see the new site:

Installing Docker Compose

Once your images are built, you need to tell Docker how to run them. Docker Engine is limited in allowing you to define how containers work together. The Docker project provides a solution called **Docker Compose**. Docker Compose is a great tool for testing out deployments, defining how containers will interact or what external storage they need, or even as a lightweight orchestration tool.

Installing Docker Compose is easy. For Windows and OS X users, `docker-compose` installs as part of the Docker Toolbox and Docker for Mac and Windows. For Linux users, `docker-compose` can be downloaded from the Docker repository on GitHub. The following command from the Docker Compose documentation shows you how:

```
# curl -L
https://github.com/docker/compose/releases/download/1.8.0  /docker-compose-
`uname -s`-`uname -m` > /usr/local/bin/docker-compose
chmod +x /usr/local/bin/docker-compose
```

- As shown, the `curl` command must be run as root in order to have the permissions to write the file to `/usr/local/bin`.
- The version number will have almost certainly changed since the time of writing. Update the command accordingly. The latest release can be found at `https://gi thub.com/docker/compose/releases/`.

Writing a Docker Compose file

A Docker Compose file defines everything about an application. The services, volumes, networks, and dependencies can all be defined in one place. The configuration can be used locally to stand up a development environment, plugged into an existing continuous integration or continuous deployment system, or even used on a server to start production services. Later chapters will show better ways to manage running services.

Docker Compose looks for a file named `docker-compose.yml` in the current directory. An alternate file can be specified with the `-f` option. The file is formatted in YAML so it can be edited in any text editor.

Let's start with a very simple compose file that starts a single `nginx` container that listens on port 80. This is an analogous container started with `docker run -p 80:80 nginx`. The value for `image` can be any image on your server or on the registry just like in the `docker run` command:

```
version: '2'
services:
  web:
    image: nginx
    ports:
      - "80:80"
```

Applications defined in Docker Compose files are started using the command `docker-compose up`. Like `docker run`, you can use the `-d` option of `docker-compose` to start your application in the background:

```
$ docker-compose up -d
Starting singleservice_web_1
```

The application has been started and is now running in the background. If you opened `http://localhost` in your web browser, you would see the Nginx welcome page. You can use `docker ps` to see the running container, but `docker-compose ps` provides a little bit of a nicer view:

```
$ docker-compose ps
      Name              Command         State           Ports
-------------------------------------------------------------------------
-----
singleservice_web_1   nginx -g daemon off;   Up      443/tcp,
0.0.0.0:80->80/tcp
```

The `singleservice` prefix is the namespace for the application. By default, it is based on the directory name that contains your `docker-compose.yml` file. It may be different on your system. A namespace can be specified by passing the `-p` flag to `docker-compose`:

```
$ docker-compose -p mynamespace up
```

When you are done, the application can be stopped by running `docker-compose stop`. To stop, as well as remove all resources created by `docker-compose` for the current context, use `docker-compose down`. Any volumes created in `docker-compose.yml` will not be removed:

```
$ docker-compose down
Stopping singleservice_web_1 ... done
Removing singleservice_web_1 ... done
Removing network singleservice_default
```

It's often useful to see the output from the containers in your application. This can be done with the `docker-compose logs` command. Adding the `-f` flag will cause `docker-compose` to *follow* the log and print messages and they appear in the log.

Multi-container applications

The example in the previous section was fun but did not really gain us anything over using the `docker` command. Most Internet applications have multiple pieces. The most common example is a web application that loads data from a database.

In `ch02/web-db` of the `docker-orchestration-examples` repository there is a very simple application that loads a list of authors and books from MySQL and displays them on a web page. Here is a `docker-compose.yml` that defines the application:

```
version: '2'

services:
  web:
    image: web-db:0.1
    build: .
    ports:
      - 80:5000
    env_file:
      - db.env
    entrypoint: ./start.pl --init --command shotgun
  db:
    image: mysql:5.7
    env_file:
      - db.env
```

The first thing that you should notice is that there are two `services` defined. The first, `web`, is the web application. The second, `db`, is a MySQL container. Let's look at them one at a time.

The `build` key tells `docker-compose` that this service will be built from a `Dockerfile` in the same directory as `docker-compose.yml`. It is possible to define a subdirectory here such as `build: ./myapp`. This is common if you have multiple custom images to build to support your application.

The name of the image to build is set with the `image` key. This is the same thing that you would pass to the `-t` flag of `docker build`. Once the image is built, you will see that name listed in `docker images`. You can run the container separately with `docker run` or `push` it into a registry.

Older versions of the `docker-compose.yml` specification did not allow you to use both `build` and `image` in the same service.

The `ports` key is the same as the `-p` flag to `docker run`. In this case, `docker-compose` will forward port `80` to `5000` in the container. The `ports` key takes a list so you can specify multiple ports to forward, if desired. Following is an example that forwards ports `80` and `443` on the host to ports `5000` and `5001` in the container, respectively:

```
ports:
  - 80:5000
  - 443:5001
```

Let's skip over the `env_file` key for the moment and go to the `entrypoint` key. The `entrypoint` key allows you to override `entrypoint` defined in the image's `Dockerfile`. It is the same as using `--entrypoint` with `docker run`. I will explain why you might want to set that later in the chapter.

The `db` service starts MySQL. Like the `web` service, the `image` option defines the image to use. In this case, however, rather than build one from a `Dockerfile`, `docker-compose` will download the official `mysql` image from the Docker Hub.

The astute reader may notice something else about the `db` service. There are no ports set. Services within a single `docker-compose` namespace can connect to the ports the other containers define with the `EXPOSE` command in their `Dockerfile`. There is no need to make the ports available to other people or containers. Even better, `docker-compose` provides name resolution for every container in the cluster so that they can find each other. In this case, the web application can connect to MySQL using the name of the service - db. Networking will be discussed in more detail a little later in this chapter.

Using environment files

Now let's turn to that mysterious `env_file` option. The `env_file` option allows you to supply one or more environment files. These files set environment variables which will be passed to the services when they start. This is the same as setting environment variables using the `-e` flag to `docker run`. The same file can be passed to the `--env-file` option to `docker run`. The `mysql` image uses environment variables to configure the name of a database to create if one does not exist, the root password, an application username and password, and many other things. This particular `env_file` contains MySQL user information:

```
MYSQL_DATABASE=db
MYSQL_USER=myapp
MYSQL_PASSWORD=password
MYSQL_ROOT_PASSWORD=root-password
```

Putting that information in an `env_file` lets you pass those same variables to the web application. The `./start.pl` script defined in the `web` service's `entrypoint` reads those environment variables and writes a configuration file for the application.

Having that information in the environment variables rather than in the web image itself makes it easier to update your running services in the event of a password change. All you need to do is update the environment file and restart any containers using it. This will save a lot of time over updating the image configuration, rebuilding, and re-deploying the image to all of the Docker hosts in the cluster.

The other major use case for environment files is to have different settings for development and production. For example, in an application like the preceding one, you could have one file that defines account credentials for a development database and one for production.

One other thing to note is that `env_file` takes a list. You can specify as many different files as you might need. For example, you might have a set of common environment variables and another set which is specific to this application. In this situation, your `env_file` might look something like the following example. Variables in later files override those set in the earlier ones:

```
env_file:
   - common.env
   - myapp.env
```

Extending compose files

We have already talked about using environment files to change your application's behavior. Another way that you can do that is to use multiple Docker Compose files. Each file builds on the previous one, extending it and possibly overriding options. This can give you great flexibility in developing your application or adjusting it to fit different environments. This can be done in one of the following two ways:

- The first way is to put your overrides in a file named `docker-compose.override.yml`. This file is read automatically by `docker-compose`. The options in `docker-compose.yml` are applied first and then the options in `docker-compose.override.yml` are applied.
- The second option is to use the `-f` flag to `docker-compose`. You may include as many compose files as you want. They will be applied in order from left to right. For example, in the `docker-compose -f docker-compose.yml -f docker-compose-prod.yml` command, `docker-compose.yml` is read first then `docker-compose-prod.yml`.

Let's go back to the sample web application. The default `docker-compose.yml` defined an `entrypoint` for the `web` service which uses the Shotgun loader for Plack. That is a great tool for debugging but it is slow because it recompiles the application on every page load. To put this into production, something that has better performance is needed. Instead, let's use the preforking loader, Starman.

Here is the relevant portion of the `docker-compose.yml` file:

```
services:
  web:
    image: web-db
    build: .
    ports:
      - 80:5000
    env_file:
      - db.env
    entrypoint: ./start.pl --init --command shotgun
```

Now create a file named `docker-compose-prod.yml` that overrides `entrypoint`:

```
version: '2'

services:
  web:
    entrypoint: ./start.pl --init –command starman
```

Start the application with `docker-compose`:

```
$ docker-compose -f docker-compose.yml -f docker-compose-prod.yml up
```

When it starts up, you should see this message in the logs:

```
web_1  | Command: starman
web_1  | Waiting 60 seconds for mysql
web_1  | Initializing database
web_1  | Starting the app
web_1  | 2016/09/08-13:11:35 Starman::Server (type Net::Server::PreFork)
starting! pid(1)
web_1  | Resolved [*]:5000 to [0.0.0.0]:5000, IPv4
web_1  | Binding to TCP port 5000 on host 0.0.0.0 with IPv4
web_1  | Setting gid to "0 0"
```

If you stop the application and run it again without the `docker-compose-prod.yml` file, you should see it go back to using Shotgun:

```
web_1  | Command: shotgun
web_1  | Waiting 60 seconds for mysql
web_1  | Initializing database
```

```
web_1  | Starting the app
web_1  | HTTP::Server::PSGI: Accepting connections at http://0:5000/
```

Using multiple compose files can be of great use, but it can also be a little confusing. You might find yourself in a situation where you are trying to debug your application configuration and ask yourself, "Why is `docker-compose` using that option?" In those cases, it may be helpful to run `docker-compose config` to see the merged configuration:

```
$ docker-compose -f docker-compose.yml -f docker-compose-prod.yml config
networks: {}
services:
  db:
    environment:`
      MYSQL_DATABASE: db
      MYSQL_PASSWORD: password
      MYSQL_ROOT_PASSWORD: root-password
      MYSQL_USER: myapp
    image: mysql
  web:
    build:
      context: /home/user/examples/ch02/web-db
      entrypoint: ./start.pl --init --command starman
      environment:
        MYSQL_DATABASE: db
        MYSQL_PASSWORD: password
        MYSQL_ROOT_PASSWORD: root-password
        MYSQL_USER: myapp
    image: web-db
    ports:
      - 80:5000
version: '2.0'
volumes: {}
```

From this, you can see that `docker-compose` did pick up our override of `entrypoint`. You can also see all of the environment variables that were added via the `env_files` options. If you see an option that does not look right, you can start hunting through your compose files for that specific option. Most likely, you will have an ordering problem.

Controlling start order

Like almost every application that uses a database, the preceding sample application will not work if it cannot connect to the database. For this to happen, the database needs to be started first. Docker Compose provides an option called `depends_on` that helps with this:

```
version: '2'

services:
  web:
    image: web-db
    build: .
    depends_on:
      - db
    ...
  db:
    image: mysql
    ...
```

In the preceding example, `docker-compose` will start the `db` service first, then start the `web` service. It will also start the `db` service if you try to start the `web` service separately with `docker-compose up web`. You can define as many additional dependencies as the service needs.

There is an important point to note here. Docker Compose will start the required service first, but it will not wait for it to be ready to accept connections before starting the services that depend on it. In this case, `docker-compose` will start `db` and then `web` immediately after. Unfortunately, MySQL takes a little time to get started. If the web application tries to connect right away, MySQL might not be ready and your application could fail to start.

There are a few ways to deal with this problem. The first, and usually the best option is for your application to keep trying to connect. Eventually, the database will be ready and your application can go about its business. The reason I like this option is because failures happen often. In large Docker environments, failure is often a feature. Containers are designed to start quickly and are often replaced quickly as new versions of services are deployed. A self-healing service means fewer headaches for the team managing the cluster.

Another option is to use a wrapper around your application's start up command. The wrapper could repeatedly poll the database, and when it sees that the database is ready, start your application. The `start.pl` script in the example application takes a much simpler approach, it just sleeps for 60 seconds to give the database time to start.

The Docker documentation points to two tools called `wait-for-it` and `dockerize`. Either can be used to delay the start of your application until another service is ready. They are available at `https://github.com/vishnubob/wait-for-it` and `https://github.com/jwilder/dockerize`, respectively.

Using Docker networks

Docker supports the concept of virtual networks. Docker Compose uses them to provide network isolation between applications. By default, every application started with Docker Compose has its own virtual network named after the application's namespace. That means, if you start two different applications with `docker-compose`, they will not be able to see each other.

Within an application's namespace, the network created by `docker-compose` provides DNS service discovery. In the case of the example multi-container application, there were DNS entries created for the web and database services called `web` and `db`, respectively. In the configuration for the web application (`MyApp/config.yml.in`), the database connection is configured to connect to a host named `db`. Docker does the rest by making sure that the `db` hostname points to the `db` service.

 When a service is restarted, it will get a new IP address but keeps the same hostname. Make sure your application can handle this situation.

Originally, networking in Docker was very limited. Recent releases have created a pluggable network stack that can be as simple or complicated as you need. Docker Compose lets you configure that with the `networks` option:

```
version: '2'

services:
  web:
    image: web-db
    build: .
    ports:
      - 80:5000
    env_file:
      - db.env
    entrypoint: ./start.pl --init --command shotgun
    networks:
      - frontend
      - backend
  db:
    image: mysql
    env_file:
      - db.env
    networks:
      - backend
```

```
networks:
  frontend:
    driver: bridge
  backend:
    driver: bridge
```

This example builds on the simple multi-container application from the earlier section. This time, there are two `networks` defined, named `frontend` and `backend`, which uses the standard Docker `bridge` network. Start the application with `docker-compose up`:

```
$ docker-compose -f docker-compose-networks.yml up
```

If you log into the `web` container, you will see that Docker has created two NICs in the container, not counting the `loopback` interface:

```
$ docker-compose exec web /bin/bash
root@2bae616b5cf1:/var/www# ip addr
1: lo: <LOOPBACK,UP,LOWER_UP> mtu 65536 qdisc noqueue state UNKNOWN group
default qlen 1
        link/loopback 00:00:00:00:00:00 brd 00:00:00:00:00:00
        inet 127.0.0.1/8 scope host lo
           valid_lft forever preferred_lft forever
        inet6 ::1/128 scope host
           valid_lft forever preferred_lft forever
    505: eth0@if506: <BROADCAST,MULTICAST,UP,LOWER_UP> mtu 1500 qdisc
noqueue state UP group default
        link/ether 02:42:ac:13:00:03 brd ff:ff:ff:ff:ff:ff link-netnsid 0
        inet 172.19.0.3/16 scope global eth0
           valid_lft forever preferred_lft forever
        inet6 fe80::42:acff:fe13:3/64 scope link
           valid_lft forever preferred_lft forever
    507: eth1@if508: <BROADCAST,MULTICAST,UP,LOWER_UP> mtu 1500 qdisc
noqueue state UP group default
        link/ether 02:42:ac:12:00:02 brd ff:ff:ff:ff:ff:ff link-netnsid 0
        inet 172.18.0.2/16 scope global eth1
           valid_lft forever preferred_lft forever
        inet6 fe80::42:acff:fe12:2/64 scope link
           valid_lft forever preferred_lft forever
```

The database container still only has one NIC. Notice that the address assigned to `eth1` in the `web` container is in a different subnet from the addresses assigned to `eth0` in both containers:

```
$ use docker-compose exec db bash
root@cc883ceac1f3:/# ip addr
1: lo: <LOOPBACK,UP,LOWER_UP> mtu 65536 qdisc noqueue state UNKNOWN group
default qlen 1
```

```
        link/loopback 00:00:00:00:00:00 brd 00:00:00:00:00:00
        inet 127.0.0.1/8 scope host lo
           valid_lft forever preferred_lft forever
        inet6 ::1/128 scope host
           valid_lft forever preferred_lft forever
    503: eth0@if504: <BROADCAST,MULTICAST,UP,LOWER_UP> mtu 1500 qdisc
 noqueue state UP group default
        link/ether 02:42:ac:13:00:02 brd ff:ff:ff:ff:ff:ff
        inet 172.19.0.2/16 scope global eth0
           valid_lft forever preferred_lft forever
        inet6 fe80::42:acff:fe13:2/64 scope link
           valid_lft forever preferred_lft forever
```

The `networks` option makes it easy to isolate services from each other within an application. For example, you may have service in the `frontend` network, such as an SSL terminating proxy, that answers requests from the Internet that you do not want to be able to connect to the database. It can also be used to connect to networks that were previously created with `docker network create`. This is especially useful when you start working with multi-host clusters. That will be covered in more detail in `Chapter 3`, *Cluster Building Blocks – Registry, Overlay Networks, and Shared Storage*.

Keeping your data safe in volumes

Adding data directly to the container image works very well for applications that you do not want to change while the applications are running. Your application code usually falls into this category. For tasks that will be updating data regularly, it is better to put the data on a volume. Volumes also provide a measure of data persistence since they stick around even after a container is removed.

Volumes are one of the keys to orchestration. Putting container data in an external volume helps to facilitate container updates and running containers across multiple hosts. Using networked, shared storage is covered in `Chapter 3`, *Cluster Building Blocks – Registry, Overlay Networks, and Shared Storage*.

Let's go back to the web database example. The way it is configured at the beginning of the chapter, the database is created every time the application starts and destroyed when the application stops. That works for an example, but it is not very practical in real life. Instead, let's reconfigure the application to put the database on a volume:

```
version: '2'

services:
  web:
```

```
image: web-db
build: .
ports:
  - 80:5000
env_file:
  - db.env
entrypoint: ./start.pl --init --command shotgun
depends_on:
  - db
db:
  image: mysql
  env_file:
    - db.env
  volumes:
    - ./mysql:/var/lib/mysql
```

This example will put the MySQL data in a directory named `mysql` in the same directory as `docker-compose.yml`. Once the application has started, you should see the MySQL data files:

```
$ ls mysql
db  mysql  performance_schema  sys  auto.cnf  ib_buffer_pool  ibdata1
ib_logfile0  ib_logfile1
```

> If you ran the previous examples, you may need to remove the containers with `docker-compose rm` before it will use the `volume` directory.

Now, when you remove the application with `docker-compose rm`, you can see that the data is still in the `mysql` directory. If you restart the application, the MySQL container will see the data from the volume and pick up where it left off. You can see it in the example in two ways. First, a warning will be displayed that **Table 'author' already exists**. Second, there will be duplicate entries. This is because `start.pl` is run with the `--init` flag which blindly tries to create the database and insert the sample author and book entries when it starts.

Any volume driver supported by Docker can be configured. To do so, a separate `volumes` entry in `docker-compose.yml` is needed. This block will let you configure any options that the driver needs:

```
version: '2'

services:
  web:
    ...
```

```
db:
    image: mysql
    env_file:
      - db.env
    volumes:
      - dbvol:/var/lib/mysql

volumes:
  dbvol:
    driver: "driver-name"
    driver_opts:
      - opt1: "foo"
      - opt2: "bar"
```

In this example, there is a volume defined, named dbvol. The driver key tells Docker which driver to use. Any options needed for the driver are set with the driver_opts key.

To use the volume in one of your services, use the volumes option as before. This time, the first part is the volume name rather than a local path, in this case dbvol. The second part is still the path within the container to mount the volume.

Docker's pluggable architecture has allowed for an explosion of plugins supporting a wide variety of storage systems. Among those available are Azure File Storage, Ceph, Gluster, and VMware vSphere. Your favorite search engine will help you find many more. Docker maintains an incomplete list at https://docs.docker.com/engine/extend/legacy_plugins/.

Summary

In this chapter, you saw how to build new Docker images and define and control applications with Docker Compose. You also learned how to use networks to isolate traffic between containers and how to keep your data safe with volumes. In the next chapter, the groundwork will be laid for a multi-host Docker cluster including using registries, overlay networks, and network storage.

3
Cluster Building Blocks – Registry, Overlay Networks, and Shared Storage

The previous two chapters covered the basics of using Docker. Now it is time to start looking forward to building a Docker cluster. Before a new cluster can be built, a foundation needs to be laid. This chapter will cover the registry, overlay networks, and shared storage. Each component is essential for the smooth operation of containers in a Docker cluster.

Docker is a highly pluggable system. Meaning, there are many options for each component. Each has its own strengths and weaknesses. Some may be better suited to your environment than others. This chapter will give a few examples of each component and explain how to use them.

The good news is that no matter your choice, you are not locked in. Docker's plugin system makes it easy to use whichever component you need, often on a per-container basis. You could start, for example, using one system for shared storage and decide that another fits your needs. New containers can start using the new storage immediately, while older ones continue to use the old system.

The following topics will be covered in this chapter:

- Registry
- Using a registry
- Docker Hub
- Docker Cloud

- Docker Datacenter and Docker Trusted Registry
- GitLab registry
- Building it yourself
- Overlay networks
- Native Docker overlay networks
- Flannel
- Weave
- Shared storage
- Storage drivers
- Ceph

Creating a Docker Registry

A **registry** is simply a place where images are stored. Already in this book, you have used a Docker Registry. In `Chapter 1`, *Getting Started with Docker Orchestration*, there was an example of starting an `nginx` container:

```
$ docker run --name webserver -p 80:80 nginx
```

The `docker` command includes the name of the image to use, in this case `nginx`. Docker first looks for that image locally, but if the image is not found locally, Docker connects to the default registry at the Docker Hub. If the image exists on the registry, it is downloaded and your container starts.

Think of how powerful having a registry can be. A registry makes it easy to quickly deploy any image to any node in your cluster. Without one, you have to manually build your image on each and every machine first. In my early days of using Docker, I did that and it was not fun. Each time I built an image, there was a chance that a library change would break my application. Using a registry gives you consistent deployments across your cluster.

Using the Docker Hub

By far, the easiest registry to use out of the box is Docker Hub. The official Docker images for most projects are hosted there. You can create an account for free and host as many public images as you need. Private repositories are available for a fee. To create an account, go to `https://hub.docker.com`.

Logging in

Once you have an account, it is time to log into the registry with `docker login`. By default, Docker will attempt to log you into Docker Hub. Once you are logged in, you will have rights to pull your private images and push new images into the repository:

```
$ docker login
Username: username
Password:
Email: username@example.com
WARNING: login credentials saved in /home/user/.docker/config.json
Login Succeeded
```

Take note of the warning in the output. Your registry login credentials will be saved in `$HOME/.docker/config.json`. This file can be pushed to your cluster servers to automate registry actions:

```
$ cat ~/.docker/config.json
{
  "auths": {
    "https://index.docker.io/v1/": {
      "auth": "cG...",
      "email": "username@example.com"
    }
  }
}
```

Once you have logged in and your credentials have been saved, you can log in again without having to specify the password. It is also possible to pass the password on the command line using the –p option:

```
$ docker login -u username
WARNING: login credentials saved in /home/user/.docker/config.json
Login Succeeded
```

Obviously, leaving your password credentials around, even when they are hashed, can be a bit scary. At the very least, make sure that `$HOME/.docker/config.json` is only readable by your user. When you are done, you can remove your credentials from `config.json` by running `docker logout`.

When you start orchestrating your cluster, you are going to have to automate registry logins from your servers if you are using private repositories. The servers will need to be able to pull the images from the registry. If they cannot, your services will not run. Whenever possible, you should have a separate, read-only user that can pull images from your repository but cannot update it. It is possible to do this in Docker Hub but takes a few steps to set up:

1. Click on **Organizations** and then click on **Create Organization**.
2. Click on the **Create Team** button, fill in the **Team Name** and **Description** fields, then click on **Add**:

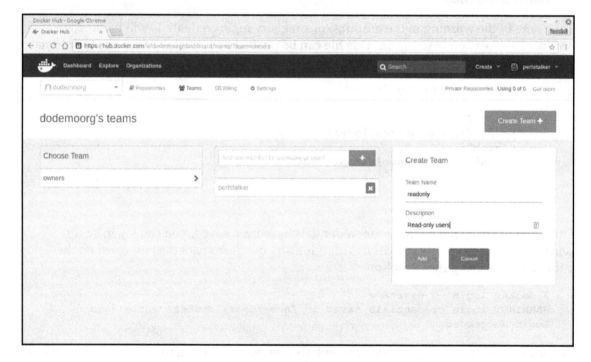

3. Click on the team from the list and add your read-only users to the team.
4. Create a repository or click on an existing repository in your organization.
5. Click on **Collaborators**. Select the team from the drop-down menu. Select **Read** and click on **Add Team**:

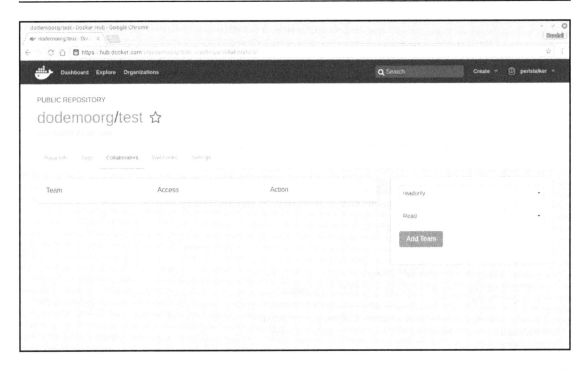

Any users that you add to the group will be able to pull images from the repository but will not be able to push to it. You can add your read-only team to as many repositories as needed. This will provide a measure of safety while still allowing your orchestration tools to pull images from the repository when needed.

Working with a repository

It is not required that a repository be created before it can be used. However, if the repository is going to be private, it should be created ahead of time. That way it can be assured that images pushed to the repository are not visible. You can create as many repositories as you need:

1. Log in to Docker Hub and click on **Create Repository**.
2. Select your namespace from the list. This will either be your username or the name of an organization.
3. Enter a name for your repository. This must be unique within the namespace.
4. Add a short description and a full description, if desired.
5. Select your **Visibility**, either **public** or **private**, and click on **Create**.

Now it is time to upload an image to Docker Hub. You must first build an image with `docker build`. The image name must be the same as the one you are pushing to. When using Docker Hub, images are named with either the username or the organization and the image name separated by a slash. For example, if your organization is `dodemoorg` and the image is named `test`, the image name would be `dodemoorg/test`. Optionally, a tag may also be included such as `dodemomode/test:0.1`. When the build is complete, push the image up to Docker Hub:

```
$ docker build -t dodemoorg/test .
[output omitted]
$ docker push dodemoorg/test
The push refers to a repository [docker.io/dodemoorg/test]
2a2c642ec5d1: Pushed
45d6c44ca123: Pushed
07066ce72cdd: Pushed
e4c7c26cda75: Pushed
0cad5e07ba33: Mounted from library/ubuntu
48373480614b: Mounted from library/ubuntu
055757a19384: Mounted from library/ubuntu
c6f2b330b60c: Mounted from library/ubuntu
c8a75145fcc4: Mounted from library/ubuntu
latest: digest:
sha256:f1af9d37d7792490f571a572bb17a21936b512b22a2d8650c11a3424f9192033
size: 2198
```

The image is now available on Docker Hub. If the repository is public, anyone can download and use the image. For that reason, do not include passwords in your image. Whenever possible, use environment variables as discussed in Chapter 2, *Building Multi-Container Applications with Docker Compose*, to keep your passwords secret.

Downloading your image from Docker Hub can be done in one of two ways. First, you could simply run a container such as `docker run dodemoorg/test`. If the image does not exist on the server, it will be downloaded automatically. Note that `docker run` will not see if an image has changed on Docker Hub. To force your system to download the image use `docker pull`:

```
$ docker pull dodemoorg/test
```

In some cases, it may be useful to use `docker pull` to download your images before you are ready to deploy it. For example, you may have a new version of an existing image that is already being used by a running container. Running `docker pull` will ensure that everything is in place before you upgrade. That will minimize potential downtime when the new container starts.

Automating image builds with Docker Hub

Docker Hub has a feature that will automatically build a new image based on updates to a Git branch hosted on GitHub or Bitbucket. To create an automated build, select **Create Automated Build** from the **Create** menu. You will be prompted to link to an account on GitHub or Bitbucket, if you have not already done so.

 Note that a linked GitHub or Bitbucket account may only be linked to a single Docker Hub account.

The wizard will walk you through the creation of a new repository. You will be asked for a name and description for the repository. Once the repository is created, go to **Build Settings** to configure the automated build. Docker Hub can track multiple branches from your Git repository and build a new tagged image every time that branch is updated.

You can also configure Docker Hub to rebuild your image if an upstream container is updated. For example, let's suppose that your container is based on the ubuntu image, in other words, you used From ubuntu at the top of your Dockerfile. Whenever the ubuntu image is rebuilt, it will trigger a rebuild of your image as well. This is one way to ensure that your images always have the latest security updates from the upstream image.

Automated builds are a great way to get started with **Continuous Integration** (**CI**) and **Continuous Deployment** (**CD**). It does not have the image testing capabilities that GitLab or Jenkins have, but you could still build an automated testing process. For example, when your developers are ready to test their application, they could push their changes to a testing branch in GitHub. That push will trigger a build on Docker Hub that builds a new image. A process could run on one of your servers that regularly pulls the testing branch, runs a test suite against it, and sends your team a build report. If the tests were successful, the team could then push their code to the master branch and trigger a build for production.

CI/CD tools are one way to ensure stability and reliability in your deployment process. The Chapter 9, *Using Continuous Integration to Build, Test, and Deploy Containers*, will show you how you can use the built-in Docker Registry in GitLab to automate testing and deployment.

Integration with Docker Cloud

Docker offers a completely cloud hosted Docker management platform called **Docker Cloud**. Docker Cloud uses Docker Hub to provide registry services. Meaning, in addition to the tight integration with the management environment, you also get the same automated build services that are available directly on Docker Hub. In addition to automated builds, Docker Cloud also provides an automated test framework. This will be covered more in Chapter 9, *Using Continuous Integration to Build, Test, and Deploy Containers*.

Another feature of Docker Cloud for private repositories is the ability to perform security scans of your images. It scans each layer of your image for known vulnerabilities and provides a report. The scans are run on image push or when an automated build is triggered. The generated reports may show a vulnerability in an image that your image is based on. In that case, you will have to rebuild with a newer version of the base image or work around the vulnerability yourself.

Using the GitLab Container Registry

GitLab is an all in one development suite. It provides Git repositories, issue tracking, CI, and a Docker Registry. The tight integration between Git, issue tracking, and Docker registries in GitLab make it an ideal solution for application development. GitLab is open source and can be installed locally. Enterprise hosting is also available at gitlab.com.

The easiest way to use GitLab is through their cloud offering, but installing it locally is straightforward. In my experience, the best way to install GitLab is to use the Omnibus installer. It installs all the software GitLab needs and manages all of the updates. The Omnibus package is available for Ubuntu, Debian, CentOS, and Raspberry Pi.

There is a Docker image available, but it is a little bit harder to work with. I recommend creating your own image using gitlab/gitlab-ce as a base to put the package configuration and SSL certificates in place. The GitLab Docker image documentation is at ht tps://docs.gitlab.com/omnibus/docker/.

Installing GitLab on Ubuntu

There are a number of dependencies that need to be installed before GitLab can be installed. Postfix is optional. If you choose not to use it, you will need to configure GitLab to use another server to send e-mail:

```
$ sudo apt-get install curl openssh-server ca-certificates postfix
```

GitLab is another one of those projects that wants you to download a script and pipe it directly through `sudo`. Again, I cannot state strongly enough how dangerous that is. Instead, download the script, review it, and if it looks okay to you, then run it:

```
$ wget -qO script.deb.sh
https://packages.gitlab.com/install/repositories/gitlab/gitlab-ce/script.de
b.sh
$ sudo bash script.deb.sh
$ sudo apt-get install gitlab-ce
```

GitLab is configured in `/etc/gitlab/gitlab.rb`. A full guide to all of the options is beyond the scope of this book. Let's, instead, focus on what is needed to configure the Docker Registry:

```
registry['enable'] = true
registry_external_url 'https://registry.example.com'
gitlab_rails['registry_path'] = "/var/opt/gitlab/gitlab-
rails/shared/registry"
registry_nginx['ssl_certificate'] =
"/etc/gitlab/ssl/registry.example.com.crt"
registry_nginx['ssl_certificate_key'] =
"/etc/gitlab/ssl/registry.example.com.key"
gitlab_rails['lfs_enabled'] = true
```

The first line enables the `registry` service in GitLab. The second line sets the URL for the registry. It can use the same address as the rest of GitLab on a different port. It is also possible to make the registry available on a separate hostname. The third line sets the location of the registry on the filesystem.

The fourth and fifth lines define the SSL certificate and key files. The certificate used for the registry must be trusted by the clients or Docker will throw an error. If the certificate you are using has an intermediate certificate, the certificate chain will need to be added to the certificate file:

```
$ cat intermediate.pem your_certificate.pem > registry.pem
```

Using GitLab Docker registry without a certificate is possible but not recommended. Add `--insecure-registry` with the address of your registry to the startup command for the Docker daemon. Full details are available at `https://docs.docker.com/registry/insecure/`.

The last line enables Git **Large File Storage** (**LFS**). It is not strictly necessary but it does allow for adding large files to the Git repository for an image. For example, I have services that require the Oracle Instant Client. The ZIP files for the client are large but they are needed to build the images. LFS allows the client to be added comfortably to Git. LFS must be installed and configured on the client to be used.

GitLab needs to be reconfigured once the changes have been made to `gitlab.rb`. This is done by running `sudo gitlab-ctl reconfigure`. This command is also run after upgrades to update the database.

> Full details on configuring the GitLab Container Registry are available at: https://docs.gitlab.com/ce/administration/container_registry.html

Enabling Docker Registry on a project

A Docker Registry can be enabled for any project created in GitLab. Click on the gear icon on the top-right and select **Edit Project**. Scroll down to the **Features** section, enable the **Container Registry** then click on **Save changes**:

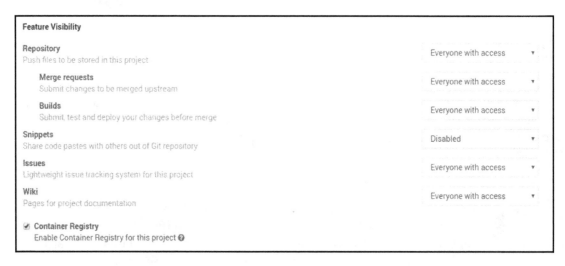

Once enabled, users with access to the repository can log in with `docker login` using their GitLab credentials. Users may have read or write access to the repository depending on their project access. Once logged in, images may be pushed, or pulled as usual. Note that the image name starts with the address of the registry:

```
$ docker pull registry.example.com/namespace/project
$ docker push registry.example.com/namespace/project
```

GitLab CI has the ability to automatically build, test, and even deploy images. This will be covered in detail in `Chapter 9`, *Using Continuous Integration to Build, Test, and Deploy Containers*.

 Full documentation on using the GitLab Container Registry on a project can be found at:
https://docs.gitlab.com/ce/user/project/container_registry.html

Introducing the Docker Trusted Registry and Docker Datacenter

The **Docker Trusted Repository** (**DTR**) is an application that is available for the Docker **Universal Control Plane** (**UCP**) and is part of Docker Datacenter. Docker Datacenter provides an on-site or cloud-based cluster management tool with **Role-Based Access Control** (**RBAC**), LDAP, and AD authentication, and monitoring of your Docker hosts. In effect, Docker Datacenter is Docker Cloud with DTR filling the role of Docker Hub running on your own network.

Docker Datacenter supports automated builds or testing of images with full CI/CD. It also has built-in support for high availability and image security. Docker Datacenter uses the integrated Docker Content Trust to digitally sign and verify images. This ensures that the image you get is the one you want.

Building it yourself

If none of those options work for you, there is the option to build it yourself. This will allow you to customize the registry for your specific needs but may require significantly more work to implement. It also works well in smaller environments that do not need the complexity of GitLab or expense of Docker Datacenter but still need a private repository.

Like so many things in the world of Docker, a new registry is just a `docker` run away:

```
$ docker run -d -p 5000:5000 --name registry registry:2
```

This command will start up a new `registry` container and is ready to use with a few caveats. First, the image data is stored in the container. Removing the container will also remove all of your images. The simplest solution is to use a volume to mount a directory from the local filesystem to `/var/lib/registry`. For greater flexibility, you will want to consider using shared storage rather than a local directory:

```
$ docker run -d -p 5000:5000 -v /data/registry:/var/lib/registry --name
registry registry:2
```

Second, this will only work with the `docker` command on the localhost unless Docker is configured to use an insecure registry. That is because `docker` requires a valid certificate for a TLS connection to the registry. You can mount a directory containing the certificates in the container and specify environment variables to tell the registry where to read the certificates from:

```
$ docker run -d -p 5000:5000 \
-v /data/registry:/var/lib/registry \
-v /data/certs:/etc/certs \
-e REGISTRY_HTTP_TLS_CERTIFICATE=/etc/certs/registry.pem \
-e REGISTRY_HTTP_TLS_KEY=/etc/certs/registry.key \
--name registry registry:2
```

The same warning about certificates in GitLab applies here as well. If your certificate is signed by an intermediate certificate, the complete certificate chain must be included in the certificate file.

Docker Registry supports basic authentication natively. If you want to do something more complex, you will need to run a proxy in front of your registry or use a token server. The proxy is simpler but a token server will give you the flexibility to control access to a minute level. Full details as well as proxy examples and a Docker Compose file to run a registry are available
at `https://github.com/docker/docker.github.io/blob/master/registry/deploying.md`.

Connecting containers with overlay networks

When Docker containers are started, they are assigned a private IP address. This avoids conflicts with addresses that may already be in use on the network and allows containers on the same host to talk to each other. It is a nice system except that containers running on different hosts cannot talk to each other unless they are exposed on the hosts. To solve this problem, various projects, including Docker, developed overlay networks.

An **overlay network** is a private network that is layered on top of an existing IP network to allow containers on multiple hosts to talk to each other. Containers connected to an overlay network are still assigned private addresses and are not accessible from outside the network. Ports can be made public using the `-p` option to `docker run` as normal.

Docker's pluggable network infrastructure has led to a growth in the number of overlay plugins. It also allows for containers to use multiple overlays networks. Using multiple networks provides for network isolation and segmentation and minimizes the risk of a compromised container sniffing network traffic that it is not supposed to see.

Using Docker native overlays

Docker's native overlay networking is a relative newcomer to the space. It provides **DNS Service Discovery** (**DNS-SD**) and the ability to use multiple overlays. When combined with Docker Swarm, it provides cross cluster connectivity. The advantage to being later to the ecosystem is that you can learn from other entries in the space. Docker has certainly done that.

The features described in this section rely heavily on Docker Swarm which will be covered in detail in `Chapter 4`, *Orchestration with Docker Swarm*. For now, a single node swarm can be created by running `docker swarm init`:

```
$ docker swarm init
```

 Docker 1.12 or higher is needed to use Docker Swarm.

Let us start by creating a network that our containers will use. Docker Swarm ensures that this network is available to all hosts connected to the swarm node:

```
$ docker network create --driver overlay external
```

The `--driver` option tells Docker that this network uses the swarm native overlay driver. At the end is the name of the overlay network. In this case, `external`. This is the name that will be used in service definitions to configure the network that will be used.

The `--opt` encrypted option is optional. If specified, it tells Docker to encrypt the connections between the containers on different nodes. To do this, Docker Swarm will automatically build IPSEC tunnels between any nodes that have containers connected to that network. The encryption key is automatically updated every twelve hours.

Using an encrypted overlay network is especially helpful if you have a network that spans providers or as a way to simplify inter-container security. For example, MySQL supports using TLS to connect. However, few containers have TLS enabled for MySQL. Using an encrypted overlay gives you the encryption that you might want when talking to the database without having to worry about certificate distribution or if TLS is supported at all.

Working with DNS-SD

One of the problems with containers is that every time they start, they get a new IP address. That makes it really hard to configure containers that connect to each other. This gets even harder when the containers are running on different hosts. Fortunately, Docker overlay networks have built-in service discovery using DNS. DNS entries are created as part of the swarm services which are described in `Chapter 4`, *Orchestration with Docker Swarm*. Consider the following command:

```
$ docker service create --network external --name nginx --replicas 2 -p
80:80 nginx
8m2wvm3n9w990kh77vf556k7i
```

This command uses Docker Swarm to create a service named `nginx` with two replicas. When the service starts, Docker creates a DNS record for `nginx` that resolves to the two containers that were started. Any other container on the network will be able to use the name `nginx` to connect to the service. Let us create a `busybox` container to test with:

```
$ docker service create --name shell --network external busybox sleep 6000
191qi81vvpnah3eqq8cvaxt4n

$ docker service ps nginx
ID                  NAME        IMAGE  NODE           DESIRED STATE   CURRENT
STATE           ERROR
```

```
da3hba7mokh0o0qr39eov9n9p   nginx.1   nginx   swarm-host2 Running
Running 30 seconds ago
4vzfcgjnujawjy6m7ngmbyiww   nginx.2   nginx   swarm-master Running
Running 30 seconds ago
$ docker service ps shell
ID                    NAME      IMAGE    NODE         DESIRED STATE  CURRENT
STATE          ERROR
ccbx21b5hs0ax06jfaeqzfjrq   shell.1   busybox   swarm-host1   Running
Running 24 seconds ago
```

This shows that the `nginx` containers are running two hosts named `swarm-master` and `swarm-host2`. The `busybox` shell service was started on `swarm-host1`. Using `docker exec`, it is possible to connect to the shell container and verify connectivity.

First, get the container name from the host with `docker ps`:

```
$ docker ps
CONTAINER ID          IMAGE               COMMAND               CREATED
STATUS                PORTS               NAMES
1148d48d5720          nginx:latest        "nginx -g 'daemon off"   2 minutes
ago        Up 2 minutes         80/tcp, 443/tcp
nginx.1.2t914z7ogcdb5nohrujd1ttln
0bc68f9957b1          busybox:latest      "sleep 6000"          2 minutes
ago        Up 2 minutes
shell.1.3wul50smhsjjhzpctnnsbeurd

$ docker exec -it shell.1.3wul50smhsjjhzpctnnsbeurd sh
/ # wget -O - nginx
Connecting to nginx (10.255.0.6:80)
<!DOCTYPE html>
<html>
  <head>
    <title>Welcome to nginx!</title>
    . . .
```

The `wget` command is requesting a web page from a host named `nginx`. The request gets forwarded to the `nginx` service and is printed on the screen.

Publishing services with mesh routing mode

Docker overlay networks support another useful feature called **mesh routing**. This is enabled automatically when the --publish or -p option is used upon service creation. The router will forward a request to any host in the cluster to the container or service listening on the requested port even if the service is not running on the host that received the request. In the preceding example, a service called nginx was started, and it used the -p flag to send port 80 on the hosts to port 80 in the containers. A request to port 80 on any of the Docker hosts will result in one of the two nginx containers answering the request.

Mesh routing load balances the requests across all the containers in the service. You could set up a round robin DNS entry for a hostname such as www.example.com that has the addresses of your hosts, or an external load balancer that points to the addresses of Docker hosts in your swarm. Doing the latter would allow you to keep your Docker nodes on private addresses.

The drawback to mesh routing in Docker Swarm, that published ports must be unique across the cluster. In other words, you cannot have services web1 and web2 that both try to publish on port 80. One would have to be on a different port.

Using Weave

Weave Net was developed by Weaveworks to provide a resilient and secure overlay network for Docker. Weave nodes form a mesh which allows traffic in the cluster to keep flowing even if a node goes down. The mesh can be encrypted to keep the data flowing across it securely. A Weave mesh can even spread between cloud providers connecting containers running on Amazon EC2, Microsoft Azure, or even locally in Docker Datacenter. Weave also supports DNS-SD allowing your containers to talk to each other by name, even on different hosts.

Full documentation on Weave Net is available at: https://www.weave.works/docs/net/latest/using-weave/.

Installing Weave

Step one is to install the `weave` tool to your desktop or other management system. The `weave` tool is just a shell script. The real guts of weave run in Docker containers. The script should also be installed directly on the Docker nodes themselves:

```
$ wget -O weave git.io/weave
$ chmod +x weave; cp weave /usr/local/bin/
```

The following examples assume a three node cluster with nodes names `swarm-master`, `swarm-host1`, and `swarm-host2`. The nodes can be created with Docker Machine as described in Chapter 1, *Getting Started with Docker Orchestration*. Any number of hosts can be added to the cluster. The greater the mesh, the more resilient it will be in the event of node failures.

The next step is to initialize Weave. Start by using Docker Machine to switch to the first server. The `consensus` flag tells Weave that there will be initially three servers. More can be added later:

```
$ eval $(docker-machine env swarm-master)
$ weave launch --ipalloc-init consensus=3
```

This will download and start three containers on `swarm-master`. Add the `--password` flag to `weave launch` if you want to encrypt your mesh. The password must be the same on every node that connects:

```
$ weave launch --password XXXXX ...
```

You can verify that they are running with `docker ps`:

```
$ docker ps
CONTAINER ID          IMAGE                            COMMAND
CREATED               STATUS            PORTS               NAMES
b645e00cde8d          weaveworks/plugin:1.6.1          "/home/weave/plugin"
42 seconds ago        Up 41 seconds                       weaveplugin
 e0bc711a0972           weaveworks/weaveexec:1.6.1     "/home/weave/weavepro"
44 seconds ago        Up 43 seconds                       weaveproxy
 89897514f42d           weaveworks/weave:1.6.1         "/home/weave/weaver -"
45 seconds ago        Up 44 seconds                       weave
```

Next, install Weave on the second host and connect it to the first:

```
$ eval $(docker-machine env swarm-host1)
$ weave launch --ipalloc-init consensus=3
$ weave connect 10.128.0.2
```

The IP address in the last command is the IP address of the `master` node. Often you can use `$(docker-machine ip swarm-master)` there. If you are running your hosts on a service such as GCE, you will want to use the internal IP address there as it does not change. Repeat the process for the third host:

```
$ eval $(docker-machine env swarm-host2)
$ weave launch --ipalloc-init consensus=3
$ weave connect 10.128.0.2
```

Once Weave is installed and running on all three nodes, check the status of the network with `weave status`:

```
$ weave status
Version: 1.6.1 (up to date; next check at 2016/09/16 23:30:55)

        Service: router
       Protocol: weave 1..2
           Name: 22:b6:71:6d:9c:d2(swarm-host2)
     Encryption: disabled
  PeerDiscovery: enabled
        Targets: 1
    Connections: 2 (2 established)
          Peers: 3 (with 6 established connections)
 TrustedSubnets: none

        Service: ipam
         Status: idle
          Range: 10.32.0.0/12
  DefaultSubnet: 10.32.0.0/12

        Service: dns
         Domain: weave.local.
       Upstream: 169.254.169.254
            TTL: 1
        Entries: 0

        Service: proxy
        Address: tcp://104.197.144.79:12375

        Service: plugin
     DriverName: weave
```

Connecting containers to Weave

Now that the network is set up, it is time to start containers that use it. The containers will use the `weave` network that was created when Weave was started. This example will start two containers named `shell1` and `shell2`. The `shell1` container will run in the background:

```
$ docker run --net=weave -h shell1.weave.local $(weave dns-args) -tdi
weaveworks/ubuntu
```

```
$ docker run --net=weave -h shell2.weave.local $(weave dns-args) -ti
weaveworks/ubuntu
```

For DNS-SD to work, the `--dns` and `--dns-search` options need to be used with `docker run`. Weave provides a helper command, `weave dns-args`, that will set those appropriately.

After the second command, you will be left at Command Prompt in the `shell2` container. From there, you should be able to ping `shell1`:

```
root@shell2:/# ping shell1
    PING shell1 (10.40.0.0) 56(84) bytes of data.
    64 bytes from 89d43b8ac937.weave (10.40.0.0): icmp_seq=1 ttl=64
time=0.180 ms
    64 bytes from 89d43b8ac937.weave (10.40.0.0): icmp_seq=2 ttl=64
time=0.099 ms
    64 bytes from 89d43b8ac937.weave (10.40.0.0): icmp_seq=3 ttl=64
time=0.069 ms
    64 bytes from 89d43b8ac937.weave (10.40.0.0): icmp_seq=4 ttl=64
time=0.104 ms
    ^C
    --- shell1 ping statistics ---
    4 packets transmitted, 4 received, 0% packet loss, time 3000ms
    rtt min/avg/max/mdev = 0.069/0.113/0.180/0.040 ms
```

Using Flannel

Flannel is an overlay network developed by CoreOS. It uses `etcd` as a data store and for network synchronization. Flannel lacks some of the features that Docker overlay and Weave support. There is no option for encryption or DNS-SD. It is, however, very simple to use once it is configured.

Configuring etcd and Flannel

CoreOS is configured through `cloud-config`. A `cloud-config` file is a YAML file that is passed to the host through the user data option. The file must start with `#cloud-config` for CoreOS to recognize it.

Before you begin, a new token must be generated for `etcd`. The `size` parameter is the initial size of your cluster. You will be able to add and remove nodes later:

```
$ wget -qO - 'https://discovery.etcd.io/new?size=3'
    https://discovery.etcd.io/c37921aac12231bf487a3ed82c464a4f
```

The discovery URL can take additional options. For full details, see `https://coreos.com/etcd/docs/latest/clustering.html`.

The generated token will be used in the `coreos` > `etcd2` > `discovery` option in the `cloud-config` file. You will need to use the same token for every host in the cluster. A new token must be generated for each cluster:

```
#cloud-config

coreos:
  etcd2:
    discovery: https://discovery.etcd.io/<token>
    advertise-client-urls:
    http://$private_ipv4:2379,http://$private_ipv4:4001
    initial-advertise-peer-urls: http://$private_ipv4:2380
    listen-client-urls:
    http://0.0.0.0:2379,http://0.0.0.0:4001
    listen-peer-urls: http://$private_ipv4:2380
  flannel:
    public_ip: $private_ipv4
    etcd_endpoints: http://$private_ipv4:2379
  fleet:
    public_ip: $private_ipv4
  units:
    - name: etcd2.service
      command: start
    - name: fleet.service
      command: start
    - name: flanneld.service
      command: start
      drop-ins:
        - name: 50-networking-config.conf
          content: |
            [Service]
            ExecStartPre=/usr/bin/etcdctl set
            /coreos.com/network
            /config '{"Network":"10.42.0.0/16"}'
    - name: docker.service
      command: start
      drop-ins:
        - name: 40-flannel.conf
          content: |
            [Unit]
            Requires=flanneld.service
            After=flanneld.service
```

This example shows how to use Flannel on CoreOS. It assumes that your CoreOS hosts have two network interfaces; one on a public network and one on a private network. The `$private_ipv4` variable is replaced with the private IP address assigned by the cloud provider. This is supported by Amazon EC2, GCE, Microsoft Azure, and OpenStack.

Flannel stores its configuration in JSON format in `etcd` in the `/coreos.com/network/config` path. Before Flannel starts, the configuration must be written to `etcd`. Since CoreOS uses `systemd` to manage services, it is possible to create a drop-in file that adds the configuration to `etcd` before Flannel is started.

The preceding example has the bare minimum needed for Flannel. All it does is set the network that will be used to assign IP addresses to each container. You should change this to something that does not conflict with anything in your environment. Docker will need to be restarted, if it is already running. A full list of options is available in the Flannel documentation at `https://github.com/coreos/flannel`.

Starting a CoreOS cluster with Flannel

The following command starts three CoreOS alpha servers on GCE. The `--can-ip-forward` flag is required for Flannel to properly forward traffic for running containers. The `cloud-config` file for the hosts is set with the `--metadata-from-file` option:

```
$ gcloud compute instances create core1 core2 core3 --image-project coreos-
cloud --image-family coreos-alpha \
--zone us-central1-a --machine-type g1-small --can-ip-forward --scopes
compute-rw --metadata-from-file \
user-data=coreos-user-data.yml
```

Ensure `sshd` started:

```
$ gcloud compute instances get-serial-port-output core1 | grep
Starting.*sshd
Starting Generate sshd host keys...
```

Once the hosts have been started, log into one of them to verify that `etcd` is healthy. Since Flannel depends on `etcd`, if that does not work, neither will Flannel:

```
$ gcloud compute ssh --zone us-central1-a core@core1
X11 forwarding request failed
Last login: Sat Sep 17 21:34:41 2016 from 162.220.127.20 core@core1 ~ $
etcdctl cluster-health
member 9817b5cb6bd4b548 is healthy: got healthy result from
http://10.128.0.4:2379
    member aa7418b2c3e34652 is healthy: got healthy result from
```

```
http://10.128.0.2:2379
    member d9402f140b10154d is healthy: got healthy result from
http://10.128.0.3:2379
    cluster is healthy
```

If etcd shows as healthy, you can check on the status of Flannel with sudo systemctl status flanneld.

When Flannel starts, it creates an environment file named /run/flannel_docker_opts.env. This file is loaded by the docker.service unit file to configure Docker's networking to use Flannel. Because the Docker daemon is configured to use Flannel, there is no need to specify any special networking options when you use docker run.

Now, verify Docker was correctly configured by Flannel to use the subnet for its Docker bridge:

```
$ sudo systemctl status docker.service
● docker.service - Docker Application Container Engine
Loaded: loaded (/usr/lib64/systemd/system/docker.service; disabled; vendor
preset: disabled)
Active: active (running) since Sun 2016-10-30 05:27:48 UTC; 22s ago
        Docs: http://docs.docker.com
    Main PID: 1881 (docker)
       Tasks: 6
      Memory: 14.1M
         CPU: 205ms
      CGroup: /system.slice/docker.service
              └─1881 docker daemon --host=fd:// --exec-opt
native.cgroupdriver=systemd --bip=10.42.88.1/24 --mtu=1432 --ip-masq=false
--selinux-enabled
```

> The first time you run Flannel, Docker might not pick up the environment file. In that case, restart Docker with sudo systemctl restart docker.service or reboot. Docker should be fine after that.

Connecting to Flannel

Connecting containers to Flannel is as simple as docker run. Start by starting a busybox container on core1 and get the IP address. If the address that is assigned is not in the subnet set in the Flannel configuration, it means that Docker did not read the environment file created by Flannel:

```
core@core1 ~ $ docker run -it -d --name test1 busybox
ee06605271b8301d27a03a6b4ae7aa32d4fc3f558888087e2047eaedd0241c7d
core@core1 ~ $ docker exec test1 -4 ip addr | grep inet
inet 127.0.0.1/8 scope host lo
inet 10.42.88.2/24 scope global eth0
```

Next, start up another `busybox` container on `core2`. This time, run the container in the foreground so that you get Command Prompt:

```
core@core2 ~ $ docker run -it --rm --name test2 busybox / # ip -4 addr |
grep inet
inet 127.0.0.1/8 scope host lo
inet 10.42.3.2/24 scope global eth0
```

As you can see, this container was also assigned an IP in the Flannel subnet. Now ping the container that was started on `core1`:

```
/ # ping 10.42.88.2
PING 10.42.88.2 (10.42.88.2): 56 data bytes
64 bytes from 10.42.88.2: seq=0 ttl=60 time=1.491 ms
64 bytes from 10.42.88.2: seq=1 ttl=60 time=0.528 ms
```

Success! Take note of something. The IP address was used to ping rather than the container name for a reason. Flannel does not support DNS-SD. Had you tried to ping the container by its name, `ping` would have reported an error:

```
/ # ping test1
ping: bad address 'test1'
```

The lack of service discovery is not the weakness it might seem at first. Orchestration tools, such as Kubernetes, that can use Flannel as the overlay network often provide their own service discovery:

```
$ gcloud compute instances delete core1 core2 core3
```

The following instances will be deleted. Attached disks configured to be auto-deleted will be deleted unless they are attached to any other instances. Deleting a disk is irreversible and any data on the disk will be lost:

```
 - [core1] in [asia-east1-a]
 - [core2] in [asia-east1-a]
 - [core3] in [asia-east1-a]
Do you want to continue (Y/n)? y
```

Using shared network storage for Docker volumes

One of the biggest challenges with running a Docker cluster is figuring out what to do with the data. Docker supports using **volumes** to store data. By default, the volumes store data on the Docker host. What happens if that container is started on another host? None of the data is available. For most applications, this is a problem.

Docker solved this problem by creating a pluggable storage system. Volumes can be created that connect to a wide variety of storage systems. Those systems can be anything from traditional network storage such as a **Network File System (NFS)** and **Internet Small Computer System Interface (iSCSI)** to cloud services such as Amazon S3 or clustered storage systems such as Gluster or Ceph.

Each storage option has its pros and cons. Some may be better suited to some workloads than others. Fortunately, you can choose the best solution on a per-container basis. A public web server may run in Amazon EC2 and need storage there while a local file server connects to a local Ceph cluster.

A volume is created using the `docker volume create` command. The following example creates a volume named `vol1` using a fictional driver named `foo`:

```
$ docker volume create --driver foo --name vol1 --opt bar=1 --opt baz=2
```

The driver a volume uses is defined by the `--driver` flag. Each driver has its own set of options that are set adding one or more `--opt` flags. Be sure to read the documentation for each storage driver you choose to use.

Introducing Ceph

Ceph is a distributed, clustered storage solution developed by Red Hat. It provides an object store, block storage, and a shared filesystem. Ceph can also provide compatibility with Amazon S3 and OpenStack Swift with the RADOS Gateway. Multiple storage pools and storage tiering are also possible. It can also self-heal when there are problems in the cluster making it an excellent choice for providing storage for network services.

There are two components of note when setting up a Ceph cluster. The first component is the Ceph Monitor. Monitors keep track of the cluster health and the **Controlled Replication Under Scalable Hashing** (**CRUSH**) map, which tells the cluster how to find data in the cluster. Second are the Ceph OSDs. These are the daemons that actually control the storage. A best practice is to run one OSD for each disk that will be used in the cluster. For more details about Ceph, refer to *Learning Ceph, Karan Singh,* published by *Packt Publishing* or `http://www.ceph.com/`.

Using Ceph with Docker

Docker can use Ceph for volumes through one of a number of storage drivers. Some orchestration systems, such as Kubernetes, have Ceph support built-in. As always, do your own research to see which plugin is right for your environment. This demonstration will use the `volplugin` driver from `contiv` which is available at: `https://github.com/contiv/volplugin`.

The `volplugin` driver uses a number of daemons. You can install them manually but the easiest way is to run them in a Docker container:

```
$ sudo docker run -it -v /var/run/docker.sock:/var/run/docker.sock
contiv/volplugin-autorun
```

Notice that the Docker socket is being passed in to the container as a volume. That is what allows the startup scripts to register and run the required containers.

The initial installation will create a policy named `policy1` that will create new images in the `rbd` storage pool. You can create additional policies if you are using another storage pool, set a different default size, or use a different filesystem on the image. These are managed through the `volcli` tool which is available through the `volplugin` image:

```
$ sudo docker exec volplugin volcli policy get policy1
{"name":"policy1","create":{"size":"10MB","filesystem":""},"runtime":{"snap
shots
":true,"snapshot":{"frequency":"30m","keep":20},"rate-limit":{"write-
iops":0,"re
    ad-iops":0,"write-bps":0,"read-
bps":0}},"driver":{"pool":"rbd"},"filesystems":{"
    ext4":"mkfs.ext4 -m0
%"},"backends":{"crud":"ceph","mount":"ceph","snapshot":"ce
    ph"}}
```

This example shows how to use the `volcli` to get the configuration for `policy1`. Notice the use of `docker exec`, which allows the `volplugin` tool to connect to the running daemon.

Creating a Docker volume

Once `volplugin` is running, you can use it to create a Docker volume. The name of the volume starts with the policy that is being used followed by a slash, then the image name:

```
$ sudo docker volume create -d volplugin --name policy1/test
```

In Ceph, a new `rbd` is created in the storage pool. Notice the name difference. Ceph does not allow slashes in the image name so the slash is changed to a dot:

```
$ sudo rbd info policy1.test
rbd image 'policy1.test':
        size 10240 kB in 3 objects
        order 22 (4096 kB objects)
        block_name_prefix: rbd_data.372d8625e32
        format: 2
        features: layering
        flags:
```

Now the volume can be used with a running container. It works just the same as mounting a local directory except that instead of a local path, the name of the volume is used:

```
$ sudo docker run --rm -v policy1/test:/mnt busybox
```

This command starts a new `busybox` container with the Ceph `rbd` image mounted at `/mnt`. Notice that since it is a new filesystem, the only thing in `/mnt` is the `lost+found` directory. To demonstrate the power of volumes with a simple example, let's create a new file in `/mnt`:

```
/ # touch /mnt/example
/ # ls /mnt
example      lost+found
```

Because this container was started with `--rm`, the container will be deleted when it exits. The data stored on the volume, however, will remain for use by the next container. If you start a new container that uses the same volume, the data will still be there:

```
$ sudo docker run --rm -v policy1/test:/mnt -it busybox
/ # ls /mnt
example      lost+found
```

The power of using a system such as Ceph for your volumes is that you can start your container on any host in the cluster and your data will be there waiting for you. Meaning, it does not matter where in the cluster your container starts or that a particular host is running.

A word of warning. Ceph `rbd` images are block devices just like any other that is available to a host. The same is true if you were to use iSCSI, OpenStack Cinder, or storage from your cloud provider. Meaning, the standard warnings about multiple hosts trying to mount the same filesystem apply. Multiple hosts mounting the same Ext4 or similar filesystem for writing will inevitably lead to data loss. That is a bad thing.

If you need multiple hosts to have access to the same filesystem, consider using NFS or SMB as an intermediary layer. You could also use containers that run a cluster aware filesystem such as OCFS2, but that adds even more complexity to an increasingly complex environment.

Other shared storage plugins

As mentioned previously, there are a lot of storage plugins. Nearly every major storage system has a plugin. Following are a few of the more interesting ones:

- **Azure file storage**: An open source plugin developed by Microsoft to support Azure. Refer to `https://github.com/Azure/azurefile-dockervolumedriver`.
- **GlusterFS**: Supports the clustered storage system GlusterFS from Red Hat. Refer to `https://github.com/calavera/docker-volume-glusterfs`.
- **REX-Ray**: Developed by Dell EMC to support ScaleIO and Isilon for Docker and Mesos. Refer to `https://github.com/emccode/rexray`.
- **Kubernetes**: The Kubernetes orchestration tool has native support for iSCSI, NFS, Ceph, and many others.

Summary

In this chapter, you saw the building blocks that are needed for a Docker cluster. No matter what orchestration tool is used, there will be the need for a registry to store your images, an overlay network for inter-container communication, and network storage so that your containers can get at their data wherever in the cluster they start. There are many options to fill each role. While the choice of solution is important, it's easy to switch between systems if needed. Some will be better in certain environments and workloads. The next chapter will dive into orchestrating a Docker cluster using Docker Swarm.

4
Orchestration with Docker Swarm

Docker Swarm is the native orchestration tool for Docker. It was rolled into the core Docker suite with version 1.12. At its simplest, using Docker Swarm is just like using Docker. All of the tools that have been covered still work. Docker Swarm adds a couple of features that make deploying and updating services very nice. You got a glimpse of them in Chapter 3, *Cluster Building Blocks – Registry, Overlay Networks, and Shared Storage*, which covered Docker overlay networks. Now it is time to dive into the details.

The following topics are covered in this chapter:

- Creating a swarm
- Adding and removing nodes
- Changing node availability
- Swarm disaster recovery
- Grouping nodes with labels
- Creating and stopping services
- Creating replicas
- Using global services
- Using constraints
- Zero downtime upgrades with rolling updates
- Using Docker Compose with swarm
- Using Docker Datacenter

Setting up a swarm

The first step for running a swarm is to have a number of hosts ready with Docker installed. It does not matter if you use the install script from `get.docker.com` or if you use Docker Machine. You also need to be sure that a few ports are open between the servers, as given here:

- 2377 TCP port for cluster management
- 7946 TCP and UDP port for node communication
- 4789 TCP and UDP port for overlay network

Take a moment to get or assign a static IP address to the hosts that will be the swarm managers. Each manager must have a static IP address so that workers know how to connect to them. Worker addresses can be dynamic but the IP of the manager must be static.

As you plan your swarm, take a moment to decide how many managers you are going to need. The minimum number to run and still maintain fault tolerance is three. For larger clusters, you may need as many as five or seven. Very rarely will you need more than that. In any case, the number of managers should be odd. Docker Swarm can maintain a quorum as long as *50% + 1* managers are running. Having two or four managers provides no additional fault tolerance than one or three.

If possible, you should spread your managers out so that a single failure will not take down your swarm. For example, make sure that they are not all running on the same VM host or connected to the same switch. The whole point is to have multiple managers to keep the swarm running in the event of a manager failure. Do not undermine your efforts by allowing a single point of failure somewhere else taking down your swarm.

Initializing a swarm

If you are installing from your desktop, it may be better to use Docker Machine to connect to the host as this will set up the necessary TLS keys. Run the `docker swarm init` command to initialize the swarm. The `--advertize-addr` flag is optional. By default, it will guess an address on the host. This may not be correct. To be sure, set it to the static IP address you have for the manager host:

```
$ docker swarm init --advertise-addr 172.31.26.152
Swarm initialized: current node (6d6e6kxlyjuo9vb9w1uug95zh) is now a
manager.
To add a worker to this swarm, run the following command:
docker swarm join \
--token
```

```
SWMTKN-1-0061dt2qjsdr4gabxryrksqs0b8fnhwg6bjhs8cxzen7tmarbi-89mmok3p
    f6dsa5n33fb60tx0m \
        172.31.26.152:2377
To add a manager to this swarm, run 'docker swarm join-token manager' and
follow the instructions.
```

Included in the output of the `init` command is the command to run on each worker host. It is also possible to run it from your desktop if you have set your environment to use the worker host. You can save the command somewhere, but you can always get it again by running `docker swarm join-token manager`.

As part of the join process, Docker Swarm will create TLS keys, which will be used to encrypt communication between the managers and the hosts. It will not, however, encrypt network traffic between containers. The certificates are updated every three months. The time period can be updated by running `docker swarm update --cert-expiry duration`. The duration is specified as number of hours and minutes. For example, setting the duration to `1000h` will tell Docker Swarm to reset the certificate every 1,000 hours.

Managing a swarm

One of the easiest pieces to overlook when it comes to orchestrating Docker is how to manage the cluster itself. In this section, you will see how to manage your swarm including adding and removing nodes, changing their availability, and backup and recovery. In `Chapter 10`, *Why Stop at Containers? Automating Your Infrastructure*, we will learn about automating node deployment in depth.

Adding a node

New worker nodes can be added at any time. Install Docker, then run `docker swarm join-token worker` to get the `docker swarm join` command to join the host to the swarm. Once added, the worker will be available to run tasks. Take note that the command to join the cluster is consistent. This makes it easy to add to a host configuration script and join the swarm on boot.

You can get a list of all of the nodes in the swarm by running `docker node ls` from a manager node:

```
$ docker node ls
ID                         HOSTNAME  STATUS  AVAILABILITY  MANAGER STATUS
1i3wtacdjz5p509bu3l3qfbei   worker1   Ready   Active        Reachable
3f2t4wwwthgcahs9089b8przv   worker2   Ready   Active        Reachable
6d6e6kxlyjuo9vb9w1uug95zh * manager   Ready   Active        Leader
```

The list will not only show the machines but it will also show if they are active in the swarm and if they are a manager. The node marked as `Leader` is the master of the swarm. It coordinates the managers.

Promoting and demoting nodes

In Docker Swarm, just like in real life, managers are also workers. This means that managers can run tasks. It also means that workers can be promoted to become managers. This can be useful to quickly replace a failed manager or to seamlessly increase the number of managers. The following command promotes the node named `worker1` to be a manager. The command must be run on a node that is already a manager:

```
$ docker node promote worker1
Node worker1 promoted to a manager in the swarm.
```

Managers can also be demoted to become plain workers. This should be done before a manager node is going to be decommissioned. The following command demotes `worker1` back to a plain worker:

```
$ docker node demote worker1
Manager worker1 demoted in the swarm.
```

Whatever your reasons for promoting or demoting node might be, make sure that when you are done, there are an odd number of managers.

Changing node availability

Docker Swarm nodes have a concept of availability. The availability of a node determines whether or not tasks can be scheduled on that node. Use the `docker node update --availability <state> <node-id>` command to set the availability state. There are three availability states that can be set—`pause`, `drain`, and `active`.

Pausing a node

Setting a node's availability to `pause` will prevent the scheduler from assigning new tasks to the node. Existing tasks will continue to run. This can be useful for troubleshooting load issues on a node or for preventing new tasks from being assigned to an already overloaded node. The following command pauses `worker2`:

```
$ docker node update --availability pause worker2
worker2

$ docker node ls
ID                            HOSTNAME   STATUS   AVAILABILITY   MANAGER STATUS
1i3wtacdjz5p509bu313qfbei     worker1    Ready    Active         Reachable
3f2t4wwwthgcahs9089b8przv     worker2    Ready    Pause          Reachable
6d6e6kxlyjuo9vb9w1uug95zh *   manager    Ready    Active         Leader
```

Do not rely on using `pause` to deal with overload issues. It is better to place reasonable resource limits on your services and let the scheduler figure things out for you. You can use `pause` to help determine what the resource limits should be. For example, you can start a task on a node, then pause the node to prevent new tasks from running while you monitor resource usage.

Draining a node

Like `pause`, setting a node's availability to `drain` will stop the scheduler from assigning new tasks to the node. In addition, `drain` will stop any running tasks and reschedule them to run elsewhere in the swarm. The `drain` mode has two common purposes.

First, it is useful for preparing a node for an upgrade. Containers will be stopped and rescheduled in an orderly fashion. Updates can then be applied and the node rebooted, if necessary, without further disruption. The node can be set to `active` again once the updates are complete.

Remember that, when draining a node, running containers have to be stopped and restarted elsewhere. This can cause disruption if your applications are not built to handle failure. The great thing about containers is that they start quickly, but some services, such as MySQL, take a few seconds to initialize.

The second use of `drain` is to prevent services from being scheduled on manager nodes. Manager processing is very reliant on messages being passed in a timely manner. An unconstrained task running on a manager node can cause a denial of service outage for the node causing problems for your cluster. It is not uncommon to leave manager nodes in a `drain` state permanently. The following command will `drain` the node named `manager`:

```
$ docker node update --availability drain manager
manager

$ docker node ls
ID                             HOSTNAME  STATUS  AVAILABILITY  MANAGER STATUS
1i3wtacdjz5p509bu3l3qfbei      worker1   Ready   Active        Reachable
3f2t4wwwthgcahs9089b8przv      worker2   Ready   Active        Reachable
6d6e6kxlyjuo9vb9w1uug95zh *    manager   Ready   Drain         Leader
```

Activating a node

When a node is ready to accept tasks again, set the state to `active`. Do not be concerned if the node does not immediately fill up with containers. Tasks are only assigned when a new scheduling event happens, such as starting a service. The following command will reactivate the `worker2` node:

```
$ docker node update --availability active worker2
worker2

$ docker node ls
ID                             HOSTNAME  STATUS  AVAILABILITY  MANAGER STATUS
1i3wtacdjz5p509bu3l3qfbei      worker1   Ready   Active        Reachable
3f2t4wwwthgcahs9089b8przv      worker2   Ready   Active        Reachable
6d6e6kxlyjuo9vb9w1uug95zh *    manager   Ready   Active        Leader
```

Removing nodes

Nodes may need to be removed for a variety of reasons including upgrades, failures, or simply eliminating capacity that is no longer needed. For example, it may be easier to upgrade nodes by building new ones rather than performing updates on the old nodes. The new node will be added and the old one removed.

Step one for a healthy node is to set the `--availability` state to `drain`. This will ensure that all scheduled tasks have been stopped and moved to other nodes in the swarm.

Step two is to run `docker swarm leave` from the node that will be leaving the swarm. This will assign the node a `Down` status. In the following example, `worker2` has left the swarm:

```
$ docker node ls
ID                              HOSTNAME   STATUS   AVAILABILITY   MANAGER STATUS
1i3wtacdjz5p509bu313qfbei       worker1    Ready    Active         Reachable
3f2t4wwwthgcahs9089b8przv       worker2    Down     Active
6d6e6kxlyjuo9vb9w1uug95zh *     manager    Ready    Active         Leader
```

If the node that is being removed is a manager, it must first be demoted to a worker as described earlier before running `docker swarm leave`. When removing managers, take care that you do not lose quorum or your cluster will stop working.

Once the node has been marked `Down`, it can be removed from the swarm. From a manager node, use `docker node rm` to remove the node from the swarm:

```
$ docker node rm worker2
```

In some cases, the node that you want to remove is unreachable so it is not possible to run `docker swarm leave`. When that happens, use the `--force` option:

```
$ docker node rm --force worker2
```

Nodes that have been removed can be re-added with `docker swarm join`.

Recovering from a disaster

Failures are a regular occurrence in large clusters. Hard drives fail, servers fail, even full data centers will go dark. Shifting services to cloud platforms such as AWS and Azure have helped, but even they have had entire regions go down. Using containers may make your applications more resistant to failure, but the hosts running those containers are still affected by any number of things. Properly engineered, your cluster should be able to cope with disaster. Here are a few things to keep in mind to keep your cluster safe.

Restarting the full cluster

There may be times when the entire swarm has to be shutdown. Hopefully, there will be time to properly shut down running services and the hosts. When the time comes to shutdown the hosts, start with the workers then shutdown the managers. When the cluster is started up again, start the managers first then the workers. Make sure that the managers have the same IP addresses or your nodes will come up and not be able to reconnect with the swarm.

Backup and recovery

Just because Docker Swarm is resilient to failure, does not mean that you should ignore backups. Good backups may be the difference between restoring services and a resume altering event. There are two major components to back up – the swarm state data and your application data.

Backing up the swarm

Each manager keeps the cluster information in `/var/lib/docker/swarm/raft`. If, for some reason, you need to completely rebuild your cluster, you will need this data. Make sure you have at least one good backup of the `raft` data directory. It does not matter which of the managers the backups are pulled from. It might be wise to pull backups from a couple of managers, just in case one is corrupted.

Recovering a swarm

In most cases, losing a failed manager is an easy fix. Restart the failed manager and everything should be good. It may be necessary to build a new manager or promote an existing worker to a manager. In most circumstances, this will bring your cluster back into a healthy state.

If you lose enough managers to lose a quorum, recovery gets more complex. The first step is to start enough managers to restore quorum. The data should be synced to the new managers, and once quorum is recovered, so is the cluster. If that does not work, you will have to rebuild the swarm. This is where your backups come in.

If the manager node you choose to rebuild on has an otherwise healthy `raft` database, you can start there. If not, or if you are rebuilding on a brand new node, stop Docker and copy the `raft` data back to `/var/lib/docker/swarm/raft`. After the `raft` data is in place, ensure that Docker is running and run the following command:

```
$ docker swarm init --force-new-cluster --advertise-addr manager
```

The address set in with `--advertise-addr` has the same meaning as what was used to create the swarm initially. The magic here is the `--force-new-cluster` option. This option will ignore the swarm membership data that is the `raft` database, but will remember things such as the worker node list, running services, and tasks.

Backing up services

Service information is backed up as part of the `raft` database, but you should have a plan to rebuild them in case the database becomes corrupted. Backing up the output of `docker swarm ls` is a start. Application information, including networks, and volumes may be sourced for Docker Compose files, which should be backed up. The container configuration, which includes the `Dockerfile` and everything needed to build the container, and your application should be in version control and backed up.

Most importantly, do not forget your data. If you have your `Dockerfile` and the application code, the applications can be rebuilt even if the registry is lost. In some cases, it is a valid choice to not back up the registry since the images can, potentially, be rebuilt. The data, however, usually cannot be. Have a strategy in place for backing up the data that works for your environment. I suggest creating a container for each application that is deployed and can properly back up data for the application. Docker Swarm does not have a native scheduled task option, but you can configure `cron` on a worker node that runs the various backup containers on a schedule.

The `pause` availability option can be helpful here. Configure a worker node that will be your designated host to pull backups. Set the availability to `pause` so that other containers are not started on the node and resources are available to perform the backups.

Using `pause` means that containers can be started in the background and will continue to run after the node is paused, allowing them to finish normally. Then `cron` can run a script that looks something like the following one. The contents of `run-backup-containers` is left as an exercise for the reader:

```
#!/bin/bash
docker node update --availability active backupworker
run-backup-containers
docker node update --availability pause
```

You can also label to designate multiple nodes for backups and schedule services to ignore those nodes, or in the case of backup containers, run on them. Labels are covered in more depth in the next section.

 Many network storage solutions provide options such as snapshots that may augment your backup strategy.

Grouping nodes with labels

It is often useful to group your nodes. For example, you may have a set of nodes that have external IP addresses and another set that only has private IP addresses. Frontend services, such as web servers, should be on the public nodes while backend services such as databases should be on the nodes with private addresses. In another case, you might have a set of nodes with SSDs while another has slower disks. Docker Swarm accomplishes this grouping with labels.

Labels are added to a node with `docker node update`. A label can be added by itself or as key/value pair. One or more labels can be set at one time:

```
$ docker node update --label-add frontend worker1
$ docker node update --label-add backend --label-add env=prod worker2
```

The `docker node inspect` command will show you everything about a node including the labels. By default, it outputs in JSON format. To make it easier to read, use the `--pretty` flag:

```
$ docker node inspect --pretty worker2
ID:                     0c9wmu7elqs8zkxe6k103k1t3
Labels:
 - backend =
 - env = prod
Hostname:               worker2
```

```
Joined at:                  2016-09-23 04:19:32.236213766
+0000 utc
Status:
   State:                   Ready
   Availability:            Active
Manager Status:
   Address:                 172.31.26.153:2377
   Raft Status:             Reachable
   Leader:                  No
Platform:
   Operating System:linux
   Architecture:            x86_64
Resources:
   CPUs:                    1
   Memory:                  990.7 MiB
Plugins:
   Network:                 bridge, host, null, overlay
   Volume:                  local
Engine Version:             1.12.1
Engine Labels:
   - provider = generic
```

It is possible to output just the labels by passing a Go template to the `--format` flag. The template uses the key names from the JSON output:

```
$ docker node inspect --format '{{ .Spec.Labels }}' worker2
map[backend: env:prod]
```

Labels are removed with the `--label-rm` flag to `docker node update`. Like `--label-add`, multiple labels can be removed at one time by specifying `--label-rm` multiple times:

```
$ docker node update --label-rm backend worker1
```

Node labels can be used as constraints for services to restrict them to certain nodes. Constraints will be covered in more detail later in this chapter.

Managing services

Now that the swarm is up and running, it is time to look at services. A **service** is a collection of one or more tasks that do something. Each **task** is a container running somewhere in the swarm. Since services are potentially composed of multiple tasks, there are different tools to manage them. In most cases, these commands will be a subcommand of `docker service`.

Running containers as services in a swarm offers a number of benefits. They are as follows:

- Services can be scaled out quickly and easily.
- Swarm can perform *zero-downtime* upgrades where updated versions of an image are added while old versions are removed.
- Easily create overlay networks to connect containers running on multiple hosts. (Overlay networks were covered in detail in Chapter 3, *Cluster Building Blocks – Registry, Overlay Networks, and Shared Storage*.)

Running services

Running tasks with Docker Swarm is a little bit different than running them under plain Docker. Instead of using docker run, the command is docker service create:

```
$ docker service create --name web nginx
```

When a service starts, a swarm manager schedules the tasks to run on active workers in the swarm. By default, swarm will spread running containers across all of the active hosts in the swarm.

Offering services to the Internet requires publishing ports with the -p flag. Multiple ports can be opened by specifying -p multiple times. When using the swarm overlay network, you also get ingress mesh routing, which was described in Chapter 3, *Cluster Building Blocks – Registry, Overlay Networks, and Shared Storage*. The mesh will route connections from any host in the cluster to the service no matter where it is running. Port publishing will also load balance across multiple containers:

```
$ docker service create --name web -p 80 -p 443 nginx
```

Creating replicas

A service can be started with multiple containers using the --replicas option. The value is the number of desired replicas. It may take a moment to start all the desired replicas:

```
$ docker service create --replicas 2 --name web -p 80 -p 443 nginx
```

This example starts two copies of the nginx container under the service name web. The great news is that you can change the number of replicas at any time:

```
$ docker service update --replicas 3 web
```

Even better, a service can be scaled up or down. This example scales the service up to three containers. It is possible to scale the number down later once the replicas are no longer needed.

Use `docker service ls` to see a summary of running services and the number of replicas for each:

```
$ docker service ls
ID              NAME    REPLICAS    IMAGE   COMMAND
4i3jsbsohkxj    web     3/3         nginx
```

If you need to see the details of a service, including where tasks are running, use the `docker service ps` command. It takes the name of the service as an argument. This example shows three `nginx` tasks that are part of the service `web`:

```
$ docker service ps web
ID                         NAME    IMAGE   NODE      DESIRED STATE   CURRENT
STATE     ERROR
d993z8o6ex6wz00xtbrv647uq  web.1   nginx   worker2   Running         Running 31
minutes ago
eueui4hw33eonsin9hfqgcvd7  web.2   nginx   worker1   Running         Preparing
4 seconds ago
djg5542upa1vq4z0ycz8blgfo  web.3   nginx   worker2   Running         Running 2
seconds ago
```

Take note of the name of the tasks. If you were to connect to `worker1` and try to use `docker exec` to access the `web.2` container, you will get an error:

```
$ docker exec -it web.2 bash
Error response from daemon: No such container: web.2
```

Tasks started with the `docker service` command are named with the name of the service, a number, and the ID of the task separated by dots. Using `docker ps` on `worker1`, you can see the actual name of the `web.2` container:

```
$ docker ps
CONTAINER ID    IMAGE           COMMAND                   CREATED
STATUS          PORTS           NAMES
b71ad831eb09    nginx:latest    "nginx -g 'daemon off"    2 days ago
Up 2 days       80/tcp, 443/tcp    web.2.eueui4hw33eonsin9hfqgcvd7
```

Running global services

There may be times when you want to run a task on every active node in the swarm. This is useful for monitoring tools:

```
$ docker service create --mode global --name monitor nginx
$ docker service ps monitor
ID                          NAME        IMAGE   NODE      DESIRED STATE
CURRENT STATE           ERROR
daxkqywp0y8bhip0f4ocpl5v1   monitor     nginx   worker2   Running
Running 6
seconds ago
a45opnrj3dcvz4skgwd8vamx8   \_ monitor  nginx   worker1   Running
Running 4
seconds ago
```

It is important to reiterate that global services only run on active nodes. The task will not start on nodes that have the availability set to pause or drain. If a paused or drained node is set to active, the global service will be started on that node immediately:

```
$ docker node update --availability active manager
manager

$ docker service ps monitor
ID                          NAME        IMAGE   NODE      DESIRED STATE
CURRENT STATE           ERROR
0mpe2zb0mn3z6fa2ioybjhqr3   monitor     nginx   manager   Running
Preparing
3 seconds ago
daxkqywp0y8bhip0f4ocpl5v1   \_ monitor  nginx   worker2   Running
Running
3 minutes ago
a45opnrj3dcvz4skgwd8vamx8   \_ monitor  nginx   worker1   Running
Running
3 minutes ago
```

Setting constraints

It is often useful to limit which nodes a service can run on. For example, a service that might be dependent on a fast disk might be limited to nodes that have SSDs. Constraints are added to the `docker service create` command with the `--constraint` flag. Multiple constraints can be added. The result will be the intersection of all of the constraints.

For this example, assume that there is a swarm with three nodes – `manager`, `worker1`, and `worker2`. The `worker1` and `worker2` nodes have the `env=prod` label while manager has the `env=dev` label. If a service is started with the constraint that `env` is `dev`, it will only run service tasks on the manager node:

```
$ docker service create --constraint "node.labels.env == dev" --name web-
dev --replicas 2 nginx
913jm3v2ytrpxejpvtdkzrfjz

$ docker service ps web-dev
ID                          NAME        IMAGE   NODE      DESIRED STATE
CURRENT STATE               ERROR
5e93f110k9x6kq013ffotd1wf   web-dev.1   nginx   manager   Running
Running 6 seconds ago
5skcigjackl6b8snpgtcjbu12   web-dev.2   nginx   manager   Running
Running 5 seconds ago
```

Even though there are two other nodes in the swarm, the service is only running on the manager because it is the only node with the `env=dev` label. If another service was started with the constraint that `env` is `prod`, the tasks will start on the worker nodes:

```
$ docker service create --constraint "node.labels.env == prod" --name web-
prod --replicas 2 nginx
88kfmfbwksklkhg92f4fkcpwx

$ docker service ps web-prod
ID                          NAME         IMAGE   NODE      DESIRED STATE
CURRENT STATE               ERROR
5f4s2536g0bmm99j7wc02s963   web-prod.1   nginx   worker2   Running
Running 3 seconds ago
5ogcsmv2bquwpbu1ndn4i9q65   web-prod.2   nginx   worker1   Running
Running 3 seconds ago
```

The constraints will be honored if the services are scaled. No matter how many replicas are requested, the containers will only be run on nodes that match the constraints:

```
$ docker service update --replicas 3 web-prod
web-prod

$ docker service ps web-prod
ID                         NAME         IMAGE  NODE     DESIRED STATE
CURRENT STATE              ERROR
5f4s2536g0bmm99j7wc02s963  web-prod.1   nginx  worker2  Running
Running about a minute ago
5ogcsmv2bquwpbu1ndn4i9q65  web-prod.2   nginx  worker1  Running
Running about a minute ago
en15vh1d7819hag4xp1qkerae  web-prod.3   nginx  worker1  Running
Running 2 seconds ago
```

As you can see from the example, the containers are all running on `worker1` and `worker2`. This leads to an important point. If the constraints cannot be satisfied, the service will be started but no containers will actually be running:

```
$ docker service create --constraint "node.labels.env == testing" --name
web-test --replicas 2 nginx
6tfeocf8g4rwk8p5erno8nyia

$ docker service ls
ID            NAME      REPLICAS  IMAGE  COMMAND
6tfeocf8g4rw  web-test  0/2       nginx
88kfmfbwkskl  web-prod  3/3       nginx
913jm3v2ytrp  web-dev   2/2       nginx
```

Notice that the number of replicas requested is two but the number of containers running is zero. Swarm cannot find a suitable node so it does not start the containers. If a node with the `env=testing` label were to be added or if that label were to be added to an existing node, swarm would immediately schedule the tasks:

```
$ docker node update --label-add env=testing worker1
worker1

$ docker service ps web-test
ID                         NAME         IMAGE  NODE     DESIRED STATE
CURRENT STATE              ERROR
7hsjs0q0pqlb6x68qos19o1b0  web-test.1   nginx  worker1  Running
Running 18 seconds ago
dqajwyqrah6zv83dsfqene3qa  web-test.2   nginx  worker1  Running
Running 18 seconds ago
```

In this example, the `env` label was changed to `testing` from `prod` on `worker1`. Since a node is now available that meets the constraints for the `web-test` service, swarm started the containers on `worker1`. However, the constraints are only checked when tasks are scheduled. Even though `worker1` no longer has the `env` label set to `prod`, the existing containers for the `web-prod` service are still running:

```
$ docker node ps worker1
ID                             NAME        IMAGE   NODE      DESIRED STATE
CURRENT STATE          ERROR
7hsjs0q0pqlb6x68qos19o1b0  web-test.1  nginx   worker1   Running
Running 5 minutes ago
dqajwyqrah6zv83dsfqene3qa  web-test.2  nginx   worker1   Running
Running 5 minutes ago
5ogcsmv2bquwpbu1ndn4i9q65  web-prod.2  nginx   worker1   Running
Running 21 minutes ago
en15vh1d7819hag4xp1qkerae  web-prod.3  nginx   worker1   Running
Running 20 minutes ago
```

Stopping services

All good things come to an end and this includes services running in a swarm. When a service is no longer needed, it can be removed with `docker service rm`. When a service is removed, all tasks associated with that service are stopped and the containers removed from the nodes they were running on. The following example removes a service named `web`:

```
$ docker service rm web
```

Docker makes the assumption that the only time services are stopped is when they are no longer needed. Because of this, there is no Docker service analog to the `docker stop` command. This might not be an issue since services are so easily recreated. That said, I have run into situations where I have needed to stop a service for a short time for testing and did not have the command at my fingertips to recreate it.

The solution is very easy but not necessarily obvious. Rather than stopping the service and recreating it, set the number of replicas to zero. This will stop all running tasks and they will be ready to start up again when needed:

```
$ docker service update --replicas 0 web
web

$ docker service ls
ID            NAME  REPLICAS  IMAGE  COMMAND
5gdgmb7afupd  web   0/0       nginx
```

The containers for the tasks are stopped, but remain on the nodes. The `docker service ps` command will show that the tasks for the service are all in the `Shutdown` state. If needed, one can inspect the containers on the nodes:

```
$ docker service ps web
ID            NAME     IMAGE    NODE      DESIRED STATE  CURRENT STATE          ERROR
68v6trav6cf2qj8gp8wgcbmhu  web.1  nginx  worker1   Shutdown       Shutdown 3
seconds ago
060wax426mtqdx79g0u1wu25r  web.2  nginx  manager   Shutdown       Shutdown 2
seconds ago
79uidx4t5rz4o7an9wtya1456  web.3  nginx  worker2   Shutdown       Shutdown 3
seconds ago
```

When it is time to bring the service back, use `docker swarm update` to set the number of replicas back to what is needed. Swarm will start the containers across in the swarm just as if you had used `docker swarm create`.

Upgrading a service with rolling updates

It is likely that services running in a swarm will need to be upgraded. Traditionally, upgrades involved stopping a service, performing the upgrade, then restarting the service. If everything goes well, the service starts and works as expected and the downtime is minimized. If not, there can be an extended outage as the administrator and developers debug what went wrong and restore the service.

Docker makes it easy to test new images before they are deployed and one can be confident that the service will work in production just as it did during testing. The question is, how does one deploy the upgraded service without a noticeable downtime for the users? For busy services, even a few seconds of downtime can be problematic. Docker Swarm provides a way to update services in the background with zero downtime.

There are three options which are passed to `docker service create` that control how rolling updates are applied. These options can also be changed after a service has been created with `docker service update`. The options are as follows:

- `--update-delay`: This option sets the delay between each container upgrade. The delay is defined by a number of hours, minutes, and seconds indicated by a number followed by `h`, `m`, or `s`, respectively. For example, a 30 second delay will be written as `30s`. A delay of 1 hour, 30 minutes, and 12 seconds will be written as `1h30m12s`.

- `--update-failure-action`: This tells swarm how to handle an upgrade failure. By default, Docker Swarm will pause the upgrade if a container fails to upgrade. You can configure swarm to continue even if a task fails to upgrade. The allowed values are `pause` and `continue`.
- `--update-parallelism`: This tells swarm how many tasks to upgrade at one time. By default, Docker Swarm will only upgrade one task at a time. If this is set to `0` (zero), all running containers will be upgraded at once.

For this example, a service named `web` is started with six replicas using the `nginx:1.10` image. The service is configured to update two tasks at a time and wait 30 seconds between updates. The list of tasks from `docker service ps` shows that all six tasks are running and that they are all running the `nginx:1.10` image:

```
$ docker service create --name web --update-delay 30s --update-parallelism
2 --replicas 6 nginx:1.10

$ docker service ps web
ID                           NAME    IMAGE        NODE      DESIRED STATE
CURRENT STATE           ERROR
83p4vi4ryw9x6kbevmplgrjp4  web.1   nginx:1.10   worker2   Running
Running 20 seconds ago
2yb1tchas244tmnrpfyzik5jw  web.2   nginx:1.10   worker1   Running
Running 20 seconds ago
f4g3nayyx5y6k65x8n31x8klk  web.3   nginx:1.10   worker2   Running
Running 20 seconds ago
6axpogx5rqlg96bqt9qn822rx  web.4   nginx:1.10   worker1   Running
Running 20 seconds ago
2d7n5nhja0efka7qy2boke813  web.5   nginx:1.10   manager   Running
Running 16 seconds ago
5sprz723zv3z779o3zcyj28p1  web.6   nginx:1.10   manager   Running
Running 16 seconds ago
```

Updates have started using the `docker service update` command and specifying a new image. In this case, the service will be upgraded from `nginx:1.10` to `nginx:1.11`. Rolling updates work by stopping a number of tasks defined by `--update-parallelism` and starting new tasks based on the new image. Swarm will then wait until the delay set by `--update-delay` elapses before upgrading the next tasks:

```
$ docker service update --image nginx:1.11 web
```

When the updates begin, two tasks will be updated at a time. If the image is not found on the node, it will be pulled from the registry, slowing down the update. You can speed up the process by writing a script to pull the new image on each node before you run the update.

The update process can be monitored by running `docker service inspect` or `docker service ps`:

```
$ docker service inspect --pretty web
ID:               4a60v04ux70qdf0fzyf3s93er
Name:             web
Mode:             Replicated
Replicas:         6
Update status:
State:            updating
Started:          about a minute ago
Message:          update in progress
Placement:
UpdateConfig:
Parallelism:      2
Delay:            30s
On failure:       pause
ContainerSpec:
Image:            nginx:1.11
Resources:

$ docker service ps web
ID                          NAME         IMAGE        NODE      DESIRED STATE
CURRENT STATE                    ERROR
83p4vi4ryw9x6kbevmplgrjp4   web.1        nginx:1.10   worker2   Running
Running 35 seconds ago
29qqk95xdrb0whcdy7abvji2p   web.2        nginx:1.11   manager   Running
Preparing 2 seconds ago
2yb1tchas244tmnrpfyzik5jw   \_ web.2     nginx:1.10   worker1   Shutdown
Shutdown 2 seconds ago
f4g3nayyx5y6k65x8n31x8klk   web.3        nginx:1.10   worker2   Running
Running 35 seconds ago
6axpogx5rqlg96bqt9qn822rx   web.4        nginx:1.10   worker1   Running
Running 35 seconds ago
3z6ees2748tqsoacy114ol183   web.5        nginx:1.11   worker1   Running
Running less than a second ago
2d7n5nhja0efka7qy2boke813   \_ web.5     nginx:1.10   manager   Shutdown
Shutdown 1 seconds ago
5sprz723zv3z779o3zcyj28p1   web.6        nginx:1.10   manager   Running
Running 30 seconds ago
```

As the upgrade starts, the `web.2` and `web.3` tasks have been updated and are now running `nginx:1.11`. The others are still running the old version. Every 30 seconds, two more tasks will be upgraded until the entire service is running `nginx:1.11`.

Docker Swarm does not care about the version that is used on the image tag. This means that you can just as easily downgrade the service. In this case, if the `docker service update --image nginx:1.10 web` command were to be run after the upgrade, swarm will go through the same update process until all tasks are running `nginx:1.10`. This can be very helpful if an upgrade does work as it was supposed to.

It is also important to note that there is nothing that says that the new image has to be the same base as the old one. You can decide to run Apache instead of Nginx by running `docker service update --image httpd web`. Swarm will happily replace all the web tasks which were running an `nginx` image with one running the `httpd` image.

Rolling updates require that your service is able to run multiple containers in parallel. This may not work for some services, such as SQL databases. Some updates may require a schema change that is incompatible with the older version. In either case, rolling updates may not work for the service. In those cases, you can set `--update-parallelism 0` to force all tasks to update at once or manually recreate the service. If you are running a lot of replicas, you should pre-pull your image to ease the load on your registry.

Using Docker Compose with swarm

Docker Compose can be used with Docker Swarm to build multi-container applications. You can configure your environment to use any node in the swarm and then use `docker-compose` just as you would when talking to a single Docker host. There are some serious issues using it for now.

Building images

One of the issues is image building. It is possible to use `docker-compose build` but the image will only appear on the node that `docker-compose` used to build the image. This is fine when running on a single host, but probably not what you want since you are running a swarm. To work around this, it is necessary to build your image manually with `docker build` and push it into a registry.

Starting an application

Starting an application with `docker-compose up` and swarm is exactly the same as running it with a single host. Unfortunately, Docker Compose does not use swarm to schedule containers. In fact, it prints a warning when you try:

```
$ docker-compose up -d
WARNING: The Docker Engine you're using is running in swarm mode.
Compose does not use swarm mode to deploy services to multiple nodes in a
swarm. All containers will be scheduled on the current node.
To deploy your application across the swarm, use the bundle feature of the
Docker experimental build.
    More info:
    https://docs.docker.com/compose/bundles
    Starting webdb_web_1
    Recreating webdb_db_1
```

The containers are started on the swarm node just as they would be if you were using a single Docker node. Scaling services within the application with `docker-compose scale` also works, but again, the additional containers are started on the same swarm node.

Bundling an application

Docker **Distributed Application Bundle** (**DAB**) and stacks are an experimental feature. The ability to build a bundle with `docker-compose` was added in Docker Compose 1.8 and Docker 1.12. At the time of writing, it is only possible to use bundles and stacks with an experimental version of Docker Engine. As such, the tools to work with bundles may change considerably before they are released.

Building a bundle is as simple as running `docker-compose bundle`. A `.dab` file will be created that corresponds to the namespace of the application. For example, an application with the `webdb` namespace will create a bundle file named `webdb.dab`. Once a bundle file is created, it can be used to create a stack.

Deploying a stack

Stacks are the collection of services and resources that are run on a swarm. When deployed to a swarm, all the required services are scheduled and started on swarm nodes. Once deployed, the list of running services can be shown with `docker service ls`:

```
$ docker deploy stackname
```

The preceding command will deploy a stack named `stackname`. All services started by `docker deploy` are prefixed with the stack name. By default, `docker deploy` will look for a `.dab` file that matches the stack name. For example, a stack named `webdb` will look for a `.dab` file named `webdb.dab`. A different file can be specified with the `--file` option:

```
$ docker deploy --file webdb.dab mystack
```

Introducing Docker Datacenter

Docker Datacenter is a commercial application from Docker. It is composed of the commercially supported Docker Engine, the UCP, and the DTR. The UCP provides a web-based interface to run containers and Docker Compose applications on a cluster.

Docker Datacenter cannot be layered on an existing swarm. Instead, each node is added in a similar manner to joining a swarm. From the first node in the new cluster, run the following command:

```
$ docker run --rm -it --name ucp -v
/var/run/docker.sock:/var/run/docker.sock docker/ucp install -i --host-
address <public ip>
```

This command uses the `docker/ucp` image to perform the installation. The Docker socket is passed in as a volume to allow the install script to start the needed containers. The `--host-address` is the public IP address that will be used to access UCP. The interactive install will prompt you for an administrative password so that you can log in to the web interface.

Applications can be run with Docker Compose just like they can with Docker Swarm. Unfortunately, similar restrictions apply here as with plain swarm. The containers are all started on the same node. There is no special scheduling as you might get with Docker Swarm. What you do get is a nice interface for seeing the state of the cluster, managing volumes and networks, and running individual containers and full applications.

Creating a new container is really easy. From the dashboard, click on **Containers** and **Deploy Container**. There will be a form that allows you set the container name, image, and any other options the container might need. Containers can also be started using the standard Docker command-like tools:

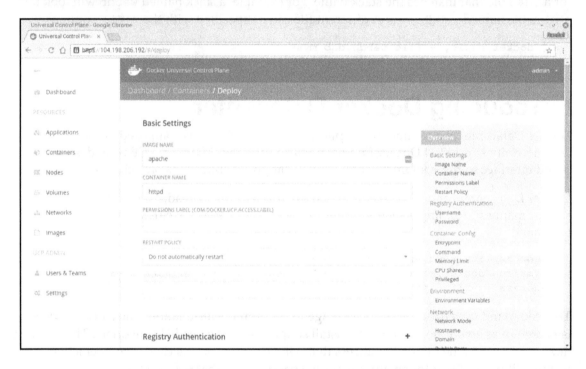

Docker Datacenter also supports running applications with Docker Compose. To run an application, go to **Applications** and click on **Compose Application**. You will be prompted for an application name and a compose file. The compose file, can be pasted into the box or uploaded from a file on your desktop. You can also use `docker-compose up` from your desktop or management server to launch applications:

Running applications appear on the **Applications** page. From there, you can scale services, restart containers, and even access the console of a running container:

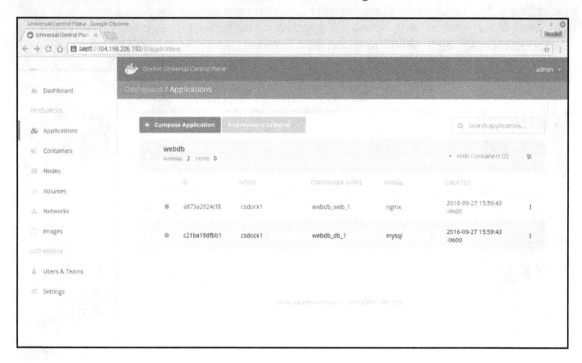

Summary

In this chapter, you have seen how to use Docker Swarm to orchestrate a Docker cluster. The same tools that are used with a single node can be used with a swarm. Additional tools available through swarm, allow for easy scale out of services and rolling updates with little to no downtime. In the next chapter, you will look at how to use Kubernetes to orchestrate your cluster.

5
Deploying and Managing Services with Kubernetes

Kubernetes was started at Google as a way for them to manage containers and was released as open source on June 2014. Other companies quickly jumped on board. Kubernetes is the backend for Red Hat OpenShift 3, Deis Workflow, and fabric8's **Platform as a Service (PaaS)** products. Everyday, more and more organizations are deploying Kubernetes to orchestrate their services.

Kubernetes is a huge project; there is no way to cover everything about it in a single chapter. This chapter will cover everything you need to get started orchestrating containers using Kubernetes. The full documentation can be found at `http://kubernetes.io/docs/`.

The following topics are covered in this chapter:

- Installing Kubernetes
- Running pods
- Managing deployments
- Using rolling updates to upgrade a deployment with zero downtime
- Using services and load balancers to expose your application to the Internet
- Using persistent volumes to preserve container data

Getting to know Kubernetes

Kubernetes is a complicated piece of software. As such, there are a number of components that an administrator needs to be aware of. Some will be used everyday while others will work quietly in the background to keep everything running.

Command-line tools

Following are the command-line tools:

- `kubeadm`: This tool was added in Kubernetes 1.4, as of this writing, still considered an alpha tool. It is the new installer for Kubernetes on Linux hosts.
- `kubectl`: This is the main tool used to interact with a running cluster. It is used to add pods and services, perform rolling updates, and much more. Nearly everyone who interacts with Kubernetes will use `kubectl`.

Master components

These components run on the master node. They are responsible for all of the high level controls of the cluster. Following are the master components:

- `etcd`: This is where Kubernetes keeps its cluster configuration. Make sure this is backed up or you will be unable to recover your cluster in the event of a total rebuild.
- `kube-apiserver`: The API server is the main point of contact for everything that interacts with the cluster. The `kubectl` tool uses it to manage services, the controllers use it for configuration, and much more. The `kube-apiserver` component is the only component on the master that needs to be accessible outside the cluster. It is also the only component that needs to connect to `etcd`.
- `kube-controller-manager`: Unsurprisingly, this manages the running controllers. This includes replication controllers, node controllers, third-party controllers, and service accounts.
- `kube-scheduler`: This schedules pods to run in the cluster. Any time new pods are started or scaled, the scheduler determines which nodes to run them on.

Node components

Node components run on the worker nodes. They control running containers, networking, and other services. They are as follows:

- `kubelet`: This is the main processing daemon on each node. It is responsible for starting containers, mounting volumes, downloading secrets, and keeping the node part of the cluster.
- `kube-proxy`: This is responsible for maintaining the network rules and forwards network requests to the correct location.

Installing Kubernetes

Kubernetes can be installed on most cloud services or locally on your own hardware or virtual machines. Unsurprisingly, since Kubernetes is a Google project, it runs best on GCE and new features tend to be supported there first.

In addition, Google has rolled out a service called **Google Container Engine** (**GKE**), which is a pre-rolled Kubernetes service. Google maintains the Kubernetes master and makes it easy to add new nodes to the cluster. You only need to worry about the containers. This is the easiest way to get started with Kubernetes.

For local installations, there are several options. The first is the new `kubeadm` tool which was released as a beta tool with Kubernetes 1.4. Second, there is the `kube-up.sh` script which is part of the Kubernetes release package which can install Kubernetes on a variety of platforms.

There are two other options worth considering. RHEL has a `kubernetes` package available which is installable with `yum`. The Rancher container management suite has an option to automatically deploy Kubernetes environments.

Installing with kubeadm

The `kubeadm` tool was introduced in Kubernetes 1.4. The goal is to provide an easy way to install Kubernetes on any platform. For now, it only supports CentOS 7 and Ubuntu 16.04. Installation using `kubeadm` is still a little messy but it is an exciting start. For more details, refer to `http://kubernetes.io/docs/getting-started-guides/kubeadm/`.

Installing with kube-up.sh

GCE is the most fully supported way of running Kubernetes. The only serious difference between running Kubernetes on GCE compared to anywhere else is how external services are mapped to running pods. GCE also does a lot of the grunt work for you such as managing firewall settings and registering new nodes with the cluster:

```
$ export KUBERNETES_PROVIDER=gce; wget -O - https://get.k8s.io | bash
```

If you do not like the security risks of piping a downloaded script directly to bash or if you want to make changes to the install options, you can download the latest release, unpack it, and run `kube-up.sh` manually:

```
$ cd kubernetes/cluster/
$ export KUBERNETES_PROVIDER=gce; ./kube-up.sh
```

The script will create a new Kubernetes master and a number of worker nodes. When it is done, it will create a `kubeconfig` file in `~/.kube/config`. You will then be able to interact with the cluster using `kubectl`.

A number of other cloud providers are available for installation with `kube-up.sh` including AWS, Azure, and GKE. It can also install a test cluster using Vagrant for local testing. For a full list and instructions on adapting `kube-up.sh` for your environment, refer to `http://kubernetes.io/docs/getting-started-guides/binary_release/`.

Installing add-ons

Kubernetes supports using add-ons to extend the functionality of the cluster. Most common are the `kube-dns` and `kube-ui` add-ons, which provide DNS-SD and a graphical view of the cluster, respectively. Add-ons can also be used to install different tools, such as Weave Net, for overlay networks. A list of available add-ons can be found at: `http://kubernetes.io/docs/admin/addons/`.

Managing resources

Every resource in Kubernetes is defined in a file in either JSON or YAML format. The two formats are completely interchangeable. YAML is usually easier for a human to read. It is possible to have some resources defined in YAML and others in JSON. As a best practice, pick a format and stick to it.

Creating resources

All resources will have at least two fields:

- `apiVersion`: This is the version of the API that is being used. As new features are added, the version may change.
- `kind`: This is the type of resource. This tells Kubernetes what type of resource is being created.

Each resource may be defined in a separate file. In some cases, it is worth combining resources into a single file. For example, it makes sense to define an ingress object in the same file as the service that it exposes. In that case, separate the resources with three dashes, ---, alone on a line. Following is an example showing how to do this:

```
apiVersion: v1
kind: Service
metadata:
  name: wp-service
  labels:
    app: wordpress
spec:
  ports:
    - port: 443
      name: https
  selector:
    app: wordpress
---
apiVersion: extensions/v1beta1
kind: Ingress
metadata:
  name: wp-ingress
spec:
  backend:
    serviceName: wp-service
    servicePort: 80
```

Once the resource is defined, it is added to Kubernetes by running `kubectl create`. The -f flag tells `kubectl` to read the resource definition from the given file. If the file name is a dash (-), the resource is read from `stdin`:

```
$ kubectl create -f multi-deployment.yml
deployment "multi-deploy" created
```

It is also possible to tell `kubectl create` to read all of the files in a directory by adding the -R flag and setting -f to a directory name. This makes it easy to put all of the resources for a specific application in a directory and load them all at once.

The Kubernetes project has created a tool called Helm which can be used to package pre-configured resources. For more information see `https://github.com/kubernetes/helm`.

Deleting resources

Resources are deleted with the `kubectl delete` command. At its simplest, `kubectl delete` is called with the type and name of the resource to delete:

```
$ kubectl delete service wp-service
service "wp-service" deleted
```

Like the `create` command, `delete` can use the -f flag to pass in a file. Every resource defined in the file will be deleted. The -R flag can also be used to delete every resource defined in a directory.

Running pods

Kubernetes organizes containers into pods. Each pod is a collection of one or more containers. A pod can be replicated, scaled, and updated independently of other pods running in the cluster. Each pod is assigned an IP address, which is used to connect to the exposed ports of containers running in the pod. Care must be taken to ensure that services within a pod do not try to use the same port, but that is much easier to coordinate than managing port usage across a Docker Swarm.

Defining a pod

Pods define one or more containers as well as all of the volumes that the containers need. The containers operate as a single unit. They are all started and stopped together. They can also communicate with each other on localhost. The pod is defined using YAML or JSON and passed to `kubectl create`. Following is a simple pod definition:

```
apiVersion: v1
kind: Pod
metadata:
  name: simple
spec:
```

```
containers:
  - name: web
    image: nginx
    ports:
      - containerPort: 80
      - containerPort: 443
```

The preceding YAML file defines a simple pod that runs a single `nginx` container. The `name` field sets the name of the pod. In this case, the pod is named `simple`. The `generateName` field may be used instead of the `name` field, this takes a prefix for an automatically generated name. This is useful if you need to run multiple, independent copies of the pod.

The `spec` field is where the pod's containers and volumes are defined. The `containers` field takes a list of one or more containers. The preceding example creates a single container named `web`. The container image is set with the `image` field. These are the only two required fields for containers.

The `ports` field defines the ports that will be exposed on the pod's IP address. This is the port in the container, not the port that will be made public. Setting the external port will be covered with service resources later in this chapter.

The `ports` field uses TCP by default. The `protocol` can be set to UDP as an additional field to the port. The following snippet shows what it would look like:

```
ports:
  - containerPort: 53
    protocol: UDP
```

There is a lot more to pods than can be covered in one chapter. For full details, refer to the pod specification at: `http://kubernetes.io/docs/api-reference/v1/definitions/#_v1_p odspec`.

Once the pod specification is written to a file, the pod can be added to Kubernetes with `kubectl create`:

```
$ kubectl create -f simple-pod.yml
pod "simple" created
```

Viewing pods

A list of running pods is available by running `kubectl get pods`. Adding `-o wide` will show the pod's IP address and the node that the pod is running on:

```
$ kubectl get pods
NAME       READY     STATUS     RESTARTS    AGE
simple     1/1       Running    0           12s
$ kubectl get pods -o wide
NAME       READY     STATUS     RESTARTS    AGE       IP              NODE
simple     1/1       Running    0           1m        10.246.46.5
kubernetes-node-1
```

The details of a pod are available using the `kubectl describe pod` command. Everything you need to know about a running pod is displayed in the output of `describe`. The following command displays the details for a pod named `simple`:

```
$ kubectl describe pod simple
Name:          simple
Namespace:     default
Node:          kubernetes-node-1/10.245.1.3
Start Time:    Wed, 05 Oct 2016 18:55:46 -0600
Labels:        <none>
Status:        Running
IP:            10.246.46.5
Controllers:   <none>
Containers:
  web:
    Container ID:    docker://6460c3565b2c0d7cb356f0d
    a2ea5e12f58017e881fb91176eafbf65b5a46bc31
    Image:           nginx
    Image ID:        docker://sha256:ba6bed934df2e644fdd34
    e9d324c80f3c615544ee9a93e4ce3cfddfcf84bdbc2
    Ports:           80/TCP, 443/TCP
    Requests:
      cpu:           100m
    State:           Running
      Started:       Wed, 05 Oct 2016 18:55:48 -0600
    Ready:           True
    Restart Count:   0
    Volume Mounts:   /var/run/secrets/kubernetes.io/
    serviceaccount from default-token-dlmur (ro)
    Environment Variables:       <none>
Conditions:
  Type         Status
  Initialized  True
  Ready        True
```

```
   PodScheduled  True
Volumes:
  default-token-dlmur:
    Type:        Secret (a volume populated by a Secret)
    SecretName: default-token-dlmur
QoS Class:       Burstable
Tolerations:     <none>
Events:
  FirstSeen      LastSeen        Count   From
SubobjectPath            Type              Reason        Message
  ---------      ---------       -----   ----                        ---
  ----------              ---------       ------        -------
     7s              7s            1         {default-scheduler }
Normal           Scheduled       Successfully assigned simple to
kubernetes-node-1
    . . .
```

Environment

Many containers use environment variables to configure how they run. The mysql image uses environment variables to initialize a database and set user passwords. The wordpress image uses environment variables to configure the location of a MySQL database and set the appropriate credentials in the configuration.

Here is an example pod that runs the mysql image and sets two environment variables. The first, MYSQL_ROOT_PASSWORD, sets the password for the root user. The second, MYSQL_DATABASE, configures the container to create a database named wordpress:

```
apiVersion: v1
kind: Pod
metadata:
  name: mysql
  labels:
    app: mysql
spec:
  containers:
    - name: db
      image: mysql:5.7
      ports:
        - containerPort: 3306
      env:
        - name: MYSQL_ROOT_PASSWORD
          value: password
        - name: MYSQL_DATABASE
          value: wordpress
```

Multi-container pods

It is possible to define pods that run multiple containers. This is especially useful when migrating legacy applications into Docker and Kubernetes.

One of the great things about pods is that every container in a pod can connect to any other container within the pod on localhost. This makes it fairly straightforward to migrate legacy applications into Kubernetes. With standalone Docker, each container is assigned its own random IP address. That can make it difficult for the containers to find each other unless a DNS-SD tool is installed. Even worse, because each container gets a different IP, a separate component such as HAProxy must be used to unify them under a single IP address for end users.

For example, suppose you had a Samba file server with a web interface and SFTP server for off-site access. Every service communicates with the others on localhost and are accessible from the same IP address and hostname. It is very convenient to be able to tell users to connect to `myfiles.example.com` no matter which service they wish to use to access their files.

By combining those services into a single pod, the application can be treated almost the same way it would as if it were on a single host. They still communicate with each other on localhost and are still available from a single IP address. Later, as work is done to decouple components and make them multiple pods, they can still be united under a single service. This service is assigned the single IP to which the hostname can be mapped. Services will be covered later in this chapter.

Let's look at an example multi-container pod that starts WordPress with a MySQL database. This example creates a pod named `multi`. This time, the `containers` field lists two containers. The first is named `wordpress` and runs the official `wordpress` image. The second is named `db` and runs the `mysql` image:

```
apiVersion: v1
kind: Pod
metadata:
  name: multi
  labels:
    app: wordpress
spec:
  containers:
    - name: wordpress
      image: wordpress
      ports:
        - containerPort: 80
        - containerPort: 443
      env:
```

```
        - name: WORDPRESS_DB_HOST
          value: 127.0.0.1
        - name: WORDPRESS_DB_USER
          value: wordpress
        - name: WORDPRESS_DB_PASSWORD
          value: password
    - name: db
      image: mysql
      env:
        - name: MYSQL_ROOT_PASSWORD
          value: password
        - name: MYSQL_DATABASE
          value: wordpress
        - name: MYSQL_USER
          value: wordpress
        - name: MYSQL_PASSWORD
          value: password
```

There are a couple of things to note with this example:

- First, the `wordpress` container is configured to look for MySQL on `127.0.0.1` which is localhost.
- Second, the `db` container has no ports defined. This is because the database does not need to be exposed on the pod's IP address.

The only containers that can connect to the database are the ones in the same pod.

Using secrets

The WordPress example in the previous section is pretty exciting, but all of your security conscious administrators are probably having a small heart attack over the plain text passwords in the pod definition. The good news is that Kubernetes makes it possible to separate out things that should be secret into a special `Secret` type. Secrets can be used to keep things such as passwords out of pod definitions or they can be used to provide different passwords, SSL certificates, or SSH keys in different namespaces without needing to change the pod definitions.

Creating secrets

Secrets are `base64` encoded strings. On Linux, the strings can be encoded with the `base64` tool. Once the string is encoded, it can be added to the YAML or JSON file that defines the secret:

```
$ echo -n "root-password" | base64
cm9vdC1wYXNzd29yZA==
```

Following is an example that defines two secret passwords for the `root` and `wordpress` users for the preceding WordPress application:

```
apiVersion: v1
kind: Secret
metadata:
  name: mysql-passwords
type: Opaque
data:
  root: cm9vdC1wYXNzd29yZA==
  wordpress: d29yZHByZXNzLXBhc3N3b3Jk
```

YAML defines a new secret named `mysql-passwords`. The secrets are in the `data` section. The `root` and `wordpress` keys will be used to reference the passwords from the node definition.

Secrets can be displayed with `kubectl describe secret`. Well, almost. The `secret` object with its associated labels and a list of keys is displayed, but the keys themselves are hidden:

```
$ kubectl describe secret mysql-passwords
Name:           mysql-passwords
Namespace:      default
Labels:         <none>
Annotations:    <none>
Type:    Opaque
Data
====
wordpress:      18 bytes
root:           13 bytes
```

It is important to note that the secrets that are not encrypted are fairly easy to get. They are hidden when the secret is described with `kubectl describe secret`, however, a user with the appropriate access can log in to a running container that is using a secret and print it out. Do not rely on secrets to keep your passwords and other sensitive secrets safe. For more details refer to `http://kubernetes.io/docs/user-guide/secrets/`.

Using secrets in environment variables

There are two ways of getting the keys into the containers. The first is through environment variables. Following is the WordPress pod definition again. This time the passwords are retrieved from the `mysql-passwords` secret object. The `key` option states which secret from the `mysql-passwords` secret object is used. The relevant sections are highlighted. Inside the containers, the `*_PASSWORD` environment variables will have the decoded values:

```
apiVersion: v1
kind: Pod
metadata:
  name: multi-secrets
  labels:
    app: wordpress
spec:
  containers:
    - name: wordpress
      image: wordpress
      ports:
        - containerPort: 80
        - containerPort: 443
      env:
        - name: WORDPRESS_DB_HOST
          value: 127.0.0.1
        - name: WORDPRESS_DB_USER
          value: wordpress
        - name: WORDPRESS_DB_PASSWORD
          valueFrom:
            secretKeyRef:
              name: mysql-passwords
              key: wordpress
    - name: db
      image: mysql
      env:
        - name: MYSQL_ROOT_PASSWORD
          valueFrom:
            secretKeyRef:
              name: mysql-passwords
              key: root
        - name: MYSQL_DATABASE
```

```
        value: wordpress
    - name: MYSQL_USER
        value: wordpress
    - name: MYSQL_PASSWORD
      valueFrom:
        secretKeyRef:
          name: mysql-passwords
          key: wordpress
```

Using secrets in files

The other option is to have the secret available as files in the container. This is done through **volumes**. A volume that contains the decoded secret values in files named after the keys is created. This can be useful for adding SSL certificates and SSH keys to a container. The application can be configured to use the mounted secrets volume, or a small wrapper script can copy the file to a place the application can find it.

Following is a simple pod running `nginx`. It creates a volume that is mounted in the container at `/etc/secrets`. This example uses the same `mysql-passwords` secret as the previous example:

```
apiVersion: v1
kind: Pod
metadata:
  name: nginx-secrets
spec:
  containers:
    - name: nginx
      image: nginx
      volumeMounts:
        - name: secrets
          mountPath: "/etc/secrets"
          readOnly: true
  volumes:
    - name: secrets
      secret:
      secretName: mysql-passwords
```

In the container, the decoded secrets are available in `/etc/secrets`. Each secret is stored in a file in the volume:

```
# cd /etc/secrets/
# ls
root    wordpress
# cat root
root-password
```

Logging into a container

It is often necessary to log in to a container to troubleshoot problems. The same functionality as `docker exec` is available in Kubernetes as `kubectl exec`. As one might expect, `kubectl exec` is a little bit different to account for the concept of pods:

```
$ kubectl exec multi-secrets -c wordpress -it bash
root@multi-secrets:/var/www/html#
```

This example starts a bash shell in the `wordpress` container from the `multi-secrets` pod. The `-i` and `-t` flags work just like in `docker exec` by telling `exec` to take input from stdin and to create a new TTY.

If the command that you want to run has flags, the command can be prefixed by two dashes (`--`). Following is an example that opens a MySQL shell in the `db` container in the `mysql-secrets` pod:

```
$ kubectl exec multi-secrets -c db -it -- mysql -u root -p
Enter password:
Welcome to the MySQL monitor.  Commands end with ; or \g.
Your MySQL connection id is 3
Server version: 5.7.15 MySQL Community Server (GPL)
Copyright (c) 2000, 2016, Oracle and/or its affiliates. All rights
reserved.
Oracle is a registered trademark of Oracle Corporation and/or its
affiliates. Other names may be trademarks of their respective owners.
Type 'help;' or '\h' for help. Type '\c' to clear the current input
statement.
mysql>
```

The `-c` flag can be omitted if the pod has only one container or if you want to connect to the first container in the pod. You can use `-c` even if the pod only has one container to avoid confusion.

Deleting a pod

When a pod is no longer needed, it can be deleted with `kubectl delete pod`. The following example deletes a pod named `simple`:

```
$ kubectl delete pod simple
pod "simple" deleted
```

Using deployments

A **deployment** is a set of pods with one or more replicas. It is responsible for ensuring that the requested number of pods are running and restarting them, if necessary. Deployments make it easy to scale out pods and update them later. Deployments supersede the `ReplicationController` resource.

Creating a single container deployment

One of the joys of Docker is the ability to start containers quickly and easily. Kubernetes can be complicated, but it is still easy to start a single container:

```
$ kubectl run web --image=nginx:1.11 --replicas=2 --port=80
deployment "web" created
```

The preceding command creates a new deployment named `web` that is running two `nginx` images. The `--replicas` flag can be used to set the number of replicas desired. If omitted, only one pod is started. The `--port` flag tells Kubernetes to expose port 80. The `--port` flag may be used multiple times to expose additional ports.

The `kubectl get deployments` command will show all of the current deployments in the cluster. In this case, it shows that both pod replicas are running, up to date, and available:

```
$ kubectl get deployments
NAME       DESIRED     CURRENT     UP-TO-DATE     AVAILABLE     AGE
web        2           2           2              2             12s
```

A list of running pods is available from the `kubectl get pods` command. The `-l` flag limits the display to pods with the given label(s). When the `run` command is used, the pods are automatically given the `run=<name>` label, where `<name>` is the name of the deployment. To limit the list to only pods from the `run` named `web`, use the following command:

```
$ kubectl get pods -l run=web
NAME                       READY       STATUS       RESTARTS     AGE web-4291803130-
haisr    1/1       Running    0              13m web-4291803130-j7y51    1/1
Running    0              13m
```

Both replicas are running and ready to serve web pages.

Creating a multi-container deployment

Multi-container deployments require that the deployment be defined in YAML or JSON. The file specifies the name of the deployment, the number of replicas, and the pod specification. This same format can also be used for single container deployments:

```
apiVersion: extensions/v1beta1
kind: Deployment
metadata:
  name: multi-deploy
spec:
  replicas: 2
  template:
    metadata:
      labels:
        app: web-deploy
    spec:
      containers:
        - name: nginx
          image: nginx:1.10.4
        - name: mysql
          image: mysql:5.5
          env:
            - name: MYSQL_ROOT_PASSWORD
              value: password
```

The example creates two pods with two containers—`nginx` and `mysql`. The pod is defined in the `template` section of the deployment definition. It works just like the pods already covered in this chapter. The biggest difference is that the pod name is omitted. Pod names will be based on the deployment name.

Take note of `apiVersion`. Deployments are a new feature and still, officially, in beta. The specification may change in later versions.

Scaling a deployment

Kubernetes makes it easy to increase or decrease the number of replicas in a deployment with the `scale` command. The following command scales the deployment named `web` to three replicas:

```
$ kubectl scale --replicas=3 deployment/web
deployment "web" scaled
```

A deployment can be scaled up or down as much as you need. The scheduler will ensure that the required pods are started across the cluster.

Rolling updates

Deployments in Kubernetes have a feature that allows all of the pods in a deployment to be updated automatically. Updates are triggered whenever a part of the pod specification in the `template` section of a deployment is changed.

Updating a deployment

Consider the following deployment which has two containers. The first, named `web`, is an `nginx:1.10.1` image. The second, named `db`, is a `mysql:5.5` image:

```
apiVersion: extensions/v1beta1
kind: Deployment
metadata:
  name: update-deploy
spec:
  replicas: 2
  template:
    metadata:
      labels:
        app: update-deploy
    spec:
      containers:
        - name: web
          image: nginx:1.10.1
        - name: db
          image: mysql:5.5
          env:
            - name: MYSQL_ROOT_PASSWORD
              value: password
```

Both containers are running older versions of their images. Let's start by upgrading the `web` container:

```
$ kubectl set image deployment/update-deploy web=nginx:1.11.4
deployment "update-deploy" image updated
```

This commands sets the `image` attribute of the `web` container in the `update-deploy` deployment to `nginx:1.11.4`. Immediately after that command is run, Kubernetes starts a new pod with the updated image. When the new pod is ready, one of the existing pods is stopped. This process is repeated until all of the replicas are updated.

A word of warning. Make sure that your container can run multiple times safely before updating a deployment. By default, Kubernetes uses the same mechanism to perform updates as it does to scale pods. If your application cannot run multiple copies, you can set the update `strategy` type to `Recreate` in the deployment definition. Kubernetes will then stop the existing pods before starting new ones. The following excerpt shows how to set the deployment strategy:

```
apiVersion: extensions/v1beta1
kind: Deployment
metadata:
  name: update-deploy
spec:
  strategy:
    type: "Recreate"
...
```

Getting the rollout history

Kubernetes remembers the changes that have been made to the deployment. The revision history is available by running the `kubectl rollout history deploy/<name>` command, where `<name>` is the name of the deployment:

```
$ kubectl rollout history deployment/update-deploy
deployments "update-deploy"
REVISION          CHANGE-CAUSE
1                 <none>
2                 <none>
```

Full details of the deployment are available by adding `--revision=N` to the history command, where `N` is revision number. In the following output, you can see that the image for the `web` container was updated to `nginx:1.11.4`:

```
$ kubectl rollout history deployment/update-deploy --revision=2 deployments
"update-deploy" with revision #2
Labels:     app=update-deploy
            pod-template-hash=1680774371
Containers:
  web:
    Image:      nginx:1.11.4
    Port:
    Volume Mounts:      <none>
    Environment Variables:      <none>
  db:
    Image:      mysql:5.5
    Port:
    Volume Mounts:      <none>
    Environment Variables:
      MYSQL_ROOT_PASSWORD:      password
No volumes.
```

Rolling back an update

You may find that, after the update, something has gone horribly wrong, and that the update needs to be rolled back. Fortunately, there is a very convenient `undo` command:

```
$ kubectl rollout undo deploy/update-deploy
deployment "update-deploy" rolled back
```

Without options, the command will revert the named deployment to the previous one in the history. The `--to-revision=N` flag will revert the deployment to revision `N` from the history.

Deleting a deployment

Remember that the job of a deployment is to ensure that the required number of pods are running. Trying to delete a deployment by deleting the pods is like Sisyphus trying to roll a rock up a hill. Kubernetes will keep recreating the pods as fast as they are deleted. When a deployment is no longer needed, it can be deleted with `kubectl delete deployment`. Make sure that you want to proceed because this will delete all running pods which are part of the deployment:

```
$ kubectl delete deployment web
deployment "web" deleted
```

It is possible to delete a deployment while leaving the pods running, using the `--cascade=false` flag. The leftover pods will have to be deleted manually.

Running pods on every node with DaemonSets

A **DaemonSet** is a type of resource that ensures a pod or set of pods runs on every node in the cluster. The format of the resource is very similar to that of a deployment. The `template` section is a pod specification just like a deployment:

```
apiVersion: extensions/v1beta1
kind: DaemonSet
metadata:
  name: daemon
spec:
  template:
...
```

DaemonSets are useful for running services such as logging or monitoring. For example, you might have a service such as `collectd` which sends performance data to a monitoring solution.

It is also possible to limit a DaemonSet to only run on a set of nodes that match a given selector. For example, your local Kubernetes cluster may have a mix of server hardware from HP and Dell. You can create a DaemonSet that runs the Dell OpenManage tools on nodes that have a `hardware` label set to `dell`:

```
apiVersion: extensions/v1beta1
kind: DaemonSet
metadata:
  name: omsa
spec:
  template:
    spec:
      nodeSelector:
        hardware: dell
...
```

Introducing scheduled jobs

Kubernetes 1.4 introduced scheduled jobs. These are sets of containers that run on a schedule. They are similar to Cron jobs in Linux and even use the Cron time format in the specification. Scheduled jobs are still considered alpha and are not available unless the `--runtime-config=batch/v2alpha1` flag is added to the API server on startup. For more details refer to `http://kubernetes.io/docs/user-guide/jobs/`.

Using labels

Nearly every resource in Kubernetes can be assigned labels. Labels are a way to organize your resources but do not change how they operate. They are completely arbitrary and should be chosen to fit your environment. For example, you may want to group resources by application, label pods that are currently in testing, or signify that certain pods should only run on frontend nodes.

Labels are set in the `metadata` section of a resource. They are a series of key/value pairs. In the following example, the pod has four labels set. The `app` label is used to show that this pod is part of the `wordpress` application. The `tier` label signifies that this pod should run on backend nodes. This pod is still in testing so the `env` label is set appropriately. Finally, the `hero` label exists in this example to show how arbitrary labels are:

```
apiVersion: v1
kind: Pod
metadata:
  name: mysql
  labels:
    app: wordpress
    tier: backend
    env: testing
    hero: darkwing-duck
...
```

By themselves, labels do nothing. When a resource is created, Kubernetes notes the labels and goes about scheduling the resource somewhere in the cluster.

Using selectors to find resources

All of the tools that list resources can take a selector with the `-l` flag to limit the list to resources with labels that match. This was used earlier in the chapter to see the list of pods started by a deployment:

```
$ kubectl get pods -l 'app=update-deploy'
NAME                      READY      STATUS      RESTARTS      AGE
update-deploy-1680774371-9x8qd    2/2      Running     0            23h
update-deploy-1680774371-y0tbf    2/2      Running     0            23h
```

This example lists all of the pods with the `app` key and the `update-deploy` value. There are several different comparison operators that can be used. Wrap the selector in single quotes to ensure that the shell handles spaces and special characters properly:

Operator	Description	Example
=, ==	The value of the key must match.	env = production
!=	The value of the key must not match.	env != production
in	The value is in a set of values.	env in (testing, development)

notin	The value is not in a set of values.	`env notin (testing, development)`
`label`	Does the resource have the label? The value is ignored.	`app`
`!label`	Resources without the given label. The value is ignored.	`!app`
, (comma)	Joins multiple queries. All queries must match.	`env in (production, testing), app=website`

There are a few resources in Kubernetes that use labels. The service resource, for example, groups pods that match a selector for load balancing and external access. Every time a pod that matches what the service is looking for is created, it is automatically added to the group.

 Full details on using labels and selectors may be found at `http://kubernetes.io/docs/user-guide/labels/`.

Using namespaces

Kubernetes uses **namespaces** as a logical separation between groups of running pods and their associated volumes, services, and controllers. By default, Kubernetes has two namespaces:

- `kube-system`: This is used for containers running Kubernetes services and add-ons
- `default`: This is where everything else runs

Namespaces can be used as a way of providing different environments for development and production, between two business units, or even multiple customers. It is also possible to define resource limits per namespace.

Viewing namespaces

It is possible to list the currently configured namespaces. Use the `kubectl get namespaces` command:

```
$ kubectl get namespaces
NAME            STATUS     AGE
default         Active     3h
kube-system     Active     3h
```

Details of a specific namespace can be displayed with `kubectl describe namespace`. This includes the overall quota on the namespace as well as resource limits on individual entities:

```
$ kubectl describe namespace default
Name:    default
Labels: <none>
Status: Active
No resource quota.
Resource Limits
Type              Resource         Min      Max      Default Request Default
Limit  Max Limit/Request Ratio
    ----              --------         ---      ---      ---------------- -------
------  ----------------------
    Container         cpu                       -        -        100m                -
    -
```

Creating namespaces

A new namespace is defined in a YAML file. This example creates a namespace named `production`:

```
apiVersion: v1
kind: Namespace
metadata:
  name: production
```

Then pass the namespace definition file to `kubectl create`:

```
$ kubectl create -f production-ns.yaml
namespace "production" created
```

Switching namespaces

Once a namespace is created, it is possible to take actions on that namespace. For one off changes, the --namespace option can be passed to kubectl:

```
$ kubectl --namespace=kube-system get pods
NAME                                      READY     STATUS     RESTARTS   AGE
    heapster-v1.2.0-3649594813-4zdoy        0/4       Pending    0
4h
    kube-dns-v19-zma1s                      3/3       Running    0
4h
    kube-proxy-kubernetes-node-1            1/1       Running    0
3h
    kubernetes-dashboard-v1.4.0-pbhe2       1/1       Running    0
4h
    monitoring-influxdb-grafana-v4-zc7x4    2/2       Running    0
4h
```

If you plan on doing a lot of work in a namespace, it is best to create a context. This example creates a context named production that uses the production namespace:

```
$ kubectl config set-context production --namespace=production
context "production" set.
```

The flags --cluster and --user can be used to set the cluster and username for the context, if they are different. Once a context is set, it is easy to switch to it whenever you need to. The following example switches to the production context. Now every command that is run with kubectl will be in the production namespace:

```
$ kubectl config use-context production
switched to context "production".
```

Deleting a namespace

A namespace may be a temporary sandbox or a long running environment. Whatever you use namespaces for, you may need to delete one. The following command will delete the production namespace:

```
$ kubectl delete namespace production
namespace "production" deleted
```

Take a deep breath before deleting a namespace. Doing so will destroy anything in that namespace including pods, services, and volumes. Make sure there is nothing important in the namespace before you delete it.

Networking

Networking in Kubernetes is different from straight Docker, in that, IP addresses are assigned per pod rather than per container. This allows containers within a pod to connect to each other on localhost. It also allows them to act as one service. This is more akin to the traditional server model than most Docker tools. In addition, Kubernetes provides tools for doing automatic load balancing for applications and can work with most cloud providers to use their existing load balancers to provide external access.

Kubernetes requires the use of an overlay network to allow pods to communicate across the cluster. It supports GCE, Weave, Flannel, OpenVSwitch, and others either out-of-the-box or with an add-on. DNS-SD is also available out-of-the-box through the `kube-dns` add-on, but other services can be used instead.

Services

Kubernetes assigns each pod an IP address, but that address will change every time the pod is restarted. In addition, the IP assigned to the pod is a private address that is not accessible outside of the cluster. Neither is helpful if you want to make the application public. The solution is a service.

Services provide load balancing and maintain a static IP address for as long as the service exists. Pods can be restarted, updated, or scaled and the service will keep track of them and route traffic appropriately. This is done using selectors.

Creating a service

As discussed previously, pods and deployments can have labels assigned. A service uses those labels to determine which pods to send traffic to. Let's look at an example:

```
apiVersion: extensions/v1beta1
kind: Deployment
metadata:
  name: wp
spec:
  replicas: 1
  template:
    metadata:
      labels:
        app: wordpress
    spec:
      containers:
```

```
        - name: wordpress
          image: wordpress
          ports:
            - containerPort: 80
            - containerPort: 443
. . .
```

This is an abbreviated deployment for a WordPress install. Notice that the label `app` has been set to `wordpress`. Now, let's take a look at a service for this application:

```
apiVersion: v1
kind: Service
metadata:
  name: wp-service
  labels:
    app: wordpress
spec:
  type: LoadBalancer
  ports:
    - port: 80
      name: http
    - port: 443
      name: https
  selector:
    app: wordpress
```

There are a couple of things to note here. The `ports` section lists all of the ports that this service will expose. If the ports match the ports set with `containerPort`, then there is nothing more to do. If not, the `targetPort` field can be added to the `port` entry with the port that the container is listening on. The following example shows how to send port 80 in the service to port 5000 in the pod:

```
ports:
  - port: 80
    name: http
    targetPort: 5000
```

The `selector` field is where the service is configured to know which pods to serve. In this case, the service is looking for pods or deployments with the `app` label set to `wordpress`. Any new pod that shows up in the namespace that matches the selector will be automatically added to the service.

> Make sure that the selectors for services do not overlap. It would be *bad*. If they do overlap, there will be contention and the possibility that your applications will appear in multiple services. Your WordPress service, for example, might suddenly be showing your accounting application.

The `Type` field tells Kubernetes how this service will be exposed:

- `ClusterIP`: This is the default type. It assigns the service an IP from a pre-configured pool. This address is almost always private and only accessible from within the cluster. Use this if your service is only servicing other applications in Kubernetes.
- `NodePort`: This allocates a random port from 30,000 to 32,767 on every node in the cluster. Any request to that node will be sent to the pods targeted by the service. A specific port can be set with the `nodePort` option on a port entry. The port must still be within the configured range. The `NodePort` type is useful if you want to run your own load balancer.
- `LoadBalancer`: This will start a cloud-specific load balancer to handle traffic for the service.

There is much more to services than can be covered here. For more details refer to `http://kubernetes.io/docs/user-guide/services/`.

Listing services

The list of services is available by running `kubectl get service`. The list will show the services, cluster IP and the external IP address if one has been assigned:

```
$ kubectl get service
NAME             CLUSTER-IP      EXTERNAL-IP        PORT(S)          AGE
kubernetes       10.3.240.1      <none>             443/TCP          2h
wp-service       10.3.242.67     104.154.253.227    80/TCP,443/TCP   1h
```

A detailed description of a service is also available by running `kubectl describe service` with the service name. The description includes the cluster IP, port list, and the ingress port:

```
$ kubectl describe service wp-service
Name:                     wp-service
Namespace:                default
Labels:                   app=wordpress
Selector:                 app=wordpress
Type:                     LoadBalancer
IP:                       10.3.242.67
LoadBalancer Ingress:     104.154.253.227
Port:                     http      80/TCP
NodePort:                 http      31342/TCP
Endpoints:                10.0.2.3:80
Port:                     https     443/TCP
```

```
NodePort:                https    30763/TCP
Endpoints:               10.0.2.3:443
Session Affinity:        None
No events.
```

Introducing DNS-SD

Kubernetes ships with an add-on called `kube-dns` which provides DNS-SD. In recent versions of Kubernetes, this is enabled by default. Names are assigned to services. It is expected that if pods need to talk to each other, they will do it through a service.

Generated hostnames are in the `service_name.namespace.svc.cluster.local` form, where `service_name` is the name of the service and `namespace` is the namespace the service is running in. For example, a service named `wordpress` in the `prod` namespace would have an `A` record that is `wordpress.prod.svc.cluster.local`.

Using volumes

Like plain Docker, Kubernetes supports volumes. The main difference is that Kubernetes supports them at the pod level. This means that a volume configured in a pod is available and may be used by every container in the pod for reading and writing. Second, Kubernetes volumes may use multiple different types of network storage at the same time.

Volumes come in two forms, the first is an **ephemeral volume** that lives only as long as the pod using it. When the pod is deleted, so is the volume. The second is a **persistent volume** that persists data even when a pod is deleted.

Using plain volumes

Volumes in Kubernetes behave a lot like volumes do in plain Docker. They are only expected to live as long as the pods using them. Every container in the pod may mount the volume and they may mount in the same or different locations. The only restriction is that volumes cannot be mounted on filesystems that are mounted from other volumes. In other words, volumes may not nest:

```
apiVersion: v1
kind: Pod
metadata:
  name: web
spec:
```

```
volumes:
  - name: test
    gcePersistentDisk:
      pdName: test-pd
      fsType: ext4
containers:
  - name: nginx
    image: nginx
    volumeMounts:
      - mountPath: /mnt
        name: test
```

This is a simple pod that uses a GCE persistent disk named `test-pd`. Volumes are defined in the `volumes` section. As many volumes as may be needed can be defined there. The `nginx` container mounts the volume in `/mnt`. The name in `volumeMounts` must match the name in volumes.

The options for the volume will vary depending on the type of disk. Note that many types of networked storage must exist before it can be used as a volume. For more details, refer to `http://kubernetes.io/docs/user-guide/volumes/`.

Storing long-lived data in persistent volumes

Persistent volumes are, as one might expect, persistent. They are designed to persist after a pod is deleted and to be used again by another pod. Typically, databases and similar systems use persistent volumes to store their data. Whenever the pod is restarted for any reason, such as after an update, the data is there waiting for it.

Persistent volumes happen in two parts. The first is the `PersistentVolume` object, which stores the connection details for physical storage that is being used. The second is a `PersistentVolumeClaim`, which tells Kubernetes that at some point, something is going to want to use that storage. A pod with a claim basically has permission to use that piece of storage.

You can think of it like a ticket to a theater. The `PersistentVolume` object is a seat in the theater. The `PersistentVolumeClaim` object is the ticket that allows one to enter the theater and sit in the seat.

Persistent volumes also allow some measure of abstraction of the volume from a pod. The `PersistentVolume` object stores all the details for accessing the physical storage. The pod does not have to care about it. It simply uses a `PersistentVolumeClaim` object to access the storage.

Creating a PersistentVolume

Let's start by creating a `PersistentVolume` object. This uses the same GCE persistent disk as the preceding volume example:

```
apiVersion: v1
kind: PersistentVolume
metadata:
  name: test-pd
  labels:
    name: test-pd
spec:
  capacity:
    storage: 10Gi
  accessModes:
    - ReadWriteOnce
  persistentVolumeReclaimPolicy: Retain
  gcePersistentDisk:
    pdName: test-pd
    fsType: ext4
```

The interesting things that happen in the `spec` section are as follows:

- If one pod claims write access on a persistent volume that already has a write claim, the second claim will be denied. A claim will also be denied if it tries to get write access on a volume that is only allowing read-only access.
- Next, `accessModes` determine what sort of access pods are allowed to claim. To continue the theater analogy, it is like saying that a pod can get a ticket on the main floor or in the balcony. There are three modes that can be set:
  - `ReadWriteOnce`: Only a single node may mount this storage read-write
  - `ReadOnlyMany`: Many nodes may mount this storage for read-only access
  - `ReadWriteMany`: Many nodes may mount this storage for read-write access
- First, the storage capacity is defined; in this case 10 GiB. It is possible to create multiple storage chunks of varying sizes ahead of time and let a pod claim the size that it needs.

- Third is `persistentVolumeReclaimPolicy`. This setting determines what will be done with the volume when the claim is released. There are three possible values. Note that not every storage type supports every reclaim policy:
  - `Retain`: Nothing is done with the volume. It is up to the cluster administrator to remove the volume if it is no longer needed.
  - `Recycle`: The physical storage remains, but Kubernetes attempts an `rm -rf *` on the volume before making it available again.
  - `Delete`: The volume will be deleted when the claim is released.

The last field configures the storage. In this case, a GCE persistent disk named `test-pd`. This will vary depending on the storage that is being used.

Creating the PersistentVolumeClaim resource

Before any pod can use a `PersistentVolume` resource, a `PersistentVolumeClaim` resource must be created:

```
apiVersion: v1
kind: PersistentVolumeClaim
metadata:
  name: test-pd-pvc
spec:
  accessModes:
    - ReadWriteOnce
  resources:
    requests:
      storage: 10Gi
  selector:
    matchLabels:
      name: test-pd
```

This example creates a claim named `test-pd-pvc`. The `accessModes` specification tells Kubernetes that this claim is for write access for only this pod. The `resources` section means that this claim is looking for a volume that is at least 10 GiB. The volume that is actually mapped to this claim may be bigger but it will not be smaller. Finally, `selector` matches the labels on `PersistentVolume`. In this case, claim is looking for a persistent volume with a name label that is `test-pd`.

It is possible for a claim to match multiple volumes. If that is the case, the volume that Kubernetes determines is the closest match provided. If you are trying to connect to a specific volume, use a unique label on the persistent volume that the claim can match.

Using a PersistentVolumeClaim as a volume

When a pod wants to use a persistent volume, a claim is listed in the `volumes` section of the pod specification. Following is the `nginx` pod from before. This time, it is using `PersistentVolumeClaim` to access the volume:

```
apiVersion: v1
kind: Pod
metadata:
  name: web-pvc
spec:
  volumes:
    - name: test-pd
      persistentVolumeClaim:
        claimName: test-pd-pvc
  containers:
    - name: nginx
      image: nginx:1.11
      volumeMounts:
        - mountPath: /mnt
          name: test-pd
```

The volume type is a `persistentVolumeClaim`. The `claimName` attribute must match the `PersistentVolumeClaim` created earlier. Like the plain volume before, the volume name in the pod, `test-pd` in this case, is used in the container definition to mount the storage in the container.

> There are number of other things that can be done with `PersistentVolumes` including dynamic provisioning of volumes for pods. For more details, refer to:
> `http://kubernetes.io/docs/user-guide/persistent-volumes/`.

Further reading

As long as this chapter is, it has only scratched the surface of what Kubernetes can do. The following is a list of a few features that were not covered:

- **Ingress resources**: The Ingress resource is a new load balancer abstraction that works with services. It provides more granular routing for web applications including host-based and path-based routing. Refer to `http://kubernetes.io/docs/user-guide/ingress/`.

- **Kubernetes Dashboard**: Kubernetes ships with the `kube-ui` add-on which provides a dashboard for viewing the cluster and quickly creating new pods and other resources. Refer to `http://kubernetes.io/docs/user-guide/ui/`.

- **Pod resource limits**: It is possible to set per-pod and per-container CPU and memory limits at the namespace level. Refer to `http://kubernetes.io/docs/admin/limitrange/`.

- **Quotas**: Quotas can be applied at a project level to ensure that the total number of pods or the amount of resources are not exceeded. Refer to `http://kubernetes.io/docs/admin/resourcequota/`.

- **Batch jobs**: Jobs are a resource type that is expected to run and terminate. Multiple jobs can be run in parallel. Refer to `http://kubernetes.io/docs/user-guide/jobs/`.

- **Health checks:** Kubernetes has the capability of running health checks against a container to verify that it is running properly. Refer to `http://kubernetes.io/docs/user-guide/liveness/`.

Summary

In this chapter, you saw how to install Kubernetes and create resources. You saw how to create pods and how to use them with deployments for replication and updates. Network features such as DNS-SD and services were discussed and it was shown how to create load balancers to make services available to the Internet. Finally, volumes were discussed and you saw how to use `PersistentVolume` to make data available across pods. The next chapter will examine how to use Apache Mesosphere as a Docker orchestration platform.

6

Working with Mesosphere

Apache Mesos is a *distributed kernel*. It allows one to work on a cluster of servers as if they were a single resource. Mesosphere and DC/OS build on this to provide a robust system for running any workload, including Docker containers. Native support for distributed workloads such as Cassandra and Jenkins, as well as Docker, make for a powerful combination.

Microsoft's **Azure Container Service** (**ACS**) is based around DC/OS. In March 2016, Mesosphere open sourced DC/OS, making it easier than ever to get started.

This chapter will look at using Mesosphere, to manage and deploy Docker-based applications. It will cover deploying, scaling, and upgrading new applications. It will also show how to use the built-in overlay with the load balancing features of Marathon. Finally, the chapter will cover the use of volumes to persist data and how to use a private registry.

This chapter will cover the following topics:

- Installing Mesos and DC/OS
- Managing containers and applications
- Scaling applications
- Using health checks
- Scaling applications
- Updating applications with zero downtime upgrades
- Connecting to the Mesos overlay network
- Using virtual IPs and the Marathon load balancer
- Using local and external volumes
- Using a private registry

Getting started with DC/OS

Installing DC/OS is a complicated process to be covered here, and the instructions differ for each environment. Be sure to read through the documentation before you start this process. There are features, such as the number of masters or external persistent storage that must be enabled at install time and cannot be changed later without reinstalling. Installation instructions are available at `https://dcos.io/docs/1.8/administration/installing/`.

 The easiest way to get Mesosphere up and running is to use the stack install on AWS or use ACS which runs Mesosphere.

There are a few things to be aware of if you are installing manually or on local hardware:

- Nodes must have at least two cores or virtual processors.
- DC/OS nodes must be running CoreOS 7, RHEL 7, or CoreOS.
- All nodes in the cluster must have NTP enabled. NTP servers are set in `/etc/systemd/timesyncd.conf`. After the NTP servers have been set, run `systemctl`, enable `systemd-timedated.service` and `systemctl`, and start `systemd-timedated.service` to enable and start the `systemd` internal NTP client. Following is a sample `timesyncd.conf` for use on GCE:

```
[Time]
NTP=time1.google.com time2.google.com
time3.google.com time4.google.com
FallbackNTP=0.pool.ntp.org 1.pool.ntp.org
0.fr.pool.ntp.org
```

Logging into the web interface

After DC/OS is installed, it will be possible to log in using the web interface. Mesosphere uses OAuth for authentication with Google, GitHub, or Microsoft accounts. After you have logged in, you will be directed to the Mesosphere **Dashboard**. From there you can start managing applications or install the command-line client, dcos:

Installing the DC/OS client

Once DC/OS is installed, log into the website. At the bottom-left corner, the popup menu has a link labeled **Install CLI**. The window that opens after clicking this link has instructions for client installation on Windows, OS X, and Linux:

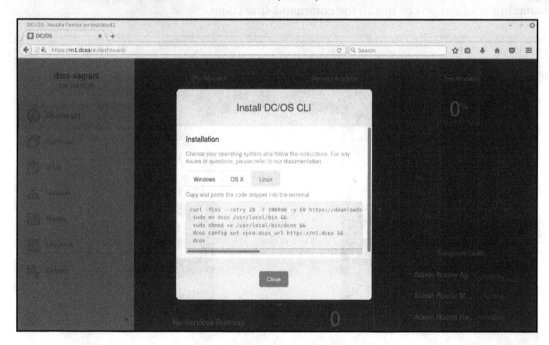

The client can also be installed manually. On Linux, the commands for installation looks like this:

```
$ wget -O dcos
https://downloads.dcos.io/binaries/cli/linux/x86-64/dcos-1.8/dcos
$ chmod +x dcos
$ sudo cp dcos /usr/local/bin/
$ dcos config set core.dcos_url https://m1.dcos
```

Change the version number in the URL to match your master server version. In this example, it is `1.8`. The last command configures the location of the DC/OS master. Change the URL passed to `dcos config` to the appropriate address for your environment. If you do not have a valid SSL certificate, `dcos` can be configured to ignore the verification:

```
$ dcos config set core.ssl_verify false
```

Once `dcos` is installed, it is time to log in:

```
$ dcos auth login
```

Now go to the following link in your browser:

```
https://m1.dcos/login?redirect_uri=urn:ietf:wg:oauth:2.0:oob
```

Enter the authentication token:

Go to the indicated URL. DC/OS will attempt to authenticate you with OAuth 2 via `https://auth0.com/`. Copy the token and paste it into the shell. You should now be logged in and ready to use the command line.

Managing applications

A Mesos cluster is managed with the `dcos` tool and the web interface. Applications in Mesos are handled by the Marathon scheduler and are defined in JSON format.

Running a simple application

Let's start with a simple container that runs Nginx. Create a file named `nginx.json` that contains the following definition:

```
{
  "id" : "simple-nginx",
  "instances" : 1,
  "cpus" : 0.25,
  "mem" : 64.0,
  "container" : {
    "type" : "DOCKER",
    "docker" : {
      "image" : "nginx:1.11",
      "network" : "HOST"
    }
  }
}
```

The `id` tag is the name of the service. It is displayed in the service list. The `instances` tag tells Marathon that only one instance is needed. It can be increased or decreased as needed later.

The `cpus` and `mem` tags are hints to Marathon as to what percentage of CPU and the amount of RAM is needed. They do not actually set resource limits in Docker. However, Marathon may kill tasks that use more than the allocated resources. In this case, the application is requesting 25 percent of a CPU and 64 MB of RAM. These settings cannot be changed after an application is created without redeploying the application.

The `container` tag is where the Docker container is defined. Because this is a Docker container, the `type` tag is set to `DOCKER`. The image is set in the `image` tag. This is the same image name that will be passed to `docker run`.

Finally, the `network` tag is set to `HOST`, which tells the Docker Engine to use host networking. Later in the chapter, other networking types will be used, but this will suffice for now.

Start the service with `dcos marathon app add nginx.json`. If everything goes well, the command will produce no output. Otherwise, an error is displayed. Use `dcos marathon app list` to verify that the application is running:

```
$ dcos marathon app list
ID             MEM  CPUS  TASKS  HEALTH  DEPLOYMENT  CONTAINER  CMD
/simple-nginx  64   0.25  1/1    ---     ---         DOCKER     None
```

Nginx is running, but how do you get to it? Because host networking was used, you can point your web browser to the external IP address of the node the container is running on. The host address is available in the service details in the web interface or by running `dcos marathon app show simple-nginx`.

Stopping an application

A service may be stopped without removing it from Marathon with the `dcos marathon app stop` command. Marathon will create a deployment to scale the service to zero tasks. The web interface refers to this as **suspending** an application:

```
$ dcos marathon app stop simple-nginx
Created deployment e5be6896-f593-4a32-852f-30bd98551a0e
$ dcos marathon app list
ID             MEM  CPUS  TASKS  HEALTH  DEPLOYMENT  CONTAINER  CMD
/simple-nginx  64   0.25  0/0    ---     ---         DOCKER     None
```

Removing an application

When the service is no longer needed, it can be removed with `dcos marathon app remove`. An application does not have to be stopped to be removed. Marathon will stop the running containers and remove the application from the list:

```
$ dcos marathon app remove simple-nginx
```

Forcing Marathon to pull images

One of the biggest problems with running containers across a cluster is ensuring that the image being run is up to date. Remember, Docker caches images are downloaded from the registry. If a container is started with the `nginx` image and a new version is released that fixes a security hole, containers on that host will continue to run the vulnerable version.

Marathon provides the `forcePullImage` option to force the node to pull a new image every time the application is started. It goes in the `docker` section of a container specification. The following example shows how it works:

```
"docker" : {
  "image" : "nginx:latest",
  "forcePullImage" : true
}
```

Ensure that your registry can handle the load. If a lot of applications that pull an image are started, there is the possibility that they will overwhelm the registry.

Using environment variables

Some Docker images require the use of environment variables to run. The official MySQL image, for example, uses them to set the initial root password. Marathon uses the `env` tag to pass environment variables to the task. In this case, the environment variables `MYSQL_ROOT_PASSWORD` and `MYSQL_DATABASE` are being set:

```
{
  "id": "/mysql",
  "instances": 1,
  "cpus": 1,
  "mem": 1024,
    "env": {
      "MYSQL_ROOT_PASSWORD": "password",
      "MYSQL_DATABASE": "mydb"
```

```
        },
        "container": {
          "docker": {
            "image": "mysql:5.7",
            "forcePullImage": true,
            "network": "HOST"
          }
        }
      }
```

Scaling applications

Marathon makes it very easy to scale up or down the number of tasks for an application. Not only does this allow one to scale out to meet increased load, it also allows for blue-green deployments, which will be covered a little later in the chapter.

Assume that there is an application named `nginx` running with one instance. All that needs to be done to increase that to two instances is to run `dcos marathon app update`:

```
$ dcos marathon app update nginx instances=2
Created deployment 8dbf3d16-44d3-4478-9366-9743658dcfcd
```

This example sets the number of instances to two. Applications can similarly be scaled up or down. Marathon will attempt to start or stop as many instances as needed to meet the new requirement.

Make sure that your application can support running multiple instances. Databases, in particular, do not react well to other processes changing their files.

Checking application health

Marathon, very similar to Kubernetes, supports the option of setting one or more health checks on a service to ensure it is running properly before making it available to handle requests. There are options to run a custom check command, check for TCP connectivity, or check the HTTP status for a specific path.

Using TCP and HTTP checks

This is an example of a TCP check for MySQL. The `protocol` option says that this is a TCP check. The `portNumber` defines the port to connect to. Instead, it can be replaced with `portIndex` which will check the index into the `ports` or `portDefintion` lists in the application definition. The index is zero based so the first entry is 0, the second is 1, and so on:

```
"healthChecks": [
  {
    "protocol": "TCP",
    "portNumber": 3306,
    "gracePeriodSeconds": 300,
    "intervalSeconds": 60,
    "timeoutSeconds": 20,
    "maxConsecutiveFailures": 3
  }
]
```

There are a number of settings that are usable for every check type. They are as follows:

- `gracePeriodSeconds`: This is the number of seconds to wait before throwing errors. It allows containers, such as MySQL, that take time to start to finish initializing before throwing errors. If the check passes before the grace period ends, the application is immediately marked as healthy.
- `intervalSeconds`: This is the number of seconds to wait between checks.
- `timeoutSeconds`: The check fails if it does not respond in these many seconds.
- `maxConsecutiveFailures`: If a health check fails these many times in a row without a success, the task is killed and restarted.
- `taskKillGracePeriodSeconds`: When a task has failed too many checks, Marathon will send a `SIGTERM` signal. If the task has not stopped by the time these many seconds have elapsed, Marathon will send the `SIGKILL` task. This defaults to three seconds.

The HTTP and HTTPS protocols check the HTTP status code for a given path. The `path` option may be set, which defines the path to test. It defaults to `/`. The HTTP and HTTPS checks also use the `portNumber` and `portIndex` options described earlier. The HTTPS protocol is used to check SSL enabled websites. It does not check the validity of the SSL certificate.

By default, only status codes in the 200-399 range are considered healthy. You can configure the check to ignore status codes from 100-199 by setting `ignoreHttp1xx` to `true`. Every other status code is considered a failure.

Using command checks

It is also possible to check the health status using a custom command. The check is considered successful if it exits with a true value, usually 0 in sh. Anything else is considered a failure. The following example adds a command check to an application:

```
{
  "id" : "nginx-health",
  "instances" : 1,
  "cpus" : 0.25,
  "mem" : 64.0,
  "labels" : {
    "HAPROXY_GROUP" : "external"
  },
  "container" : {
    "type" : "DOCKER",
    "docker" : {
      "image" : "nginx",
      "network" : "BRIDGE",
      "portMappings" : [
        {
          "hostPort" : 0,
          "containerPort" : 80,
          "servicePort" : 80,
          "name" : "web"
        }
      ]
    }
  },
  "upgradeStrategy" : {
    "minimumHealthCapacity" : 1,
    "maximumOverCapacity" : 1
  },
  "healthChecks" : [
    {
      "protocol" : "COMMAND",
      "command" :
      {
        "value" : "your_check_health_command.sh"
      }
    }
  ]
}
```

The `command` is passed to `/bin/sh -c ""`. Any double quotes in the `command` must be escaped. To complicate matters, the escape character (\) must also be escaped. A command that includes a double quoted component looks something like this:

```
"healthChecks" : [
  {
    "protocol" : "COMMAND",
    "command" : {
      "value" : "your_check_health_command.sh "Foo""
    }
  }
]
```

Deploying rolling updates

Existing applications are updated with `dcos marathon update`. Previously, this command was used to scale the number of instances of an application. It can also be used to update an application to use a new image:

```
{
  "id" : "nginx",
  "instances" : 1,
  "cpus" : 0.25,
  "mem" : 64.0,
  "container" : {
    "type" : "DOCKER",
    "docker" : {
      "image" : "nginx:1.10",
      "network" : "HOST"
    }
  }
}
```

This is a simple Ngnix application.

Note that the `image` tag is set to `nginx:1.10`. It just so happens that 1.11 has been released and now it is time to update the application. There are two ways to do it.

The easiest way is to edit the application in the web interface. In **Container Settings**, change **Container Image** to `nginx:1.11` and click on **Deploy Changes**. A new deployment will be created that will create a new task running the `nginx:1.11` image and end the old task:

The second way is to use `dcos marathon update`. This works best if you already have your applications defined in JSON files. Create a new file or edit the existing one that defines the Nginx application. Change the `image` tag to `nginx:1.11`:

```
{
  "id" : "nginx",
  "instances" : 1,
  "cpus" : 0.25,
  "mem" : 64.0,
  "container" : {
    "type" : "DOCKER",
      "docker" : {
        "image" : "nginx:1.11",
        "network" : "HOST"
      }
  }
}
```

Once the file is changed, it can be passed to `dcos`:

```
$ dcos marathon app update nginx < nginx-1.11.json
Created deployment 2c28f5db-0fcd-4605-9d5b-b1abd5986579
```

Once again, Marathon will proceed to replace the old tasks with ones running the updated image. When the deployment finishes, you can verify that the application is running the new image:

```
$ dcos marathon app show nginx | grep image
"image": "nginx:1.11",
```

Setting an upgrade strategy

An application can define an upgrade strategy to control how application tasks are replaced. By default, Marathon will start all of the new tasks before stopping the old ones. This can be problematic for two reasons:

- First, the update could corrupt data if the application cannot handle multiple tasks writing to the same volume
- Second, you need to have enough capacity to run all of those extra tasks

To solve this problem, Marathon allows one to set an `upgradeStrategy` for an application:

```
"upgradeStrategy": {
    "minimumHealthCapacity": 1
}
```

The `minimumHealthCapacity` option is a value from zero to one. When set to `1`, the new instances are started before the old ones have been stopped. When set to `0`, all of the old instances are stopped before the new ones start. This solves the first problem. It also, technically, solves the second, but there could be noticeable downtime when the number instances gets too low to serve the clients trying to access it.

To smoothly update the application while minimizing client impact, `minimumHealthCapacity` can be set to a fraction between `0` and `1`. This value represents a percentage of running instances to scale the application down to. For example, if there are ten instances and `minimumHealthCapacity` is set to `0.4` (40 percent capacity), the application will be scaled down to four instances and six new instances will be started. Anything over `0.5` means that additional capacity will be needed for the upgrade. If the new instances have no errors, the rest of the old instances will be shut down and the new instances will be started to take their place.

Testing updates with blue-green deployments

The built-in update mechanism is great for automatically deploying a new version of the application. In some cases, however, it may be desirable to roll out an update more slowly to verify that there is no impact on end users. This is especially useful if the updates make significant changes.

A **blue-green deployment** slowly replaces the old application, called blue, with a new version, called green. In Marathon, this manual process is done by creating a new application which uses the updated image. Give the new application a title that makes it obvious that it is the new one.

The green application is started with a small number of tasks; often just one. Once the health checks show that everything is ready, the green application is added to the load balancer for the service. Assuming there are a larger number of the old, blue tasks running, most of the requests will go there. A small number, however, will be sent to the green application.

Once requests start going to the green application, one can watch for errors or other issues that might require a rollback. As tests pass, the green application can be scaled up and the blue application can be scaled down. This is a manual process that can take as much or as little time as needed. It is not unusual to wait hours or days before choosing to scale up the green application. If anything goes wrong, the green application can be scaled back down or removed from the load balancer completely.

When you are satisfied that the green application is fully ready for production, the green application can be scaled up to the desired number of tasks and the blue application can be scaled to zero and removed from the load balancer. At that point, the application is fully upgraded. The blue application can be removed from the system once it is clear that it will no longer be needed for rollback.

More information on blue-green deployments and how they may be scripted is available at
https://mesosphere.github.io/marathon/docs/blue-green-deploy.htm l.

Introducing pods

With the 1.9 release, DC/OS introduces pods. Pods in DC/OS and Marathon are very similar to those found in Kubernetes. They allow multiple containers to be grouped together into a single object. All of the containers can share volumes and communicate with each other over localhost.

Using network services and load balancing

Mesosphere provides a number of networking services that make orchestration easier. These services provide service discovery and load balancing for running applications.

Discovering services with DNS

Every service that is created is assigned a hostname in Mesos DNS. The entries are `service-name.marathon.mesos`, where `service-name` is the name of the service in the `id` field. The following snippet is from a service with `id` set to `simple-nginx`. Mesos DNS would create a record named `simple-nginx.marathon.mesos`:

```
{
  "id" : "simple-nginx",
  ...
}
```

Because the services are translated directly into DNS hostnames, there are a few restrictions, as follows:

- First, names must only contain letters, numbers, and dash (–).
- Second, the names must be shorter than 24 characters. Longer names will be shortened. This can lead to problems if two services end up with the same hostname. Tasks running in one service may be returned for the other service.

The DNS service can also be queried over HTTP using REST API. Entries are returned in JSON format. The following example gets the IP information for the `simple-nginx` service:

```
$ curl http://master.mesos:8123/v1/hosts/simple-nginx.marathon.mesos
[
  {
    "host": "simple-nginx.marathon.mesos.",
    "ip": "10.128.0.4"
  }
]
```

Connecting to the overlay network

So far, the examples have used host networking. DC/OS creates a Docker overlay network when it is installed. Connecting applications to the overlay network enables the use of load balancing as well as the ability to connect to other services across the network:

```
{
    "id" : "nginx-overlay",
    "instances" : 1,
    "cpus" : 0.25,
    "mem" : 64.0,
    "container" : {
      "type" : "DOCKER",
        "docker" : {
          "image" : "nginx",
          "network" : "USER"
        }
    },
    "ipAddress":{
      "networkName":"dcos"
    }
}
```

The preceding example creates a service named `nginx-overlay` that connects to an overlay network. The `network` tag is set to `USER` and the `networkName` tag is set to the name of the overlay network, in this case, `dcos`.

Using virtual IPs

Marathon can assign a name-based virtual IP to a service. Virtual IPs provide layer four load balancing for the services they are attached to. Tasks across the cluster can then use the virtual IP to access the service.

To add a virtual IP, click on the service in the web interface then click on the **Edit** button. Go to the **Network** section. Select **Virtual Network**. This is the same as connecting the service to an overlay network. Enter **Container Port**, **Name**, and **Protocol**, then click on the checkbox next to **Load Balanced**. If additional ports are needed, click on the **Add an endpoint** link. When you are done, click on **Deploy Changes**:

The service will be assigned a name that looks like `service-name.marathon.l4lb.thisdcos.discovery` where `service-name` is the name of the service. For a service named `nginx`, the name is `nginx.marathon.l4lb.thisdcos.discovery`. The service can then be accessed with the virtual IP anywhere in the cluster:

```
$ curl nginx.marathon.l4lb.thisdcos.directory:80
<!DOCTYPE html>
<html>
...
```

Using the Marathon load balancer

Marathon provides a second load balancer by the name of Marathon-LB. It is a HAProxy-based service that can handle multiple services as well as proxy based on the hostname for a web service. Marathon-LB is an add-on installed with the DC/OS package manager:

```
$ dcos package install marathon-lb
We recommend a minimum of 0.5 CPUs and 256 MB of RAM available for the
Marathon-
LB DCOS Service.
Continue installing? [yes/no] yes
Installing Marathon app for package [marathon-lb] version [1.4.1]
Marathon-lb DC/OS Service has been successfully installed!
See https://github.com/mesosphere/marathon-lb for documentation.
```

The `dcos` command will install Marathon-LB. By default, the installation is configured to serve external requests. The load balancer is visible in DC/OS as a service named `marathon-lb`.

Adding a new service to the load balancer is pretty easy. Following is a service that runs `nginx`:

```
{
  "id" : "nginx-mlb",
  "instances" : 1,
  "cpus" : 0.25,
  "mem" : 64.0,
  "labels" : {
    "HAPROXY_GROUP" : "external"
  },
  "container" : {
    "type" : "DOCKER",
    "docker" : {
      "image" : "nginx",
      "network" : "BRIDGE",
      "portMappings" : [
        {
          "hostPort" : 0,
          "containerPort" : 80,
          "servicePort" : 10001,
          "name" : "web"
        }
      ]
    }
  },
  "upgradeStrategy": {
    "minimumHealthCapacity": 1,
```

```
      "maximumOverCapacity": 1
  }
}
```

The `HAPROXY_GROUP` label tells Marathon that this service will use the external HAProxy group, which is served by the `marathon-lb` service.

The other important settings are in the `portMappings` list. This example defines a single port to make available through the load balancer. The `containerPort` is the port that the container is listening on. `hostPort` is the port on the host that the container will listen on. If it is missing or set to `0`, the container is assigned a random port. A `hostPort` is required, even if set to `0`, to make the container's service available outside the cluster.

Finally, `servicePort` is the port on the load balancer that will service this application. In this case, external clients will connect to the load balancer on port `10001` to access this application. In practice, an external load balancer, such as an ELB on AWS, will be used to provide mapping from a standard port to the one configured in the load balancer.

By default, Marathon-LB is configured to use service ports 10000 through 10100, 80, and 443. Any service that will use this load balancer must select an available port from these for `servicePort`. Make sure that the ports do not overlap.

It is possible to run multiple load balancers. However, the load balancers run in the host mode on the nodes, which means that it is only possible to run as many load balancers as there are worker nodes.

Running an additional load balancer is straightforward. First, create a file called `options.json` that contains the following:

```
{
  "marathon-lb":{
    "name":"marathon-lb-internal",
    "haproxy-group":"internal",
    "bind-http-https":false,
    "role":""
  }
}
```

The name option is the name of the new service. The haproxy-group option sets the HAProxy group. This group is what goes in the HAPROXY_GROUP label in the service. Marathon will use whichever load balancer that matches the group. Create the new load balancer by running the following command:

```
$ dcos package install --options=lb-options.json marathon-lb
We recommend a minimum of 0.5 CPUs and 256 MB of RAM available for the
Marathon-LB DCOS Service.
Continue installing? [yes/no] yes
```

If there are resources available, the load balancer will start and be ready to serve requests.

Providing persistent storage

Running ephemeral containers like these is all well and good, but more complicated workloads will require some form of additional storage. DC/OS and Marathon provide two options. The first is local storage, which is only available on the node that the task starts on. The second is external volumes, which are available anywhere in the cluster.

 As of this writing, volumes are considered experimental. The functionality may change.

Using local volumes

Local persistent volumes are blocks of data allocated on a node that persists across application upgrades and restarts. Because the volume is located on a single node, the application is pinned to that node and will always start there. This means that the data will always be available for the application, but it also means that if that node goes away, the application will not be able to start. The following example shows how to add a local volume:

```
{
  "id" : "nginx-volume",
  "instances" : 1,
  "cpus" : 0.25,
  "mem" : 64.0,
  "container" : {
    "type" : "DOCKER",
    "docker" : {
      "image" : "nginx",
```

```
            "network" : "USER"
        },
        "volumes" : [
            {
                "containerPath" : "website",
                "mode" : "RW",
                "persistent" : {
                    "size" : 20
                }
            }
        ]
    },
    "ipAddress" : {
        "networkName" : "dcos"
    },
    "residency": {
        "taskLostBehavior": "WAIT_FOREVER"
    }
}
```

This example creates an application with a local persistent volume. Volumes are created with the `volumes` block within the `container` definition. The path of the volume is set by `containerPath`. The path may not contain forward slashes (`/`). Within the container, the volume will be available in `/mnt/mesos/sandbox/containerPath`. In this case, the `website` volume will be `/mnt/mesos/sandbox/website`.

The `mode` option can only be `RW`, which gives the container read-write access to the volume. Other modes may be added as the volumes feature is developed. The `persistent` block only has the `size` option which defines the amount of space to be allocated in MiB.

Finally, a `residency` block must be defined with `taskLostBehavior` set to `WAIT_FOREVER`. This signals Marathon that this application is stateful.

Some applications do not allow you to change the path where the data lives. This could be a problem for applications such as MySQL. Since it is not possible to specify a specific path, Marathon has a workaround. The trick is to specify a second volume:

```
{
    "id" : "nginx-volume",
    "instances" : 1,
    "cpus" : 0.25,
    "mem" : 64.0,
    "container" : {
        "type" : "DOCKER",
        "docker" : {
            "image" : "nginx",
```

```
        "network" : "USER"
      },
      "volumes" : [
        {
          "containerPath" : "website",
          "mode" : "RW",
          "persistent" : {
            "size" : 20
          }
        },
        {
          "containerPath" : "/var/lib/www",
          "mode" : "RW",
          "hostPath" : "website"
        }
      ]
    },
    "ipAddress" : {
      "networkName" : "dcos"
    },
    "residency": {
      "taskLostBehavior": "WAIT_FOREVER"
    }
  }
```

This example extends the previous one to mount the `website` volume in `/var/lib/www`. The second volume uses `hostPath`, which matches `containerPath` of the persistent volume. Since `hostPath` is being used, `containerPath` can point to any location in the container's file system. The data stored on the volume is available in both `/mnt/mesos/sandbox/website` and `/var/lib/www`.

Using external volumes

The biggest failing with local persistent volumes is that the data is stuck on a single node. If that node fails, the data is no longer accessible. External volumes allow an application to store data off the node where the application is run. An application can be started anywhere in the cluster and still access its data.

Mesosphere uses REX-Ray to manage access to external storage. REX-Ray supports Amazon EC2, GCE, OpenStack, and more. A complete list of supported storage drivers is available at `https://rexray.readthedocs.io/en/v0.3.3/user-guide/storage-providers/`.

External storage must be enabled when Mesosphere is installed. The configuration is
enabled in `genconf/config.yaml` in the installation package. The specifics will depend on
the driver used. Following is an example for GCE:

```
rexray_config:
  rexray:
    loglevel: info
  modules:
    default-admin:
      host: tcp://127.0.0.1:61003
  storageDrivers:
    - gce
  gce:
    keyfile: /path/to/gce-auth.json
```

Multiple storage drivers can be set in the `storageDrivers` section. Each storage driver will
have its own section for configuration. In the case of GCE, `keyfile` is the JSON formatted
credentials from the API portal.

The following example shows how one would use an external volume. The only option for
provider is `dvdi` with the `dvdi/driver` option set to `rexray`. The value for `name` is the
name of the volume from the provider. In the following example, the `testpd` volume will
be loaded from the storage provider:

```
{
  "id" : "nginx-volume",
  "instances" : 1,
  "cpus" : 0.25,
  "mem" : 64.0,
  "container" : {
    "type" : "DOCKER",
    "docker" : {
      "image" : "nginx",
      "network" : "USER"
    },
    "volumes" : [
      {
        "containerPath" : "website",
        "mode" : "RW",
        "external" : {
          "size" : 200,
          "name" : "testpd",
          "provider" : "dvdi",
          "options" : {
            "dvdi/driver" : "rexray"
          }
        }
```

```
      }
    ]
  },
  "ipAddress" : {
    "networkName" : "dcos"
  },
  "residency": {
    "taskLostBehavior": "WAIT_FOREVER"
  }
}
```

The rules for volume names with local volumes also apply to external volumes as well. If the volume is to be mounted in a specific path, a second volume must be used as demonstrated earlier.

Mesosphere only allows a single instance of an application to mount a specific external volume. A task may be scaled down to zero. The volume will persist and will be ready for use when the application is scaled back up.

Here are a few other things to keep in mind when using external persistent volumes:

- The volume will not be destroyed when the associated cluster is destroyed. You are responsible for volume clean up.
- For some providers, images that are created in a certain zone or region are only available to hosts running in that same zone.
- Ensure that your volume names are unique to avoid conflicts.
- Make sure that a compatible version of Docker is used. The REX-Ray documentations recommends Docker 1.10.2 or higher.

Using a private registry

Mesosphere has the ability to use a private Docker Registry for images. Images can be pulled from a local registry in the same way one would with Docker; using the registry address followed by the image. For example, to use the `myapp` image that is on `registry.example.com`, you would set the `image` to `registry.example.com/myapp`.

It is also possible to host a private registry on your Mesosphere cluster. The registry can be set up using host networking or with either VIP or Marathon-LB as the load balancer. The following example creates an insecure registry which uses Marathon-LB:

```
{
  "id" : "registry",
  "cpus" : 0.5,
  "mem" : 128,
  "instances" : 1,
  "labels" : {
    "HAPROXY_GROUP" : "external"
  },
  "container" : {
    "type" : "DOCKER",
    "docker" : {
      "network" : "BRIDGE",
      "image" : "registry:2",
      "portMappings" : [
        {
          "containerPort" : 5000,
          "hostPort" : 0,
          "servicePort" : 10003
        }
      ]
    },
    "volumes" : [
      {
        "containerPath" : "registry",
        "mode" : "RW",
        "persistent" : {
          "size" : 2048
        }
      }
    ]
  },
  "env" : {
    "STORAGE_PATH" : "/mnt/mesos/sandbox/registry"
  },
  "residency" : {
    "taskLostBehavior": "WAIT_FOREVER"
  }
}
```

This example does not use TLS keys to secure the registry. To use them, the Docker daemon must be configured with the `--insecure-registry` flag. Certificates can be added through a volume. The `REGISTRY_HTTP_TLS_CERTIFICATE` and `REGISTRY_HTTP_TLS_KEY` environment variables can then be used to set the path to the certificate and the key, respectively.

In the preceding example, the registry is stored on a volume. The `STORAGE_PATH` environment variable is used to configure the registry to use that location. While this example uses a local persistent volume, an external volume should be set up for the registry. The registry should not be dependent on running on a specific node.

For more details on running a private registry, refer to the DC/OS documentation and the registry documentation at `https://dcos.io/docs/1.8/usage/tutorials/registry/` and `https://hub.docker.com/_/registry/`, respectively.

Summary

This chapter covered the basics of using Mesosphere to manage your applications. It showed how to create applications, scale them, upgrade them without downtime, and delete them. It also showed how to use the built-in load balancers and how to run a private registry. The next chapter will look at other less well-known orchestration tools, including CoreOS Fleet and Rancher Cattle.

7
Using Simpler Orchestration Tools – Fleet and Cattle

Docker Swarm, Kubernetes, and Mesosphere are the big players in Docker orchestration, but they are hardly the only ones. In some cases, they are overkill. This chapter will look at two of the other options—Fleet and Cattle. Each tool has its own strengths and weaknesses. Fleet is a lower-level tool that is great for small environments or as a base for other tools. Cattle is a fully featured orchestration suite that is simpler to use than Kubernetes or Mesosphere.

This chapter will cover the following topics:

- Using Fleet
    - Installing Fleet
    - Using `fleetctl` to start, stop, and remove services
    - Using environment variables with Fleet unit files to configure containers
    - Setting service affinity and anti-affinity for high availability
    - Using sidekick services
    - Running global services
- Using Rancher Cattle
    - Installing Rancher Server, agents, and clients
    - Managing application stacks with `rancher-compose`
    - Perform zero downtime upgrades
    - Configuring health checks
    - Using the built-in DNS discovery and load balancing services

Using Fleet

Fleet was developed by the CoreOS company as a way of managing containers in CoreOS clusters. It is a low-level tool that other tools can build upon. Fleet has limits of approximately 100 nodes and 1,000 services. Having said that, for a small cluster, it can be just enough orchestration to meet the needs of your organization. It can also provide a solid base to build in-house processes.

Like all Docker orchestration tools, Fleet requires an overlay network. CoreOS ships with Flannel installed, but any Docker overlay network can be used. This includes the Docker native overlay and Weave Net. Overlay networks were described in Chapter 3, *Cluster Building Blocks – Registry, Overlay Networks, and Shared Storage*. It is important to note that neither Flannel nor Fleet provide any sort of service discovery. If that feature is needed, an overlay network which provides service discovery, such as Weave Net, may be used instead.

Starting Fleet

Since Fleet was developed by CoreOS, that is the easiest way to use it. As mentioned in Chapter 1, *Getting Started with Docker Orchestration*, Linux Container by CoreOS is a Linux distribution specifically designed to run containers. It uses Cloud-Init to configure the entire system on boot. This includes Fleet.

Fleet uses etcd to store the cluster configuration and for communication. Chapter 3, *Cluster Building Blocks – Registry, Overlay Networks, and Shared Storage* covered setting up etcd on CoreOS for the Flannel overlay network. The exact same process is used with Fleet. All that needs to happen is to ensure that Fleet is enabled in the cloud-config file:

```
#cloud-config

coreos:
  etcd2:
    discovery: https://discovery.etcd.io/<token>
    advertise-client-urls:
    http://$private_ipv4:2379,http://$private_ipv4:4001
    initial-advertise-peer-urls: http://$private_ipv4:2380
    listen-client-urls:
    http://0.0.0.0:2379,http://0.0.0.0:4001
    listen-peer-urls: http://$private_ipv4:2380
  flannel:
    public_ip: $private_ipv4
    etcd_endpoints: http://$private_ipv4:2379
  fleet:
```

```
    public_ip: $private_ipv4
    etcd_servers: http://$private_ipv4:2379
units:
  - name: etcd2.service
    command: start
  - name: fleet.service
    command: start
  - name: flanneld.service
    command: start
    drop-ins:
      - name: 50-networking-config.conf
        content: |
          [Service]
          ExecStartPre=/usr/bin/etcdctl set
          /coreos.com/network/config
          '{"Network":"10.42.0.0/16"}'
  - name: docker.service
    command: start
    drop-ins:
      - name: 40-flannel.conf
        content: |
          [Unit]
          Requires=flanneld.service
          After=flanneld.service
```

This is the sample `cloud-config` file from `Chapter 3`, *Cluster Building Blocks – Registry, Overlay Networks, and Shared Storage,* with the configuration to ensure that the `fleet` service is started when CoreOS boots, highlighted.

For new clusters, replace `<token>` with the one generated by `wget -qO - 'https://discovery.etcd.io/new?size=3'`, where size is the initial number of hosts in your cluster. If you are adding hosts, use the same token that was used for the original hosts in the cluster.

Verifying the cluster

Once the nodes have started, there are two commands that will verify that all the nodes are communicating as they should. First, use `etcdctl cluster-health` to ensure that `etcd` sees all the nodes in the cluster:

```
$ etcdctl cluster-health
member 577728b97424518 is healthy: got healthy result from
http://172.17.8.103:2379
member 82f8a69dac8afeb3 is healthy: got healthy result from
http://172.17.8.102:2379
```

```
member d263b74b628b0458 is healthy: got healthy result from
http://172.17.8.101:2379
cluster is healthy
```

This example is from a three node cluster. The output of `etcdctl` will list each host in the cluster and their state. The important part is the last line that shows that the cluster is healthy.

The other command is `fleetctl list-machines`. This command will list every machine in the cluster and any metadata that has been set on them:

```
$ fleetctl list-machines
MACHINE        IP             METADATA
86bceaea...    172.17.8.103   -
9c07271b...    172.17.8.102   -
acbccfa4...    172.17.8.101   -
```

The `fleetctl` tool uses SSH to communicate with the other nodes in the cluster. Make sure that your public key is in `~core/.ssh/authorized_keys` on every server. It also requires that you have an SSH-agent running. You can use an existing agent from your own desktop by passing `-A` to your `ssh` command. For example, `ssh -A core@core-01` will connect to the `core-01` server as the `core` user and forward your existing agent to the server. This will allow you to use your own SSH key without the need to copy the private key to all the Fleet nodes. Be aware that this is a potential security hole.

Starting a container

Services in Fleet are defined by `systemd` unit files. These files work like any other unit file in `systemd`, but there are a few Fleet-specific extensions to allow for scheduling services across the cluster. Let's start with a simple `nginx` service.

Create the `nginx.service` file in the current working directory with the following contents:

```
[Unit]
Description=Nginx
After=docker.service
Requires=docker.service

[Service]
TimeoutStartSec=infinity
ExecStartPre=-/usr/bin/docker kill nginx
ExecStartPre=-/usr/bin/docker rm nginx
ExecStartPre=-/usr/bin/docker pull nginx
```

```
ExecStart=/usr/bin/docker run --name nginx -p 80:80 nginx
ExecStop=/usr/bin/docker stop nginx
```

The `[Unit]` section sets the description and some meta information about the service. The `Description` option is a short, freeform description of the service. The `After` option tells Fleet that this service must start after Docker. Since it does not make sense to run a Docker container without Docker, the `Requires` option is set. For both `After` and `Requires`, the value is the name of a `systemd` unit. Additional units can be added to both by adding additional `After` or `Requires` lines or by adding additional units to the existing lines, separated by spaces.

The steps needed to start a service that is set in the `[Service]` section. The `TimeoutStartSec` option is the number of seconds to wait for a service to start. If the service does not complete start up within the timeout window, Fleet assumes the service failed and kills it.

Each `ExecStartPre` line combines to form a script that runs prior to starting the actual service. Prefixing a command with a minus (–) tells `systemd` that it is okay for this step to fail. Otherwise, any command that exits with a non-zero error code will prevent the service from starting.

The first command kills the existing `nginx` is container. If it is not running, this command will fail, but that is just fine. Killing the service might seem a little extreme. If the service stops cleanly, then the running container will be in a stopped state and kill will do nothing. If the service did not stop cleanly, `docker kill` ensures that the service is stopped so that it can be restarted.

The second command removes the container from Docker. A container cannot start if a container with the same name already exists. Removing the container ensures that the container will be recreated with all the right options later.

The third and final `ExecStartPre` line pulls a new copy of the image. This ensures that the service is not running a stale image. One might think that this would be a command that should prevent the service from starting if it fails. Letting it fail means that the service can still start if the registry is down, assuming that the image has already been downloaded.

The ExecStart command is the command that actually starts the service. Multiple lines can be specified, but that does not make as much sense when using Docker containers. It is important that the -d flag is not passed to docker run. If it is, Fleet loses track of the container and stops the service.

Finally, ExecStop is the command to run to stop the service. Remember that docker stop leaves the container around. This is why docker rm is needed in ExecStartPre. You could remove the container here. Keeping it around makes it easier to troubleshoot if there are problems:

```
$ fleetctl start nginx.service
Unit nginx.service inactive
Unit nginx.service launched on 86bceaea.../172.17.8.103
```

The preceding command loads the given unit file and starts it. In this case, the nginx.service file is in the current directory.

A unit file can be added to the Fleet registry without starting with the fleetctl submit command. The service can be started at a later time with fleetctl start:

```
$ fleetctl submit nginx.service
Unit nginx.service inactive
```

Monitoring services

There are two ways to check the status of a service. The first is the same fleetctl list-units command, which will also show the unit name, the machine where it is assigned, and the current status of each unit:

```
$ fleetctl list-units
UNIT            MACHINE                     ACTIVE  SUB
nginx.service   86bceaea.../172.17.8.103    active  running
```

The other option is to use fleetctl status. This will not only show the status of the container but also the most recent log entries for the service and the status codes of the ExecStartPre commands:

```
$ fleetctl status nginx.service
● nginx.service - Nginx
    Loaded: loaded (/run/fleet/units/nginx.service;
    linked-runtime; vendor preset
    Active: active (running) since Fri 2016-10-21 02:59:31
    UTC; 1min 24s ago
    Process: 3947 ExecStartPre=/usr/bin/docker pull nginx
```

```
        (code=exited, status=0/S
  Process: 3942 ExecStartPre=/usr/bin/docker rm nginx
        (code=exited, status=0/SUC
  Process: 3933 ExecStartPre=/usr/bin/docker kill nginx
        (code=exited, status=1/F
 Main PID: 3953 (docker)
    Tasks: 7
   Memory: 3.7M
      CPU: 40ms
   CGroup: /system.slice/nginx.service
           └─3953 /usr/bin/docker run --name nginx -p
             80:80 nginx
Oct 21 02:59:27 core-03 systemd[1]: Starting Nginx...
Oct 21 02:59:27 core-03 docker[3933]: Error response
from daemon: Cannot kill co
Oct 21 02:59:27 core-03 docker[3942]: nginx
Oct 21 02:59:28 core-03 docker[3947]: Using default
tag: latest
Oct 21 02:59:31 core-03 docker[3947]: latest: Pulling
from library/nginx
Oct 21 02:59:31 core-03 docker[3947]: Digest:
sha256:e40499ca855c9edfb212e1c3ee1
Oct 21 02:59:31 core-03 docker[3947]: Status: Image is
up to date for nginx:late
Oct 21 02:59:31 core-03 systemd[1]: Started Nginx.
```

Viewing service logs

It is possible to view the logs from a service by viewing the journal for the unit with `fleetctl journal`. The command takes the name of the unit of interest. The lines marked as coming from Docker are both the output from the `docker` command as well as the output of `docker logs`. The `-f` flag can be added to follow the logs as new entries are added:

```
$ fleetctl journal nginx.service
-- Logs begin at Thu 2016-10-20 00:35:44 UTC, end at Fri 2016-10-21
03:12:36 UTC. --
Oct 21 02:56:45 core-03 systemd[1]: Stopped Nginx.
Oct 21 02:59:27 core-03 systemd[1]: Starting Nginx...
Oct 21 02:59:27 core-03 docker[3933]: Error response
from daemon: Cannot kill container nginx: Container
816e99e3ec3de47cf48f5ab19900db4a162905a133078f4fbc3bd91b27b5c24b is not
running
Oct 21 02:59:27 core-03 docker[3942]: nginx
Oct 21 02:59:28 core-03 docker[3947]: Using default tag: latest
Oct 21 02:59:31 core-03 docker[3947]: latest: Pulling from library/nginx
```

```
Oct 21 02:59:31 core-03 docker[3947]: Digest:
sha256:e40499ca855c9edfb212e1c3ee1a6ba8b2d873a294d897b4840d49f94d20487c
Oct 21 02:59:31 core-03 docker[3947]: Status: Image is up to date for
nginx:latest
Oct 21 02:59:31 core-03 systemd[1]: Started Nginx.
Oct 21 03:12:32 core-03 docker[3953]: 172.16.69.1 - - [21/Oct/2016:03:12:32
+0000] "GET / HTTP/1.1" 200 612 "-" "Wget/1.18 (linux-gnu)" "-"
```

Stopping a service

A running service is stopped with `fleetctl stop`. It takes the name of the service as the only argument:

```
$ fleetctl stop nginx.service
Unit nginx.service loaded on 86bceaea.../172.17.8.103
```

The `stop` command stops the running container, but it leaves it scheduled on a node in the cluster. When the service is restarted, it will start on the same node that it was running on before.

To unschedule a service, use the `fleetctl unload` command. This will remove the service from the list of active units. It will remain in the Fleet registry and can be started again with `fleetctl start`:

```
$ fleetctl unload nginx.service
Unit nginx.service inactive
```

A service can be permanently removed from the cluster with the command `fleetctl destroy`:

```
$ fleetctl destroy nginx.service
Destroyed nginx.service
```

The `destroy` command is also used when changing a unit. The service must be removed with `fleetctl destroy` then it can be recreated with the required changes.

Using environment variables

Many Docker images use environment variables to configure them and control how they run. Fleet can define those variables in the unit file for the service, using the `Environment` option:

```
[Unit]
Description=MySQL
After=docker.service
Requires=docker.service

[Service]
Environment=MYSQL_ROOT_PASSWORD=password
Environment=MYSQL_DATABASE=myapp
TimeoutStartSec=infinity
ExecStartPre=-/usr/bin/docker kill mysql
ExecStartPre=-/usr/bin/docker rm mysql
ExecStartPre=-/usr/bin/docker pull mysql
ExecStart=/usr/bin/docker run --name mysql -e MYSQL_ROOT_PASSWORD -e
MYSQL_DATABASE -p 3306:3306 mysql
ExecStop=/usr/bin/docker stop mysql
```

This example starts a MySQL image and defines the MySQL root password and an initial database. The values of the variables do not need to be defined in the `docker run` command. Docker will use the values set in the `Environment` lines.

Rather than specifying all of the environment variables in the unit as was done earlier, they can all be placed into an `EnvironmentFile`. Variables and their values are defined, one per line:

```
MYSQL_ROOT_PASSWORD=password
MYSQL_DATABASE=myapp
```

The file is then specified in the `EnvironmentFile` option in the `[Service]` section of the unit:

```
...
[Service]
EnvironmentFile=/etc/mysql.env
...
```

The file must exist on every node in the cluster where the service may run. If it does not exist, the service will be unable to start.

Scheduling services with affinity

It is often desirable to ensure that a service runs on the same host as another service. Contrarily, it may be better to force services to run on separate hosts. This process, known as affinity, is configured in a special `[X-Fleet]` section of the unit file.

Setting positive affinity

There are two options that control affinity between containers. The first, MachineOf, is the name of a unit file in Fleet. Fleet will attempt to place the unit with the MachineOf option on the same node that is running the named service.

For example, let's assume that the MySQL service described in the previous section is running somewhere in the Fleet cluster. For performance reasons, it is desirable to run a certain web application that uses the database on the same node. In this example, nginx will be the web application:

```
[Unit]
Description=Nginx Affinity
After=docker.service
Requires=docker.service
Requires=mysql.service

[Service]
TimeoutStartSec=infinity
ExecStartPre=-/usr/bin/docker kill nginx
ExecStartPre=-/usr/bin/docker rm nginx
ExecStartPre=-/usr/bin/docker pull nginx
ExecStart=/usr/bin/docker run --name nginx -p 80:80 nginx
ExecStop=/usr/bin/docker stop nginx

[X-Fleet]
MachineOf=mysql.service
```

This is the same basic nginx service defined earlier in the chapter. There are two things to note here. First, a Requires option was added to ensure that mysql.service is running. If it is not running and is defined, Fleet will start it. Next is the [X-Fleet] section and the MachineOf option which ensures that Fleet will try to run nginx.service on the same host as mysql.service.

It is important to keep in mind that affinity definitions should always be one way. If they are not, a race condition develops. In this example, if mysql.service also had MachineOf=nginx.service, Fleet would be unable to start either service. It would not be possible to determine where to start the first service because the other one has not been started yet.

Using negative affinity

Sometimes it is important that two services never run on the same node. Generally, this is for redundancy and high availability reasons. Fleet provides the `Conflicts` option for those occasions. The `Conflicts` option can match an exact unit name or a group of services using glob-matching.

With glob-matching, an asterisk (*) is used to match zero or more characters. For example, to match any service that starts with `nginx`, the pattern would be `nginx*`. The following snippet shows a unit that is configured not to start on any node that is running a service that starts with `nginx`:

```
[Unit]
Description=Nginx Affinity
After=docker.service
Requires=docker.service
...
[X-Fleet]
Conflicts=nginx*
```

High availability

As mentioned earlier, negative affinity is often used for high availability. Fleet uses `systemd` template units, which make it easy to start multiple, identical services. To start, create a file named `nginxha@.service`:

```
[Unit]
Description=Nginx HA
After=docker.service
Requires=docker.service

[Service]
TimeoutStartSec=infinity
ExecStartPre=-/usr/bin/docker kill nginx
ExecStartPre=-/usr/bin/docker rm nginx
ExecStartPre=-/usr/bin/docker pull nginx
ExecStart=/usr/bin/docker run --name nginx -p 80:80 nginx
ExecStop=/usr/bin/docker stop nginx

[X-Fleet]
Conflicts=nginxha@*.service
```

For the most part, this is identical to the `nginx.service` unit that was used before. The `Conflicts` option is set to ensure that any unit that uses this template.

Each instance of the template is named `nginxha@id.service`, where `id` is whatever makes sense for the service. Usually, `id` is a number, but it does not have to be:

```
$ fleetctl start nginxha@1.service
Unit nginxha@1.service inactive
Unit nginxha@1.service launched on 86bceaea.../172.17.8.103

$ fleetctl start nginxha@2.service
Unit nginxha@2.service inactive
Unit nginxha@2.service launched on 9c07271b.../172.17.8.102

$ fleetctl start nginxha@3.service
Unit nginxha@3.service inactive
Unit nginxha@3.service launched on acbccfa4.../172.17.8.101

$ fleetctl list-units
UNIT                    MACHINE                        ACTIVE  SUB
nginxha@1.service       86bceaea.../172.17.8.103       active  running
nginxha@2.service       9c07271b.../172.17.8.102       active  running
nginxha@3.service       acbccfa4.../172.17.8.101       active  running
```

In this example, three instances of the `nginxha@.service` template were started. They were named `nginxha@1`, `nginxha@2`, and `nginxha@3`. Notice; all of them were started on different machines. A load balancer could then be used to spread the load across all the instances. If any of the units fail, the overall service will remain up.

Sidekick services

Most services are not aware of what else is happening in the cluster, by design. How does a service let other things know that it is up and ready to answer requests? To do that, a separate service called **sidekick** is started. The sidekick will notify the other services that the container has started or stopped. The specifics will vary depending on the environment. For example, it might issue API calls to an external load balancer.

Fleet does not have a native way to inform other services that a new unit has started. What it does have is `etcd`. The `etcd` key value store is designed for exactly this sort of message passing. The following example is a simple sidekick that updates `etcd` when `nginx.service` starts:

```
[Unit]
Description=Nginx Sidekick
BindsTo=nginx.service
After=nginx.service
```

```
[Service]
ExecStart=/bin/sh -c "while [ true ]; do etcdctl set
/services/websites/nginx '{ "host": "%H", "port": 80 }' --ttl 60; sleep 50;
done"
ExecStop=/usr/bin/etcdctl rm /services/websites/nginx

[X-Fleet]
MachineOf=nginx.service
```

The `BindsTo` option works like `Requires`, but it tells Fleet to stop the sidekick if `nginx.service` stops for any reason. The `ExecStart` option runs an infinite loop that updates the `/services/websites/nginx` key in `etcd` with a bit of JSON. A TTL is added to the key with the `--ttl` flag to ensure that it disappears if the sidekick fails. The `sleep` command waits 50 seconds before updating the key again. The times can be adjusted to the needs of the environment, but the sleep should always be less than the TTL minus the time it takes to update `etcd`.

The `%H` variable in the JSON is replaced with the hostname of the node that `nginx-sidekick.service` is running on. This could be problematic if the sidekick were to be started on a different host from `nginx.service`. However, the Fleet affinity option, `MachineOf`, ensures that Fleet always schedules the sidekick on the same host as `nginx.service`.

Another service can monitor the specific files or directories within the `etcd` tree and take actions based on updates to the tree. The Confd tool does exactly that, and based on the contents of the tree, can update a configuration template and restart a service. The implementation of Confd is left as an exercise for the reader. Confd is available at `https://github.com/kelseyhightower/confd`.

Starting global units

There are often times when it is desirable to run containers for logging or monitoring on every node in the cluster. Fleet accomplishes this with the `Global` option in `[X-Fleet]`:

```
[Unit]
Description=Monitor
After=docker.service
Requires=docker.service

[Service]
TimeoutStartSec=infinity
ExecStartPre=-/usr/bin/docker kill monitor
ExecStartPre=-/usr/bin/docker rm monitor
```

```
ExecStartPre=-/usr/bin/docker pull monitor
ExecStartPre=-mkdir -p /var/lib/monitor
ExecStart=/usr/bin/docker run -v /var/lib/monitor:/var/www/rrd --net=host -
-name=monitor hyper/host-monitor
ExecStop=/usr/bin/docker stop monitor

[X-Fleet]
Global=true
```

This example starts a simple container that creates RRD files and images which chart CPU, memory, and network data. The `Global` option tells Fleet to start a copy of the service on every node in the cluster:

```
$ fleetctl start monitor.service
Unit monitor.serviceTriggered global unit monitor.service start

$ fleetctl list-units
UNIT                MACHINE                         ACTIVE  SUB
monitor.service     86bceaea.../172.17.8.103        active  running
monitor.service     9c07271b.../172.17.8.102        active  running
monitor.service     acbccfa4.../172.17.8.101        active  running
```

There they are. One `monitor.service` for each node in this cluster. This can be done for as many global services as needed.

Using Rancher Cattle

The word "Simpler" in the title is a bit of a misnomer when applied to Rancher Cattle. Cattle is a fully featured orchestration system available with Rancher. It is simpler to set up than Kubernetes or Mesosphere. It is also easier to use due to a robust web interface and command-line tool based on Docker Compose. If you have already used Docker Compose, you may be quite comfortable with Cattle.

Installing Rancher

Rancher and its components run in Docker containers. This makes it very easy to install almost anywhere.

Installing Rancher server

The Rancher server can be added to any existing Docker cluster. The only requirement is that it is running Docker 1.10.3 or higher. A quick and dirty install for testing is as simple as running `docker run -d -p 8080:8080 rancher/server`. The web interface will then be available at port 8080 on your Docker host.

For a permanent solution, the Rancher data will need to be stored in a volume or connected to an external MySQL database. The volume can be any Docker volume including a directory on the host server. The following example will store the MySQL data in `/var/lib/rancherdb`:

```
$ docker run -d -v /var/lib/rancherdb:/var/lib/mysql -p 8080:8080
rancher/server
```

For an external database, create an environment file that contains the connection information. The database set in `CATTLE_DB_CATTLE_MYSQL_NAME` must have already been created and the user set in `CATTLE_DB_CATTLE_USERNAME` must have been granted all rights to the Cattle database. The schema will be created automatically by Rancher if it does not already exist:

```
CATTLE_DB_CATTLE_MYSQL_HOST=mysql-host
CATTLE_DB_CATTLE_MYSQL_PORT=3306
CATTLE_DB_CATTLE_MYSQL_NAME=cattle
CATTLE_DB_CATTLE_USERNAME=cattle
CATTLE_DB_CATTLE_PASSWORD=cattle-password
```

The Rancher Server can be started with the environment file. In this example, it is named `cattle.env`:

```
$ docker run -d --env-file cattle.env --name rancher-server -p 8080:8080
rancher/server
```

 The Rancher Server can be installed on multiple nodes for high availability. For more information, refer to `http://docs.rancher.com/rancher/v1.2/en/installing-rancher/installing-server/`.

Installing Rancher agents

Once Rancher has been started, it can create new hosts using any upstream provider that is supported by `docker-machine`. Log in to the web UI, go to **Hosts** in the **INFRASTRUCTURE** menu, and click on **Add Host**. A wizard will walk you through adding the host to the cloud environment:

It is also possible to add the agent manually. Select the **Custom** option in **Add Host**. There will be a Docker command that will need to be run on each Docker host that is being added to the cluster. It will look something like the command listed here:

```
sudo docker run -d --privileged -v
/var/run/docker.sock:/var/run/docker.sock -v
/var/lib/rancher:/var/lib/rancher rancher/agent:v1.0.2
http://172.17.8.101:8080/v1/scripts/781E07FE518B7181D563:1477180800000:N3gZ
UQgoo3mFPCgkQEimBOnEXFc
```

The Rancher agent creates IPSEC links between all the hosts in the environment to provide a secure overlay network. It also listens for Docker events and sends regular updates to the Rancher server with information on running containers and performance statistics.

Installing Rancher Compose

Nearly anything that needs to be done to create and manage services in Rancher can be done through the web interface. However, there is a command-line tool called `rancher-compose` that can be used as well. It is available for Windows, OS X, and Linux. To install Rancher Compose follow these steps:

1. To download it, click on **Download CLI** in the bottom right corner of the web interface and select your operating system.
2. Unpack the downloaded archive and place the `rancher-compose` tool in your path.
3. Rancher Compose requires an API key to authenticate the Rancher server. A new key for the environment or for a specific user can be created in the API section at the top of the page.

4. Click on **Add Environment API Key** or **Add Account API Key** to create the appropriate key. You will be presented with an access key and a secret key.

5. Copy them to a safe location. There is no way to get the secret key after it has been created:

The access key, secret key, and Rancher URL are passed to `rancher-compose` using the `--access-key`, `--secret-key`, and `--url` flags, respectively:

```
$ rancher-compose --url http://rancher:8080/ --access-key=CA... --secret-key=C4G...
```

It is also possible to set the keys and URL with the `RANCHER_ACCESS_KEY`, `RANCHER_SECRET_KEY`, and `RANCHER_URL` environment variables. Add them to the equivalent of `.bash_profile` for your client system:

```
export RANCHER_URL=http://rancher:8080/
export RANCHER_ACCESS_KEY=CA...
export RANCHER_SECRET_KEY=C4G...
```

Introducing environments

Rancher supports running multiple environments. After installation, a single environment named `default` will be created that runs the Cattle orchestration suite. Additional environments can be created as needed. The environments are isolated from each other. This makes it easy to create environments for development, testing, production, or environments for different business units.

While Cattle is the default orchestration tool, Rancher also has the ability to create new environments running Docker Swarm, Kubernetes, and Mesosphere. This is probably the easiest way to install either of those systems in a local environment. Once the new environment is created, add a new host. The services for the environment, such as `kubectl` or the Swarm agent, will be added automatically.

For more information on using Docker Swarm refer to `Chapter 4`, *Orchestration with Docker Swarm*, for Kubernetes refer to `Chapter 5`, *Deploying and Managing Services with Kubernetes*, and for Mesosphere refer to `Chapter 6`, *Working with Mesosphere*.

Managing services

Cattle uses Docker Compose files to define services. As of the 1.1.4 release, only version 1 of the Docker Compose specification is supported. Version 2 support is being added in Rancher 1.2.

Rancher Compose builds on the standard `docker-compose.yml` file in two ways. First, special labels can be added to services to define things such as affinity. Second, another file called `rancher-compose.yml` can be used to define Rancher-specific settings such as health checks.

 The following sections discuss using the Rancher CLI. All of the following actions can also be done through the web interface.

Starting a stack

By design, the `rancher-compose` tool is very similar to `docker-compose`. A **stack** is a collection of services defined in a `docker-compose.yml` file and an optional `rancher-compose.yml` file. There are pre-built stacks for many applications in the Rancher catalog. In addition to quickly deploying services, they can be great examples for building your own stacks.

To create your own stack, make a directory for your application that contains the `docker-compose.yml` file. The stack name is derived from the directory name, but may be overridden with the `-s` flag. When the compose files have been created, run `rancher-compose up` in the directory. The following is a `docker-compose.yml` file that starts a WordPress stack:

```
wordpress:
  image: wordpress
  env_file:
    - db.env
db:
  image: mysql:5.6
  env_file:
    - db.env
lb:
  image: rancher/load-balancer-service
  ports:
    - 80:80
  links:
    - wordpress:wordpress
```

This example starts three services. The first, `wordpress`, starts the WordPress application. The second, `db`, is a MySQL database. Both services use the `db.env` environment file to load the environment variables needed to start. Environment files were covered in Chapter 2, *Building Multi-Container Applications with Docker Compose*.

The `lb` service configures a Rancher load balancer service for this application. Load balancers will be covered in more detail later in this chapter. For now, it is enough to know that it is configured to send port 80 to the `wordpress` service.

As with `docker-compose`, multiple `docker-compose.yml` files may be specified on the command line with the `-f` flag. The `-d` flag can also be set to start the stack in the background:

```
$ rancher-compose up -f docker-compose.yml -f production.yml -d
```

Stopping a stack

Services are stopped with `rancher-compose stop`. This must be run in the same directory that contains the `docker-compose.yml` file. By default, `rancher-compose` will stop all running services:

```
$ rancher-compose stop
INFO[0000] [0/3] [lb]: Stopping
INFO[0000] [0/3] [db]: Stopping
INFO[0000] [0/3] [wordpress]: Stopping
INFO[0001] [0/3] [lb]: Stopped
INFO[0001] [0/3] [db]: Stopped
INFO[0001] [0/3] [wordpress]: Stopped
```

Individual services may be stopped by specifying the service name on the command line:

```
$ rancher-compose stop wordpress
INFO[0000] [0/3] [wordpress]: Stopping
INFO[0001] [0/3] [wordpress]: Stopped
```

Removing a stack

A service can be removed with `rancher-compose rm`. A single service can be removed by specifying the service name on the command line. The following command removes the `lb` service:

```
$ rancher-compose rm lb
INFO[0000] [0/3] [lb]: Deleting
INFO[0000] [0/3] [lb]: Deleted
```

Removing an entire stack requires that the `--force` flag be added to the command line. If `--force` is not included, `rancher-compose` will exit with an error and a reminder to add it:

```
$ rancher-compose rm --force
INFO[0000] [0/3] [lb]: Deleting
INFO[0000] [0/3] [wordpress]: Deleting
INFO[0000] [0/3] [db]: Deleting
INFO[0000] [0/3] [db]: Deleted
INFO[0000] [0/3] [wordpress]: Deleted
INFO[0000] [0/3] [lb]: Deleted
```

Upgrading a stack

There are two ways to upgrade a stack. The first is an **in-service** upgrade and the second is a **rolling upgrade**. Both options can provide zero-downtime upgrades. An in-service upgrade will replace the service running in a stack without changing the name of the service. In the WordPress example, the `wordpress` service remains `wordpress`. With a rolling upgrade, a new service must be defined which requires changing the service name in `docker-compose.yml`. In-service upgrades are recommended by Rancher and the only upgrade option available through the web interface.

In-service upgrades are performed with `rancher-compose up -upgrade`:

```
$ rancher-compose up --upgrade -d
INFO[0006] [0/3] [db]: Starting
INFO[0006] [0/3] [wordpress]: Starting
INFO[0009] [1/3] [db]: Started
INFO[0009] Updating wordpress
INFO[0011] Upgrading wordpress
INFO[0029] [2/3] [wordpress]: Started
INFO[0029] [2/3] [lb]: Starting
INFO[0034] [3/3] [lb]: Started
```

Any changes to existing services will be applied. If an upgrade requires a change to a running service, the containers are stopped and then the new containers for the service are started. This behavior is controlled on a per-service basis with the `upgrade_strategy` option in `rancher-compose.yml`. The following example configures Rancher to start new `wordpress` services before stopping the old ones. The `db` service, which runs MySQL, continue to use the default behavior and will still stop the container first before starting a new one:

```
wordpress:
  upgrade_strategy:
    start_first: true
```

There are a couple of additional flags to `rancher-compose` that are commonly used with upgrades. The first is the `--pull` flag, which forces Rancher to pull a new copy of the image, even if it has it already. This is especially useful if you are using the latest tag for an image and need to ensure that the latest copy is available.

The second flag is the `--force-upgrade` flag. This will force Rancher to perform an upgrade even if the `docker-compose.yml` and `rancher-compose.yml` files have not changed. When combined with the `--pull` flag, this can be used to upgrade all containers in the stack to the latest version of whichever image tag they are running. Again, this is most useful when using the latest tag or a tag that gets updated with point releases.

By default, `rancher-compose` will follow the logs of all the services in the stack. The `-d` flag will perform the upgrade in the background without displaying the logs.

Rolling back and confirming upgrades

At this point in the process, there is still an opportunity to rollback an upgrade. If the upgrade goes badly, it can be rolled back by running `rancher-compose up --upgrade --rollback`. The rollback can be done at any time as long as the update has not been confirmed.

Once you are sure that the upgrade is successful, it can be confirmed by running `rancher-compose up --upgrade --confirm-upgrade`. Remember that once an upgrade has been confirmed, it cannot be rolled back:

```
$ rancher-compose up --upgrade -d --confirm-upgrade
INFO[0005] [0/3] [db]: Starting
INFO[0005] [0/3] [wordpress]: Starting
INFO[0009] [1/3] [db]: Started
INFO[0013] [2/3] [wordpress]: Started
INFO[0013] [2/3] [lb]: Starting
INFO[0016] [3/3] [lb]: Started
```

In both cases, `rancher-compose` will follow the logs of the services in the stack. This can be suppressed by passing the `-d` flag to `rancher-compose`:

Checking service health

Rancher supports adding health checks to a service. A check can be configured to query a TCP port or to make an HTTP request. For TCP, the service just needs to accept a connection. For HTTP, the request must return a status code between 200 and 399. Anything else will trigger an error. The following is a `rancher-compose.yml` file that defines an HTTP check for WordPress and a TCP check for MySQL:

```
wordpress:
  upgrade_strategy:
    start_first: true
  health_check:
    port: 80
    request_line: GET / HTTP/1.0
    interval: 3000
    initializing_timeout: 60000
    unhealthy_threshold: 3
    strategy: recreate
    response_timeout: 2000
db:
  health_check:
    port: 3306
    interval: 3000
```

```
initializing_timeout: 60000
unhealthy_threshold: 3
strategy: recreate
response_timeout: 2000
```

For an HTTP check, `request_line` must be set. If it is empty or absent, the check will only test the TCP connection. The `initializing_timeout` option defines the time in milliseconds to wait for a service to start. The number of milliseconds between checks is defined by the `interval` setting. If the check is not successful in the number of milliseconds defined in `response_timeout`, the check will fail.

The `unhealthy_threshold` option sets the number of failures before Rancher does something about it. That something is defined by the `strategy` option. When set to `recreate`, as in the example, Rancher will recreate the service. There are two other options for strategy. The first option is `none`, which tells Rancher to do nothing. The second is `recreateOnQuorum`, which tells Rancher to restart the service if there is a given number of healthy containers in the service. The number is defined in the `recreate_on_quorum_strategy_config` section. An example is shown here:

```
recreate_on_quorum_strategy_config:
  quorum: 1
```

Health checks can be updated by upgrading the stack with `rancher-compose up --upgrade`.

Scheduling and affinity

Rancher supports scheduling services manually on specific hosts, running them globally on all hosts in the environment, or setting service affinity or anti-affinity. Rancher does this with labels on the service in `docker-compose.yml`. A full list of the labels that can be used for scheduling is available at `http://docs.rancher.com/rancher/v1.2/en/cattle/scheduling/`.

Using networking services

Rancher provides a couple of useful services. First of all, Rancher uses IPSEC to create a secure overlay network for services running on the cluster. Second, it provides DNS-SD for services within a stack and for referencing services across stacks. Finally, Rancher can create load balancers, which can spread the requests across containers in a service or redirect traffic based on HTTP request information.

Discovering services

Rancher provides DNS-SD for all services running in the cluster. Within a stack, all services are accessible by the service name. In the preceding WordPress example, the `wordpress` container can access the MySQL service with the `db` hostname. Services running other stacks are accessible with `<service name>.<stack name>`. For example, if the preceding WordPress stack was named `wordpress`, the MySQL service would be `db.wordpress`.

Each service can specify an alias to refer to another service using the `links` option. In the following example, an alias is created in the `wordpress` service. That link makes the `db` service accessible with the name `mysql`:

```
wordpress:
  image: wordpress
  env_file:
    - db.env
  links:
    - db:mysql
db:
  ...
```

Load balancer

Rancher provides a HAproxy-based load balancer. It can proxy at layer four by simply forwarding connections to the appropriate port or at layer seven, where it can route traffic based on HTTP information. The load balancer can also provide SSL termination for any service.

The easiest way to create a load balancer is through the web interface. Click on the down arrow next to **Add Service** and select **Add Load Balancer**. A window will open providing configuration options:

If the load balancer is providing SSL termination, a certificate must be created in **INFRASTRUCTURE | SSL**. Multiple certificates can be configured for web services. The load balancer will use SNI to provide the correct certificate based on the requested server name.

As seen in the preceding WordPress example, a load balancer may be created as part of a `docker-compose.yml` file. In that example, a simple load balancer is created that proxies HTTP connections on port 80 to port 80 in the `wordpress` service. To use plain TCP, append `/tcp` to the target port number. For example, to forward port 25 to TCP port 25 on a container, the port entry would be `25:25/tcp`.

> All of the load balancer settings from the web interface are also possible through `docker-compse.yml`. For more details, refer to `http://docs.rancher.com/rancher/v1.2/en/cattle/adding-load-balancers/`.

Further reading

This chapter and the preceding three showed just a few of the orchestration platforms out there. There are many others and it seems as if another one is released every day. Here are some other orchestration tools to look at:

- Google, Amazon, and Microsoft all have container services as part of their cloud offerings. These are often the easiest ways to use containers in the cloud.
- Red Hat OpenShift is a PaaS platform built on top of Kubernetes. It is available as a hosted platform or it can be installed on-site. There is also an open source variant called OpenShift Origin. For more details, refer to `https://www.openshift.com/`.
- Panamax is an open source project developed by CenturyLink based on Fleet and CoreOS. It provides an easy to use web interface for managing applications. For more details, refer to `http://panamax.io/`.
- Modera Cloud is an open source package that works with Docker Swarm. It bills itself as being, *by developers for developers*. It uses a command line interface to manage applications. For more details, refer to `https://mcloud.io/`.
- Microsoft Azure Stack unifies management of containers with the rest of your on premise cloud. Windows Server 2016 released with container support, which is compatible with Docker. Windows Server is capable of running Windows-based containers as well as Linux-based containers in light weight VMs. As of this writing, Azure Stack is still a technical preview. For more details, refer to `https://azure.microsoft.com/en-us/overview/azure-stack/`.

Summary

This chapter looked at two different tools—Fleet and Rancher. Fleet is a lower level system that is great for small environments or as a base for a higher level tool. It was shown how to start and stop services, set service affinity, run highly available services, and run global services across the cluster.

Rancher makes it easy to run multiple environments using different orchestration tools, including Docker Swarm, Kubernetes, Mesos, and Rancher Cattle. This chapter also showed how to use `rancher-compose` to manage applications, create health checks, and load balance services.

The next chapter will cover logging and monitoring of Docker clusters.

8
Monitoring Your Cluster

Setting up orchestration for a Docker cluster is only half the battle. One also needs visibility into the cluster. Why is data retrieval slow? Is it disk or network? What is being logged by the web server for an application? How much memory is being used by an application? At some point, these or similar questions will come up and it will be up to you, as the administrator, to have the answers for these.

This chapter will look at different tools that can be deployed to assist in monitoring and troubleshooting. Some, such as Kibana, can provide a summary of the cluster health while others, such as Sysdig, can provide deep dive information on applications or individual containers.

This chapter will cover the following topics:

- Docker logging drivers
- Logging for containers that do not send logs to standard out or standard error
- Logging and viewing logs with the ELK stack
- Using remote logging with Kubernetes, Mesosphere, and Docker Datacenter
- Collecting performance metrics
- Graphing metrics with Kibana and Grafana
- Considerations for logging and troubleshooting
- Using Sysdig to view container metrics in real time

Logging with containers

Nearly every application generates logs of some sort. They might track usage such as web server access logs or they may only show start up or error messages. In every case, logs have their use and not being able to see them can be a serious problem.

Logging in Docker is a strange beast. Containers are, by design, transitory. They are designed to be created and destroyed often. This becomes a problem for application logs because log files are deleted right along with a container.

The solution to the problem is two-fold. First, Docker provides a plugin system for logging, which takes everything an application prints to standard out or standard error and logs it somewhere. Second, a *somewhere* is needed for those logs to go to. In other words, a log aggregation server is needed.

Using Docker logging plugins

Docker assumes that everything that is printed to standard out or standard error is a log. These logs can be accessed by running `docker logs <container name>` where `<container name>` is the name of the container. Unfortunately, these logs only exist as long as the container does. Docker solved this problem by creating a logging plugin system that allows an administrator to configure Docker to send those logs elsewhere.

In an orchestrated environment, logs should be sent to a log aggregation server. If they are kept local, it becomes a challenge to find the logs when they are needed. There are several options for remote logging available. Following are a few of them:

- `syslog`: This is the tried and true remote logging solution on Unix and Linux systems. This is a fine solution if a remote Syslog infrastructure is already available. The biggest drawback is that Syslog logs are unformatted making it difficult to automatically mine useful data from the logs.
- `gelf`: The **Graylog Extended Log Format (GELF)** was developed by the Graylog project to overcome the deficiencies in Syslog by providing a structured log format. It works hand-in-hand with NoSQL style databases that can automatically index and search based on the keys in the GELF entry.
- `fluentd`: This takes the concept of structured logs one step further by making it easy to send different logs to different logging and analytics services, including Elasticsearch, MySQL, and Nagios. No matter what the environment is, it is a good bet that Fluentd can work with it.
- `awslogs` and `gcplogs`: These plugins send logs to Amazon CloudWatch and Google Cloud Logging, respectively. They are a great option if a Docker cluster is running exclusively on AWS or GCE.
- `etwlogs`: This Windows-only plugin sends Docker logs to **Event Tracing for Windows (ETW)**. From there, standard Windows tools such as **System Center Operations Manager (SCOM)** can be used to aggregate and alert based on the logs.

A complete list of logging drivers and their settings may be found at `https://docs.docker`
`.com/engine/admin/logging/overview/`.

A log driver may be specified for the Docker daemon with the `--log-driver` flag. The
driver will apply to any containers started on the server. It is also possible to pass `--log-`
`driver` as an argument to `docker run` to override the logging options for that container.

Each logging driver takes a number of options specific to the driver. The `syslog` driver, for
example, has options for the remote Syslog server address, log facility, and TLS options.
The following example configures the Docker daemon to use the `gelf` driver to send logs to
a Graylog server. The address name is set with the `gelf-address` option:

```
$ docker daemon --log-driver=gelf --log-opt gelf-
address=udp://graylog:12201 ...
```

Setting the logging driver for a specific container works the same way. This example uses
the `syslog` driver for a container:

```
$ docker run --log-driver=syslog ...
```

Nearly all of the logging plugins prevent the use of the `docker logs` command. The only
way to see the logs for those containers will be through the aggregation server. During
container testing, it may be helpful to set the log driver to the default `json-file` driver.

Warning: All output from a container is sent to the log server. This
includes all of the command output from containers running a shell such
as `docker run -it busybox`. The output of commands run through
`docker exec` are not included. Specify a local logging driver if you are
running commands that will output sensitive information that should not
be in the logs.

Logging containers that do not play by the rules

There may be times when an application in a container does not output logs to standard
output or standard error. This is common for traditional applications that are being
transitioned to run in containers. There are a couple of options for handling the logs
depending on the application.

The first option is to run a service such as Logstash or Filebeat inside the container. Logstash is configured to watch the application's log files and send them to the appropriate server. A service controller such as `supervisord` is used as the `entrypoint` in the `Dockerfile` to start the application and Logstash. Be careful with this because it is possible that the logging service could stop and not be restarted.

A second option is to configure a volume in the `Dockerfile` for the logs. Logstash could then be run in a sidekick container to read the logs and send them to the aggregation server. If the service is running in a Kubernetes cluster, a pod could be used to group the containers. This is a better option, in general, because it keeps the logging tools separate from the application making it easier to upgrade or replace each of them.

Logging with the ELK stack

The combination of Elasticsearch, Logstash, and Kibana make up the ELK stack. Each component makes up a single part of the whole. Elasticsearch is the database. All log information will end up here. Logstash is what puts (or stashes) the logs in Elasticsearch. Logstash has a number of input plugins including `gelf` and `syslog`. Finally, Kibana provides a simple way to search the logs and create dashboards based on the log information.

Starting Elasticsearch

Elasticsearch is a NoSQL style database that can be used by a number of tools. It is very fast and was designed from the beginning to be able to run in a multi-master environment. The following example starts a new Elasticsearch container:

```
$ docker run -d --name es -p 9200:9200 -p 9300:9300 elasticsearch -E
node.name="Node1"
```

Single configuration settings can be set with the `-E` flag. The value of `node.name` is the name of this node in the Elasticsearch cluster. If you plan to run more than one Elasticsearch container, two more options are needed. The first is `cluster.name` which is the name of the cluster and must be the same for all nodes. The second is `discovery.zen.ping.unicast.hosts` which contains a list of hosts to connect to. It may also be a DNS name that resolves to multiple hosts. This is a good place to use the hostname from an overlay network's DNS-SD.

If a more involved configuration is needed, the configuration settings can be added to `/usr/share/elasticsearch/config` in the container either as a volume or by building a new image. The following `Dockerfile` shows how it might be done. This has the advantage of letting you build an image with your configuration *baked in* and allowing you to version your images for more controlled deployments in the cluster:

```
FROM elasticsearch:5.0
COPY config /usr/share/elasticsearch/config
```

The `elasticsearch` image stores its data in `/usr/share/elasticsearch/data`. This should be a persistent, network volume. The exact configuration of the volume will depend on what is being used for shared storage.

Starting Logstash

Logstash is a tool that takes logs from various sources and stores them in Elasticsearch. The simplest way to use it with Docker is to configure it to listen for GELF logs. The configuration will look similar to the one shown here:

```
input {
  gelf { }
}
output {
  elasticsearch {
    hosts => [ 'es.weave.local' ]
  }
}
```

The `gelf` block tells Logstash to listen for GELF logs. The `elasticsearch` block tells Logstash that output is going to Elasticsearch. The `hosts` option is a comma delimited list of hosts. It can also be a DNS entry that returns one or more IP addresses:

```
$ docker run -d --name logstash -p 9200:9200 -p 12201:12201/udp logstash -f
/config/logstash.conf
```

The configuration file to use is set with the `-f` flag. This file can be added to the container as a volume or added to a custom `logstash` image. Adding the configuration to the image prevents configuration drift and ensures that every Logstash service is doing the same thing:

```
FROM logstash:5.0
COPY logstash.conf /config/logstash.conf
```

There are two options for using Logstash with Docker:

- The first is to run a central Logstash service that every Docker host uses.
- The second option is to run Logstash on every host and configure Docker to send logs to the local Logstash container. This option will scale better on large clusters.

The following example shows how to configure the Docker daemon to send GELF logs to a service running on localhost. If a central Logstash server is used instead, replace localhost with the address of the server:

```
$ docker daemon --log-driver=gelf --log-opt gelf-
address=udp://localhost:12201
```

Viewing the logs with Kibana

Sending the logs to a remote server is great, but does not do any good unless there is a way to view them. This is where Kibana comes in. Kibana provides an interface to view and search the logs in Elasticsearch. It can also create graphs and charts based on any information in the Elasticsearch database.

The easiest way to get started with Kibana is with the official Docker image. The following example shows how to run it. The value of ELASTICSEARCH_URL is the address of the Elasticsearch API service:

```
$ docker run -d --name kibana:5.0 -e
ELASTICSEARCH_URL=http://elasticsearch:9200 -p 5601:5601 kibana
```

Once Kibana is running, you can connect to the Docker host where Kibana is running. For example, if Kibana is running on 172.17.8.101, the address of the web interface is http://172.17.8.101:5601. There is no authentication, by default:

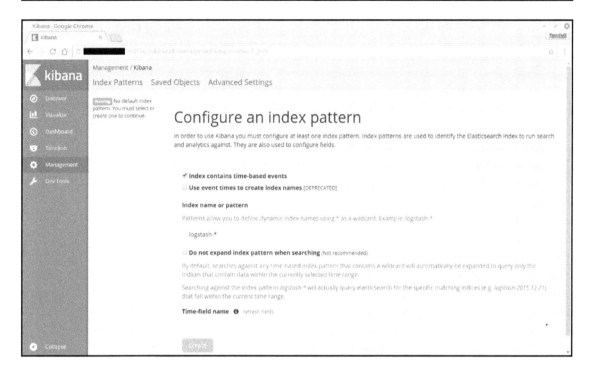

The first time that you log in, you will be prompted for an index that Kibana will run analytics against. Logs from Logstash are available under the `logstash-*` index. Entries in the selected index must exist before an index can be configured. The **Time-field name** field must be set to `@timestamp`.

Once the index pattern has been configured, the logs can be viewed on the **Discover** page. Once a lot of logs from a large number of services start arriving, viewing all of the logs at once becomes an exercise in futility. Fortunately, Elasticsearch is very good at searching. For example, one can see the logs for a single container with the `container_name:<container>` query, where `<container>` is the name of the container. It is also possible to search based on the image name using `image_name:<name>` in the query.

The field names `container_name` and `image_name` may be different if a different logging driver is used to add the logs to Elasticsearch.

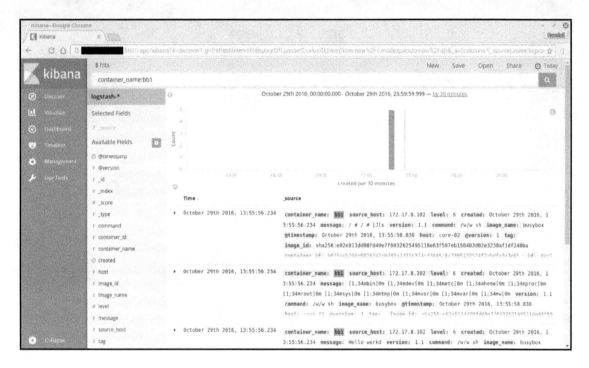

Individual logs are made up of a number of fields. Each field can be used as a query term. This makes it possible to drill down to exactly what is needed. The following screenshot shows the fields for a single log from Docker:

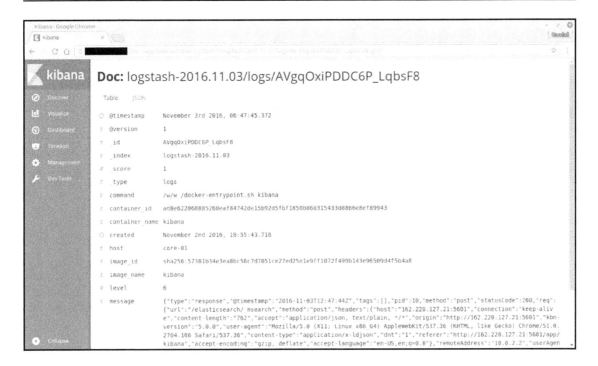

Among the more useful fields for `docker logs` are the following:

- `container_name`: This is the name of the container as specified by the `--name` flag to `docker run`.
- `container_id`: This is the full ID of the container. This can be particularly useful if multiple containers are running with the same name.
- `image_name`: This is the name of the image being used. This makes it possible to find logs for all containers running a specific image.
- `host`: This is the name of the host that the container is running on.
- `message`: This is the actual log message. This is whatever would have been printed by the `docker logs` command.

 Queries in Kibana are built using Elasticsearch syntax. Documentation may be found at
`https://www.elastic.co/guide/en/elasticsearch/reference/5.0/quer y-dsl-query-string-query.html#query-string-syntax`.

Search queries can be saved. This makes it easy to rerun queries that are needed often. Saved searches can also be added to dashboards to bring multiple sets of logs into a single view.

Remote logging in Docker Datacenter

Docker hosts managed by Docker Datacenter can be configured to use log drivers just like any other Docker host. Docker Datacenter, itself, supports logging to a remote Syslog server. Go to **Settings** and then to **LOGS**. From there, the remote Syslog server, protocol, and log level can be set. Click on **Enable Remote Logging** when you are done:

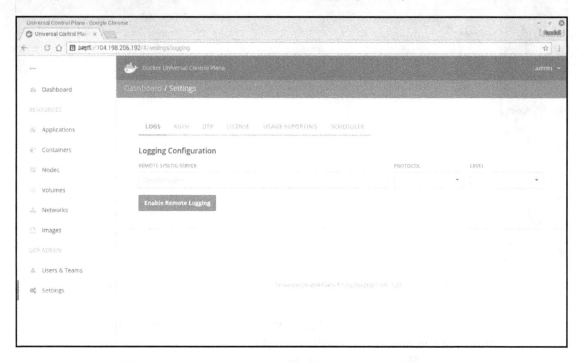

Logging from Kubernetes

Kubernetes was designed with centralized logging in mind. It can send logs to Google Cloud Logging or to Elasticsearch running as a Kubernetes service. Kibana is also started to provide an easy way to access logs sent to Elasticsearch. To enable Elasticsearch on installation, set the `KUBE_LOGGING_DESTINATION` environment variable to `elasticsearch` before running `kube-up.sh`:

```
$ KUBE_LOGGING_DESTINATION=elasticsearch kube-up.sh
```

For full details, refer to `http://kubernetes.io/docs/getting-started-guides/`.

Logging from Mesosphere

Mesosphere makes logs from every running service available through the Marathon web interface. Unfortunately, it can be cumbersome to access logs for more than one service at a time. There is no native way to send service logs to an aggregation server.

There are a couple of options to work around that. The first option is to configure the Docker daemon to send logs to Elasticsearch using the GELF logging driver as described earlier. The other option is to use Logstash or Elastic Filebeat to read the service logs directly and send them to Elasticsearch.

To use Filebeat, install it on each host from Elastic's `yum` repository. Then add the following to `/etc/filebeat/filebeat.yml`. Be sure to change the name of the Elasticsearch hosts in the `hosts` key:

```
filebeat.prospectors:
- input_type: log
  paths:
    - /var/lib/mesos/slave/slaves/*/frameworks/*
      /executors/*/runs/latest/stdout
    - /var/lib/mesos/slave/slaves/*/frameworks/*
      /executors/*/runs/latest/stderr
output.elasticsearch:
  hosts: ["elasticsearch:9200"]
```

Logging your Docker hosts

Remember that the cluster logs should include the Docker hosts as well as Docker, itself. When considering a logging solution for Docker, it is worth ensuring that logs from the hosts can be sent there as well. Logstash, for example, has an option to act as a Syslog server. Each host can be configured to send logs through Logstash which will add them to Elasticsearch.

Adding the logs from the Docker hosts to the same logging solution as Docker will aid in troubleshooting and root cause analysis. A viewer such as Kibana becomes the *single pane of glass* to see everything that is happening in the cluster. Imagine getting alerts warning that certain containers cannot talk to a database and seeing in the same view as the Docker logs, a log message that an interface on a Docker host is disconnected. The faster problems can be found, the faster services can be restored.

Collecting and graphing performance data

Logs are great, but sometimes what is really needed is a summary of system performance. A quick view of performance graphs can often tell an administrator much more than sifting through hundreds or thousands of log entries. A simple question such as "Why is this application slow?" can often require looking at performance data for the disks on the storage nodes, network utilization between each storage node and between the storage and the Docker host, memory and CPU utilization, and host disk performance. That does not even include things such as database speed and application inefficiencies. The good news is that all of this data can be collected and graphed.

Collecting data with collectd

The collectd daemon is a powerful tool that can collect data from many different sources and send the data to a number of databases. Two of those databases are Elasticsearch and InfluxDB. Using Elasticsearch means that the data is available for Kibana to build visualizations and to include in dashboards. InfluxDB is a high-speed database designed specifically for storing time series data. There are a number of tools which can create graphs and charts from InfluxDB, including Grafana, which will be discussed a little later.

Sometimes, the right answer to the question of which database to use to store cluster metrics is *both*. Elasticsearch and InfluxDB have their strengths and weaknesses but they compliment each other well. Try running them both for a while. It is always possible to stop sending data to one or the other at a later date.

Running collectd

There are packages for collectd available for most major Linux distributions. In Debian and Ubuntu, installation is as simple as `apt-get install collectd`. Packages and installation instructions for other distributions are available at `https://collectd.org/download.shtml`.

The `collectd` daemon can be run manually from the command line as in the following example. The `-f` flag will keep `collectd` in the foreground. The `-C` flag is used to provide a path to the configuration file:

```
$ collectd -f -C /etc/collectd/collectd.conf
```

There is no official Docker container for collectd. Some plugins make assumptions that makes running it in a container problematic. For example, the memory plugin hardcodes /proc as the source for memory information. In a container, /proc only contains the information for the container rather than for the entire system.

Interface data is odd when collectd is run in a container because of the virtual interfaces created for a container. This can be worked around using --net=host with docker run.

Configuring collectd

Data is collected through a series of plugins. Each plugin is loaded with the LoadPlugin option. If the plugin has options, they are set using a <Plugin name> block, where name is the name of the plugin. A complete list of plugins with links to their options is available in the collectd.conf(5) man page or at https://collectd.org/wiki/index.php/Table_of_Plugins.

The following example shows a basic configuration that reads CPU usage metrics, load average, and disk usage:

```
BaseDir "/var/lib/collectd"
PIDFile "/run/collectd.pid"
Interval 10.0

LoadPlugin cpu
LoadPlugin load
LoadPlugin disk
```

The Interval option is the number of seconds between data collection runs. Be sure that this is not set so low that it overwhelms the server. The interval can be set per plugin using the <LoadPlugin> tag and specifying the Interval option there:

```
<LoadPlugin foo>
   Interval 60
</LoadPlugin>
```

The preceding base example reads the data but does not do anything with it. In a clustered environment, it is most likely that the data will be sent to a database. The `network` plugin can be configured to send collected data to one or more servers. The following snippet loads the `network` plugin and configures collectd to send the data to two servers. The number after the IP address is the UDP port number:

```
LoadPlugin network
<Plugin network>
 Server "172.17.8.102" "25826"
 Server "172.17.8.101" "12203"
</Plugin>
```

Storing performance data in Elasticsearch

The collectd daemon data is added to Elasticsearch through Logstash. The following example adds a UDP `input` plugin to the `input` block. Logstash will listen for collectd connections on the port specified by the `port` option. The `buffer_size` option sets the maximum packet size. For performance reasons, this should be set small enough to fit in a single network frame.

The `codec` option tells Logstash that the incoming packets are in binary network format of `collectd`. In order to properly map the data types, Logstash needs a copy of `types.db` from `collectd`. The collectd daemon usually installs `types.db` in `/usr/share/collectd/`.

This example does one last thing. It sets the type for each `input` plugin. This makes it easy to see only logs in queries in Kibana by adding `_type:log` to a query:

```
input {
  gelf {
    type => log
  }
  udp {
    port => 12203
    buffer_size => 1452
    codec => collectd {
      typesdb => [ '/usr/share/collectd/types.db' ]
    }
    type => perf
  }
}
```

If you are going to run Logstash in a container, create a custom image that adds `types.db`. An example `Dockerfile` is shown here:

```
FROM logstash:5.0
COPY types.db /usr/share/collectd/types.db
```

Storing performance data in InfluxDB

InfluxDB was built from the ground up to handle time-series data. It is very fast with several options for high availability. Best of all, there is an official Docker container available. Starting InfluxDB is as simple as running the following command:

```
docker run -d -p 8083:8083 -p 8086:8086 -p 25826:25826/udp --name influxdb \
-v /usr/share/collectd/types.db:/usr/share/collectd /types.db:ro \
-e INFLUXDB_COLLECTD_ENABLED=true \
-e INFLUXDB_COLLECTD_port=25826 \
-e INFLUXDB_COLLECTD_DATABASE=collectd_db \
-e INFLUXDB_COLLECTD_TYPESDB=/usr/share/collectd/types.db\
influxdb
```

The environment variables configure InfluxDB to do the following in this order:

- Enabling collectd support
- Listening for collectd connections on UDP port `25826`
- Setting the database for collectd data to `collectd_db`
- Setting the path within the container to the collectd `types.db`

The `influxdb` image stores the database in `/var/lib/influxdb`. When run in production this should be on an external volume.

Graphing data with Kibana

The **Visualize** page provides options for creating graphs and charts of data in Elasticsearch. Visualizations that are created can then be saved for later viewing, or combined on dashboards to provide a more complete view of a cluster or service.

Creating a new chart

To create a new graph, click on **Visualize**, select the chart type, and then select the name of the index. Logstash data will be in the indices matching the `logstash-*` pattern. You will then be taken to a page to create the graph:

1. Click on the arrow next to **Y-Axis** to show the options.
2. Select the **Aggregation** method. The **Average** method works well in most cases.
3. Select a **Field**. Obviously, this will vary depending on the data that is being graphed.
4. Optionally, set the **Custom Label** for the axis.
5. Additional metrics can be added:

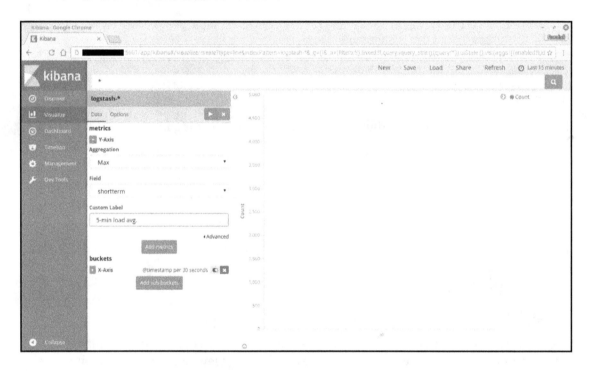

6. In the **buckets** section, click on the arrow next to **X-Axis**.
7. Select the **Aggregation** method. In most cases this will be **Date Histogram**.
8. The **Field** should be **@timestamp** unless there is a custom timestamp field set:

9. Click on the arrow at the top of the configuration panel to apply the changes and see the graph.
10. Click on **Save** from the menu at the top of the page to save the chart.

By default, Kibana will aggregate all of the data for the chosen field into the graph. Often, it makes more sense to see the data broken out based on the host or other metadata. To do that, click on **Add sub-buckets**. Then click on **Split Lines** or **Split Chart**. **Split Lines** shows a line for each sub-bucket. **Split Chart** creates a separate chart for each sub-bucket. **Split Chart** is better if there are many metrics being graphed.

To break the data out by hostname, set **Sub Aggregation** to **Significant Terms**, set **Field** to **host.keyword**, and **Size** to 1. Click on the arrow at the top to apply any changes and see what the graph looks like.

Adding charts to a dashboard

Dashboards provide a way to show saved charts and searches together in one place. To create a new dashboard, follow the steps mentioned here:

1. Click on **Dashboard** from the menu on the left and click on **New** from the menu at the top. Click on **Add** at the top of the page to add a new panel to the dashboard.

2. Click on the saved visualization or search and it will be added to the dashboard:

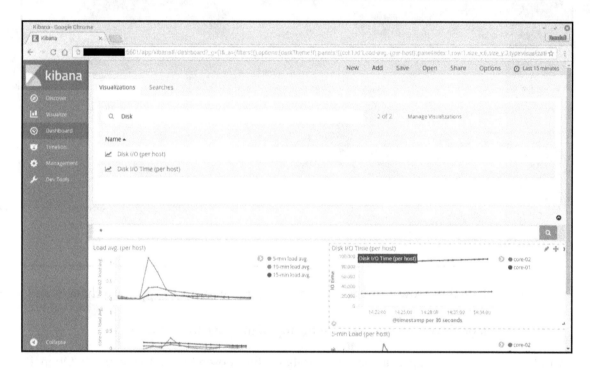

Panels can be resized and moved around the dashboard to present the information in a way that makes the most sense. When the dashboard is ready, click on the **Save** option at the top of the page. Give the dashboard a name and click on the **Save** button. Previously saved dashboards can be opened by clicking on the **Open** option from the menu at the top of the page.

Graphing data with Grafana

Grafana is a very powerful tool for graphing data. It can use Elasticsearch and InfluxDB as data sources, but InfluxDB has more query options for manipulating the data.

One of Grafana's biggest features is the ability to create dashboard templates that allow one to build groupings of datasets for easy display. For example, you could choose to display just web servers, database servers, or all servers tagged with *frontend*. For more details, refer to http://docs.grafana.org/reference/templating/.

Installing Grafana

The Grafana project has created a Docker image to make deploying Grafana easier. The basic command to get started is given here. The default username and password are both `admin`.

```
$ docker run -d -p 3000:3000 --name grafana grafana/grafana
```

By default, Grafana stores database and session information in `/var/lib/grafana` using SQLite. It can be configured to use MySQL or PostgreSQL instead. If you choose to stick with SQLite, make sure that `/var/lib/grafana` is mounted as an external volume. Full configuration documentation may be found at
http://docs.grafana.org/installation/configuration/.

Adding data source

Before Grafana can be used to graph data, it must know where the data is. To add a new data source select **Data Sources** from the drop-down menu at the top left. Click on the **Add new** button. The specifics will vary depending on the data source chosen with the **Type** option. When you are finished setting the connection information for the data source, click on **Save & Test**. Grafana will attempt to connect to the data source and will print a warning if there is a problem. Multiple data sources may be added and used within a single graph:

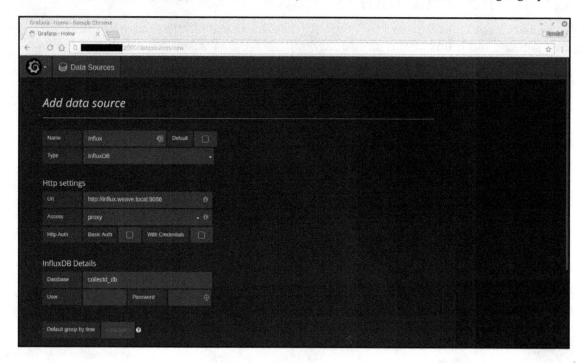

Creating a new dashboard

A new dashboard can be created by selecting Dashboard from the drop-down menu and choosing the **+New** option. The new dashboard will be blank with a very small pop-out menu to the left of the row. From that pop-out menu, new panels can be added. The menu on an example dashboard is shown here:

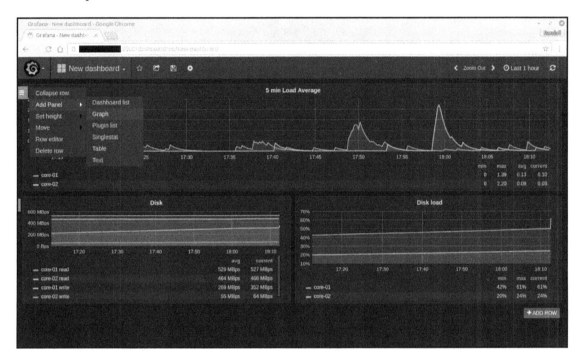

Creating a graph

Open the pop-out menu for a row and go first to **Add Panel** then to **Graph**. The graph editor will then be displayed. There are a lot of options. Do not panic. Most of them are simple with obvious functions. The most complicated is the **Metrics** tab. This is where the metrics are chosen to be displayed on the graph.

Click on the button that says **select metric** and choose the metric that will be used for this graph. In the following screenshot, the **load_shortterm** metric has been selected. Additional metrics can be added to the graph with the **Add query** button:

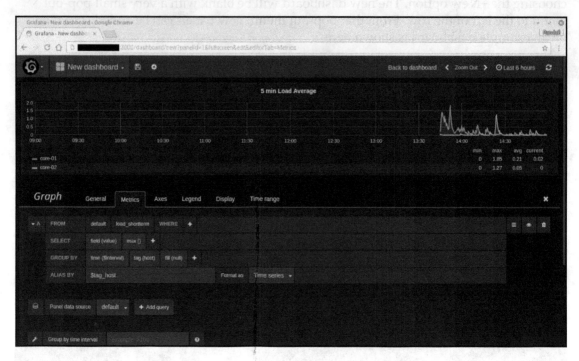

A number of options are available including options to manipulate the chosen metric. One useful option is the ability to group the metric by a tag. Click on the plus sign in the **GROUP BY** row and select **tag(host)** to break each host out into its own line.

When the graph is done, click on **Back to dashboard** to return to the dashboard. Click on the disk icon at the top or press *Ctrl + S* to save the dashboard. The dashboard will be available from the drop-down menu at the top of the page.

Using Heapster in Kubernetes

Heapster is a Kubernetes service that collects node and pod metrics and makes them available through InfluxDB and Grafana or through Google Cloud Monitoring. It is installed by default when Kubernetes is installed with `kube-up.sh`. Full details on accessing metrics from Heapster are available at
`http://kubernetes.io/docs/user-guide/monitoring/`.

One of the things Heapster does is group container metrics by pod. It adds labels to the metrics based on the labels set in the pod. This makes it easy to create charts in Grafana that focus on a single pod or a single application made up of multiple pods.

Considerations for monitoring system health

One of the things a system administrator learns early in his or her career is that it is better to find out about problems and fix them before the customer or the boss notices them. Log collection and performance graphs are essential when it comes to troubleshooting problems. Rarely, however, is someone watching every log message and every piece of performance data. There is just too much information and some administrators even have lives outside of the office. Fortunately, computers are very good at sifting through lots of data and rarely ask for time off.

Most of the tools that have been used for years to monitor server and service health still apply. However, a fully orchestrated environment offers some unique challenges when compared to the old standalone server model. For example, a service does not live on a single host. It could run anywhere in the cluster. In addition, the ability to quickly add or remove capacity to the Docker cluster through AWS, GCE, or even a VM in a local data center makes adding specific hosts in a monitoring suite a challenge.

There are too many variations to provide specific solutions that will work in all circumstances, but here are some general guidelines.

Monitor services

Remember that the most important thing your clients care about when using your service is; "Does it work?", For the administrator, the question is not just; "Is it up?", but; "How can I keep it that way?". There are several things that can be done to ensure that the administrators know that there are problems before the clients do:

- **Use health checks**: Some orchestration tools, such as Kubernetes, can run checks to monitor the health of a service. Use them and make them meaningful. It is not enough to know that a web server is accepting connections on port 80. You also need to know if it is returning a good status code and showing what is expected.
- **Monitor all of the moving parts**: A web application is usually more than a web server. Is there a database and is it responding properly? Do not be afraid to write a health check that logs into the database with the credentials of the web application and performs queries.

- **Do not forget the network**: When running a cluster locally, it can be easy to overlook, or take for granted, the network infrastructure. Where feasible, add the networking stack to your monitoring. Some organizations split the network and server operations teams which may make adding the network stack to the Docker monitors politically problematic. In that case, make friends with the network team.
- **Create useful dashboards**: Being able to see the logs and metrics from related components in one place can simplify troubleshooting. The trick is to know what is worth looking at and what is not. Too much information can be just as much a problem as too little.

Watching services in real time with Sysdig

Sysdig is a real-time command-line monitoring tool. It can monitor most host components and has support for reporting container statistics. It also has support for viewing metrics based on Kubernetes pods, replication controllers, services, and more.

When possible, Sysdig should be installed and run directly on the host machine. This will provide it the most visibility into the system. Packages are available for Debian and Red Hat-based systems. Installation instructions may be found at `http://www.sysdig.org/install/`.

It is also possible to run Sysdig in a container. This is especially useful if the Docker hosts are running a Linux distribution that is not directly supported or systems such as CoreOS which run everything in containers. The command to start the container is as follows:

```
$ docker run -it --rm --name=sysdig --privileged=true \
--volume=/var/run/docker.sock:/host/var/run/docker.sock \
--volume=/dev:/host/dev \
--volume=/proc:/host/proc:ro \
--volume=/boot:/host/boot:ro \
--volume=/lib/modules:/host/lib/modules:ro \
--volume=/usr:/host/usr:ro \
sysdig/sysdig
```

There are a couple of things to note:

- First of all, running `sysdig` in a container requires the use of the `--privileged` flag. It needs the access in order to load the `sysdig` kernel module and to be able to access all of the required information.
- Second, the command maps through a number of important file systems such as `/proc` for visibility reasons.

- Third, `/var/run/docker.sock` is mapped into the container so that `sysdig` can retrieve information about running Docker containers.

Once `sysdig` has been installed, run the command `csysdig` to start the curses interface. This provides a top-like interface which lets you see what is happening on the server. Use *F2* to switch views. The `-pc` flag adds container information to many of the views that are available:

```
$ csysdig -pc
```

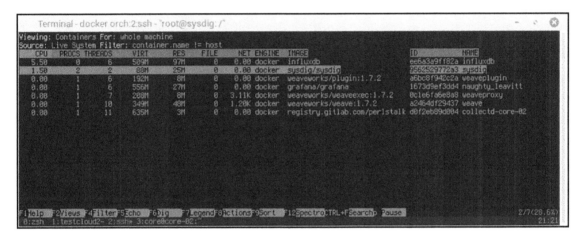

Sysdig can be invaluable in troubleshooting a problem on a system in real time. Each view has options to drill down and see more information about a specific thing, which may be a container, network connection, host process, or any number of other items.

Summary

This chapter showed how to send Docker logs and metrics to remote services. It showed how to use Kibana to view logs stored in Elasticsearch and how to use Kibana and Grafana to build charts and dashboards based on metrics stored in Elasticsearch and InfluxDB to provide useful information quickly. Some general tips were presented for monitoring services in a Docker cluster. Finally, Sysdig was introduced which can provide live monitoring of a host and containers. The next chapter will cover how to use continuous integration to build, test, and deploy containers.

9

Using Continuous Integration to Build, Test, and Deploy Containers

One of the most important parts of running containers is building the images those containers are based on. After all, without an image, there is no container. One of the challenges is to ensure that the Docker images actually, not only build, but also work *before* being deployed.

This chapter will demonstrate how to use GitLab to implement **Continuous Integration** (**CI**) for Docker images. It will show how to automatically build an image, run a test suite against it, push the new image into a Docker Registry, and even deploy the new image to a Docker cluster.

The following topics will be covered in the chapter:

- The importance of using CI
- Setting up a project in GitLab for CI
- Automatically building a new image
- Running tests against an image
- Releasing a tested image
- Automatically deploying the image
- Using GitLab CI to create DAB files
- Using Docker Cloud for image testing

The importance of using CI

It is worth keeping in mind how a Docker application is defined. At its most basic level, a Docker application is really no different from any software project. It is simply a `Dockerfile` and the resources needed for the image are most likely stored in version control. It is software.

Treating Docker applications like code means that an administrator or team of administrators can benefit from all of the advances in software development methodologies. One of those is the automated building and testing of a project. This process is called CI. Any time a change is made to an application, whether it is a small change to a configuration file or the upgrade of the actual application, the image can be automatically rebuilt and tested to ensure that the image will work as intended when it is deployed.

I often joke that my job as a system administrator is to get other people or things to do my work for me. The reality is that the more I can empower other people in my organization, the more effective we can all be. For example, imagine a development team that is working on a web application. In a traditional model, these developers must wait for an administrator to deploy any changes into the testing and production environments and hope that nothing breaks in the process. Using a proper CI workflow means that whenever the developers are ready to deploy, the CI tools can safely deploy the application without waiting for an administrator to get around to it. The end result is faster, more consistent, and more reliable deployments.

Using GitLab for CI

GitLab is a wonderful tool for CI and deployment for Docker images and services. It combines Git with issue tracking, a Docker Registry, and CI to provide a unified experience. However, this process is not unique to GitLab. The lessons learned in this section should be applicable regardless of the systems used.

Setting up GitLab for CI

GitLab CI is available for free as part of the offerings at GitLab.com. It is also possible to pay for an enterprise license which provides more resources. The free community and commercial enterprise editions of GitLab can also be installed locally. In Chapter 3, *Cluster Building Blocks – Registry, Overlay Networks, and Shared Storage* we showed how to install GitLab and how to enable the Docker Registry.

A **registry** is an important part of making CI work. It provides a place for finished images to be stored for use in the cluster. Another registry could be used instead of GitLab. For example, an organization may choose to use the Docker Hub or the secure registry in Docker Datacenter.

As of GitLab 8.0, GitLab CI is fully integrated into the main package. There is nothing else to install or enable in GitLab to make those features available, with one exception. The last component that is needed is a GitLab Runner.

Installing the GitLab Runner on Ubuntu

It is the job of the GitLab Runner to perform the actual image builds. Each build is queued up and processed in turn. It is possible to use multiple runners to allow multiple builds to be performed in parallel. Runners can be tagged to run specific tasks such as building Docker images or building an application for Microsoft Windows.

The GitLab.com provides a shared runner that can be used to build images. This is great for smaller projects or for testing. Larger organizations should consider paying for an enterprise license or installing their own runner locally. A local runner may also be desired if the image tests contain sensitive information or if they need to connect to resources that are not accessible from the Internet.

The preferred method of running the GitLab Runner is to install it natively on Debian, Ubuntu, RHEL, or CentOS. However, there is an official Docker image. For details on using the image, refer to
https://gitlab.com/gitlab-org/gitlab-ci-multi-runner/blob/master/docs/install/docker.md.

The first step in installing a runner that will build Docker images is to have Docker installed. The build process will need to be able to pull images, build new ones, and push the completed build into the repository.

GitLab provides a script to add their `apt` repository to the server. Download the script, double check that it will do what is expected, and then run it. For security reasons, do not pipe the download directly to `sudo` bash:

```
$ wget -O script.deb.sh
https://packages.gitlab.com/install/repositories/runner/gitlab-ci-multi-run
ner/script.deb.sh
$ sudo bash script.deb.sh
```

The script will add GitLab's GPG key to the `apt` keyring, add the repository, and run `apt-get update`. When it is complete, the runner can be installed:

```
$ apt-get install gitlab-ci-multi-runner
```

The runner does not have to be on the GitLab server. If load is an issue, runners can be installed on multiple servers or on cloud providers. It is also possible to have GitLab automatically scale up the number runners on any provider supported by Docker Machine. For details, refer to `https://docs.gitlab.com/runner/install/autoscaling.html`.

Registering a runner

Once the runner is installed, it must be registered with GitLab. There are two ways to do it. The first is to register it for a single project. In that case, the runner will only run for the builds of the specific project. The other option is to register it globally. This will make the runner available for every project in GitLab. There are pros and cons to both approaches, but they are not mutually exclusive. It is possible to configure one or more global runners for general use and others specifically for a project.

A registration token is needed before the runner can be registered with GitLab. For project specific runners, go to the **Runners** settings page of the project. The **Specific Runners** section will show the URL and token to use when registering a runner:

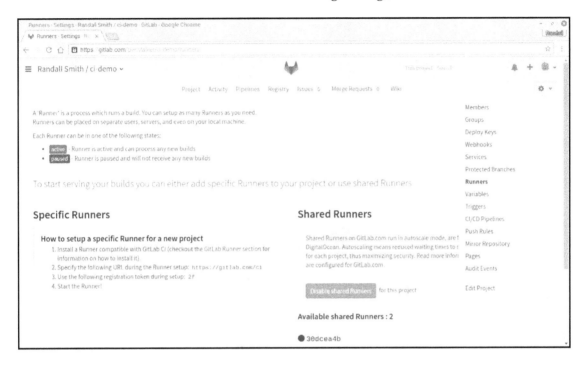

For shared runners, the registration token is in the **Runners** page in the **Admin Area** (the wrench icon) when logged in as an administrator. The URL is the same as for the project specific runner:

There are multiple ways of creating a runner that can be used to build Docker images. The simplest is to use the shell executor. It is designed to run any shell commands to build the project. It works well for almost any sort of project including Docker. The `gitlab-runner` user must be in the `docker` group or otherwise have rights to run `docker`.

The following command is used to register the runner. Replace $GITLAB_URL with the CI URL for the GitLab install listed on the project's **Runners** page. If you are using GitLab.com, the URL would be `https://gitlab.com/ci`. The $REGISTRATION_TOKEN token is the token from either the project specific or global **Runner** pages:

```
$ sudo gitlab-ci-multi-runner register -n \
--url $GITLAB_URL \
--registration-token $REGISTRATION_TOKEN \
--executor shell \
--description "Shell Runner"
```

The other option is to run the docker-in-docker executor. This executor builds the project in a Docker container which contains Docker and Docker Compose:

```
$ sudo gitlab-ci-multi-runner register -n \
--url $GITLAB_URL \
--registration-token $REGISTRATION_TOKEN \
--executor docker \
--description "Docker Runner" \
--docker-image "docker:latest" \
--docker-privileged
```

The runner container must run in privileged mode in order to run the build containers.

Enabling a Docker Repository

The next thing to set up before beginning the build process is to enable a Docker Registry. GitLab provides a registry service that can be enabled on a per project basis. Instructions for setting it up are in `Chapter 3`, *Cluster Building Blocks – Registry, Overlay Networks, and Shared Storage*. If it is already set up or you are using `GitLab.com`, go to **Edit Project** and ensure that the box next to **Container Registry** is checked.

The GitLab registry is a great choice because of the integration with GitLab and the CI process. Other registries can be used, if desired. If another registry is used, set up an account for the runner that has rights to push new images into the registry.

Adding the project to the repository

Finally, the project needs to be added to the Git repository in GitLab. This is done with standard `git` commands. Following is the basic script. If the Docker configuration is already in Git, only the last two commands are needed. Be sure to change the URL of the remote to match your repository:

```
$ git init
$ git add .
$ git commit -m 'initial commit'
$ git remote add origin http://gitlab.example.com/project/repo
$ git push -u origin master
```

The following examples will use a very simple Docker image. It is an Nginx web server with a single page website. Following is the Dockerfile:

```
FROM nginx:1.10
COPY index.html /usr/share/nginx/html/
```

Full examples of the CI process described in this section are available on GitLab. Each branch is a complete example for each step. Download the examples from `https://gitlab.com/perlstalker/ci-demo`.

Creating .gitlab-ci.yml

CI is configured through a file named `.gitlab-ci.yml` in the root of the repository. This YAML file defines the build stages, variables, and jobs needed to build, test, and deploy the image. Any number of jobs can be defined and jobs can be run in parallel. For full details on the options available in `.gitlab-ci.yml`, refer to `https://docs.gitlab.com/ce/ci/yaml/README.html`.

The following `.gitlab-ci.yml` example is a simple configuration that can build the image and push it into the registry. This example uses the docker-in-docker executor. The first three lines can be omitted when using the shell executor with a local runner:

```yaml
image: docker:latest
services:
  - docker:dind

stages:
  - build
  - test
  - release
  - deploy

variables:
  DOCKER_CI_IMAGE: registry.gitlab.com/perlstalker/ci-
demo:$CI_BUILD_REF_NAME

before_script:
  - docker login -u gitlab-ci-token -p $CI_BUILD_TOKEN registry.gitlab.com

build-image:
  stage: build
  tags:
    - docker
  script:
    - docker build --pull -t $DOCKER_CI_IMAGE .
    - docker push $DOCKER_CI_IMAGE
```

The `stages` option defines the list of stages that jobs can be configured to run in. Any number of stages can be defined to fit the needs of the project. The four listed here, `build`, `test`, `release`, and `deploy`, are typical. Each stage is run in the order it is listed. Jobs for the `build` stage are run first, then `test`, and so on. If there are multiple jobs in each stage, they are run in parallel.

The `variables` option allows one to define variables for use in the rest of the build process. In the example, a variable named `$DOCKER_CI_IMAGE` is set to the name of the image that will be built. The image name includes the `$CI_BUILD_REF_NAME` variable, which is a built-in variable that is set to the branch or tag name. The value of `$DOCKER_CI_IMAGE` should be changed for the specific project.

Using `$CI_BUILD_REF_NAME` can be very helpful, especially when testing a new image or preparing a new release. During testing, creating a new branch means that the generated image will be tagged with the branch name. For example, if a branch named `foo` is created, the new image will be `image:foo`.

 GitLab provides a number of useful variables that can be used in the CI configuration. A full list is available at `https://docs.gitlab.com/ce/ci/variables/README.html`.

Git tags will also generate an image with that tag. For example, if the `1.1` tag is added to a commit, a new image named `image:1.1` is created. This makes it easy to create versioned images for deployment. Remember that using `image:version` instead of `image:latest` makes it easier to track exactly what is running on the cluster and makes it easy to roll back to the previous image version in the event of a failure.

The `before_script` option contains a list of commands to run to prepare the environment before each job. In this example, it logs into the GitLab Docker registry using a special CI account and build token. The build token temporarily gives the builder the rights of the user who triggered the build. If a different registry is being used, the login credentials for that registry would be used instead.

The last block is a job named `build-image`. The `stage` option gives the stage at which this job will run. In this case, the `build-image` job runs in the `build` stage. If multiple jobs are defined in the same stage, they are run in parallel.

Jobs can define a list of `tags` which are used to define which runner is used. In the preceding example, the image will be built by a runner with the `docker` tag. If multiple tags are set, the runner must match all of them to be used. This makes it possible to create runners that can build certain types of projects and not others.

Finally, the `script` option is a list of commands to run to build the project. Each command must succeed before the next command is run. If any of them fail, the build stops and it is marked as having failed. The commands can be regular system commands as in the example or scripts from the repository.

In this example, the runner first builds the image. The `--pull` flag is used with `docker build` to ensure that the latest copy of the base image is used to build the new image. If the build succeeds, the new image is pushed back into the repository. A list of available images is available in the **Registry** section on the project page:

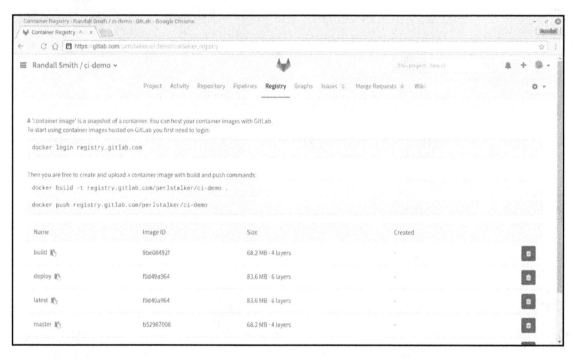

The status of the current build, as well as previous builds, is available in the **Pipelines** section of the project. Click on any build to drill down and see the status of each build stage. Clicking on the stage will show the build log for the stage. Any errors generated by a failed build will appear there:

Testing the image

One of the reasons that CI is so popular among software developers is that it provides a way to automatically run a test suite against the new build to ensure that it works properly. The tests provide a level of security in knowing that whatever changes the developers made, these did not break the functionality of the software. This is just as valuable for Docker images that are going to be deployed to, potentially, hundreds or thousands of servers.

There are several ways of implementing the tests:

- The first is to include the tests in the `git` repository, but not adding them to the image. This keeps the image small, but requires that all of the tools needed for testing are installed on the runner. Some runners, such as the docker-in-docker executor may not include the tools needed to run the tests.

- The second way is to include the tests in the Docker image. The tests can then be run from within the container with either `docker run` or `docker exec`. This leads to a larger image, but ensures that all of the tools needed to test the image are available. It also makes it possible to run the tests on a running image at anytime. This could be useful if there are problems that only show up when the image is running in production.
- A third option is to create a separate image that contains all of the tests needed to validate the image. This image can be downloaded and run by GitLab during the test stage to test the application image. The nice thing about this approach is that the tests and test image can be updated independently as new test cases come up.

Let's take a look at the very simple web page that is being used in this example:

```html
<html>
  <head><title>Docker Orchestration</title></head>
  <body>
    <h1>Docker Orchestration is fun!</h1>
    <p>Automate all the things!</p>
  </body>
</html>
```

The boss has decided that the web page must always proclaim how much fun Docker orchestration is. To this end, a test is created to ensure that it remains fun. In this example, it is placed in a `tests` directory and named `run-tests.sh`:

```sh
#!/bin/sh
curl -s http://localhost | grep 'fun!</h1>' > /dev/null
```

This test is very simple. It accesses the web page and checks to see if `fun!` is the last thing in the heading. To simplify things, the test will be added to the image. The updated `Dockerfile` is listed here. It does two things. First, it adds `curl`, which is needed for the test. Second, it adds the tests to the `/tests` directory in the image:

```
FROM nginx:1.11
RUN apt-get update && apt-get install -y curl && apt-get clean
COPY index.html /usr/share/nginx/html/
COPY tests /tests
```

To run the test, a new job needs to be added to `.gitlab-ci.yml`. The following snippet shows the job. Once `.gitlab-ci.yml` is updated in the repository, future commits will run the tests:

```
test-image:
  stage: test
  tags:
    - docker
  script:
    - docker pull $DOCKER_CI_IMAGE
    - docker run -d -P --name $CI_BUILD_ID $DOCKER_CI_IMAGE
    - docker run --rm --network container:$CI_BUILD_ID --name $CI_BUILD_ID-
test
      --entrypoint /tests/run-tests.sh $DOCKER_CI_IMAGE
    - docker stop $CI_BUILD_ID; docker rm -f $CI_BUILD_ID
```

The `stage` option is set so that the job will run in the `test` stage. This job will not run if the `build` stage fails. It also includes the `docker` tag so that GitLab will use a runner that is also tagged with `docker`.

The `script` section lists the commands that are run to test the image. The first two commands download the image and run it in the background. The container name is set to `$CI_BUILD_ID`, which is the unique build ID assigned to the build by GitLab. It is important to set the name because it will be needed when the test is run.

The third entry in the `script` block runs the actual test. It starts a new container that shares the target container's network. This allows the tests to connect to the web server on localhost. The test container runs the test script which was shown earlier. The `grep` in the script will fail if the pattern is not matched and the test will return a non-zero exit code, which GitLab interprets as a failure. If the pattern in the script is found, the test succeeds and the process moves on.

The last line stops the target container and removes it. The container running the tests is removed automatically when the test is done because `--rm` was used when it was started.

Cleanup jobs

The preceding test job works great when the tests succeed, but when it fails, it can leave the `test` container running. This is not an issue when using the shared runner on `GitLab.com` because a new VM is started for every test and removed immediately after the build process has been completed. However, it could be a problem when using a local runner. In that case, a job may be needed for cleanup after the test.

To start, create a new `cleanup_test` stage and a job named `cleanup_tests` is defined to run in the `cleanup_test` stage. Normally, if a job in the `test` stage fails, nothing after it would run. The `cleanup_tests` job gets around that using the `when` option. By setting it to `always`, the job will run no matter what happens in the `test` stage. The `when` option can also be set to `on_success` or `on_failure` to run the job only when the jobs succeed or fail, respectively. There is a fourth option, `manual`, that will be covered later in the chapter. The following snippet shows how to create a job that cleans up after the CI process completes:

```
stages:
  - build
  - test
  - cleanup_test
  - release
  - deploy
...
test-image:
  stage: test
  tags:
    - docker
  script:
    - docker pull $DOCKER_CI_IMAGE
    - docker run -d -P --name $CI_BUILD_ID $DOCKER_CI_IMAGE
    - sh tests/run-tests.sh $CI_BUILD_ID

cleanup_tests:
  stage: cleanup_test
  script:
    - docker stop $CI_BUILD_ID; docker rm -f $CI_BUILD_ID
  when: always
```

Releasing the image

The `build-image` job has been creating an updated image every time changes are pushed to the `git` repository. Let's take a closer look at what is being created. The `docker build` command in the example is creating an image that is named `registry.gitlab.com/perlstalker/ci-demo:$CI_BUILD_REF_NAME`. The `$CI_BUILD_REF_NAME` variable is the name of the branch or tag. This means that, at this point, the only image that is created is `registry.gitlab.com/perlstalker/ci-demo:master`. There is no `:latest` image. If someone were to try and run `docker run registry.gitlab.com/perlstalker/ci-demo`, the command would fail because the image with its implied `latest` tag does not exist.

The fact that GitLab does not automatically tag the image with the `latest` tag is a feature. The idea is for the CI plan in `.gitlab-ci.yml` to explicitly tag the image. This is done by creating a new job. A snippet of `.gitlab-ci.yml` is shown here:

```
variables:
  DOCKER_CI_IMAGE: registry.gitlab.com/perlstalker/ci-
demo:$CI_BUILD_REF_NAME
  DOCKER_RELEASE_IMAGE: registry.gitlab.com/perlstalker/ci-demo:latest
...
release-image:
  stage: release
  tags:
    - docker
  script:
    - docker pull $DOCKER_CI_IMAGE
    - docker tag $DOCKER_CI_IMAGE $DOCKER_RELEASE_IMAGE
    - docker push $DOCKER_RELEASE_IMAGE
  only:
    - master
```

The first difference is that a new variable, `$DOCKER_RELEASE_IMAGE`, was added with the name of the release image.

 Note that the image tag is `latest`.

As always, the work is done in the `script` block. The first step is to pull the latest copy of the image for this branch. Next, `docker` tag tags that image with the release image name. Specifically, it is given the `latest` tag. Finally, the `docker push` command pushes the newly tagged image back into the registry.

The `only` block is important. It tells GitLab that this job must only be run when building one of the listed branches. In this case, `master`. Without the `only` block, any newly built image from any branch would replace the `latest` image.

The nice thing about this configuration is that new images can be worked on in different branches and images for those branches will be created. Those images can be individually run, tested, and debugged without modifying the released image. When the changes are ready, the development branch can be merged back into the `master` branch and a new `latest` image is created.

Deploying the image

Let's take a moment and see where things stand. At this point, new Docker images for a project are being automatically built any time changes are pushed to the Git repository in GitLab. A test suite is being run against the new image to ensure that it will function as expected. If the changes are pushed to the `master` branch, a new release image is created. The only thing left to do is to deploy the image to the cluster.

How the image is deployed will depend on the orchestration suite chosen. In most cases, all that is needed is to run the command that performs a rolling update of the service. A snippet of an automated deployment job is as follows:

```
deploy-to-dev:
  stage: deploy
  tags:
    - docker
  environment: development
  script:
    - ./deploy.sh $DOCKER_CI_IMAGE development
  only:
    - master
```

There are a couple of things to note here. First, the `stage` is set to `deploy`. The job will only run if the `build`, `test`, and `release` stages are completed successfully; `environment` is optional. The **Environments** page in the **Pipelines** section in the project makes it easy to track deployments to different environments:

The `deploy.sh` script in the snippet is a placeholder. The script can contain whatever is needed to deploy the image in your environment. The script could also be included directly in the `script` block. Later in the chapter, it will be shown how to deploy an image to a Kubernetes cluster.

Consider using the `tags` keyword instead of a branch name in the `only` section for deployments. This will limit deployments only to commits that have been tagged. It will ensure that all images that are deployed use the tag. It will be easier to tell which version of the image a container is running based on the tag on the image.

Deploying the image manually

Automatically deploying an image to the cluster is exciting. Perhaps too exciting. Not everyone wants services to be updated automatically. This does not mean that GitLab cannot be used for deployments. GitLab provides a way of configuring a job to run manually. The build process will run as it normally does, but when it gets to a manual job, it will wait until someone tells GitLab that it is okay to proceed. This provides the consistency of an automated deployment while still allowing a human to decide whether the deployment happens or not.

The following `.gitlab-ci.yml` snippet shows how to create a job with a `manual` trigger. It is basically the same as the preceding automated deployment. The only functional change is the `when` tag:

```
deploy-to-prod:
  stage: deploy
  tags:
    - docker
  environment: production
  script:
    - ./deploy.sh $DOCKER_CI_IMAGE production
  only:
    - master
  when: manual
```

Setting `when` to `manual` will pause the build and deployment process until someone goes to **Pipelines**, clicks on the build, and clicks on the deployment. The following screenshot shows the build pipeline:

Note that all of the jobs have succeeded. Only the `deploy-to-prod` job has not. The triangle play button shows that the `deploy-to-prod` job is awaiting `manual` action. When that button is pushed, the deployment will begin.

Any number of deployment jobs may be defined to fit a variety of needs. For example, a fully automatic job could deploy new images to a development environment. A manual job could then trigger the deployment to a QA or canary environment. Finally, another manual job could deploy the image fully into production. This could be done with parallel jobs as shown here or as separate build stages. Using separate stages ensures that each previous deployment is done before finally being pushed into production.

Deploying to Kubernetes

The preceding examples used a dummy deploy script. Let's a take a look at how one might use GitLab CI to deploy a new image to Kubernetes. In Chapter 5, *Deploying and Managing Services with Kubernetes* we covered managing deployments in Kubernetes.

The following `.gitlab-ci.yml` snippet makes a couple of assumptions:

- First, `kubectl` is installed on the runner machine and that the `gitlab-runner` user has permissions to make changes to the Kubernetes cluster
- Second, a deployment has already been created which will be updated by the build process:

```
variables:
  DOCKER_CI_IMAGE: registry.gitlab.com/perlstalker
    /ci-demo:$CI_BUILD_REF_NAME
  DOCKER_RELEASE_IMAGE: registry.gitlab.com/perlstalker
    /ci-demo:latest
  DEPLOYMENT: ci-demo
  CONTAINER: web
...
deploy-to-kube:
  stage: deploy
  tags:
    - kubectl
  environment: production
  script:
    - kubectl set image deployment/$DEPLOYMENT
      $CONTAINER=$DOCKER_CI_IMAGE
  only:
    - tags
```

```
        when: manual
```

Two new variables, DEPLOYMENT and CONTAINER are added to the configuration. They contain the name of the deployment and the container within that deployment that will be updated, respectively.

As an example, the kubectl tag is set on the job. The expectation is that a runner with the kubectl tag is available, which has kubectl configured to manage the cluster. This makes it easy to create a runner that is only used for deployments and is not used for other build jobs.

The script contains only the command to update an image in the deployment. It is not necessary to do anything with the image in the runner. The Kubernetes nodes that are running the deployment will perform the update on the container based on the deployment strategy of the pod.

Finally, the only block tells GitLab to only run this job if the build has a git tag set. This will ensure that the built image has a different tag than what was running previously. If the image name is the same as what the deployment currently uses, Kubernetes will not know that the image needs to be updated.

Building DAB files

Docker Swarm is moving to **Distributed Application Bundles (DAB)** to define stacks for deployment. GitLab CI can be used to automatically build DAB files for a project. The following snippet assumes that docker-compose.yml is in the root directory of the project:

```
build-dab:
  stage: release
  tags:
    - docker
  script:
    - docker-compose bundle
  artifacts:
    paths:
      - *.dab
    name: "${PROJECT_NAME}-${CI_BUILD_REF_NAME}"
```

The script block runs docker-compose bundle which will generate the .dab file. Additional options can be added to the command, if needed. The artifacts block tells GitLab that the build process generates files that are important. In this example, the .dab files will be saved if the build is successful. All of the files matching the entries in the path list will be added to the artifacts archive file.

Finally, the `name` option provides the name of the artifact archive. In this example, it is the name of the archive and the build reference name separated by a hyphen. For example, if the project is named `ci-demo` and the `master` branch is being built, the name would be `ci-demo-master`. The artifact archive file would be named `ci-demo-master.zip`.

Using Docker Cloud for CI

Docker Hub and Docker Cloud can automatically update images when a linked Git repository is updated. This can be used for lightweight CI, if GitLab is too involved a tool for the job. In either case, custom tools could be written to run the newly generated images against a test suite or they could be run and tested by hand.

Docker Cloud, in particular, can be useful for testing images. It can auto build an image every time the project is updated in GitHub or Bitbucket. Once the image is built, it can be started as a service in a test cluster from the web interface.

To start, click on the **Repositories** link and click on **Create** to create a new repository. Link the new repository to GitLab or Bitbucket by clicking on the appropriate icon at the bottom of the creation page. When everything is ready, click on **Create**:

Enabling autobuilds

Autobuilds can be created any time after a repository is created by selecting the repository from the **Repositories** page and clicking on the **Builds** tab. Configure the build settings and click on **Save** to save the settings or **Save and Build** to save and immediately build the project.

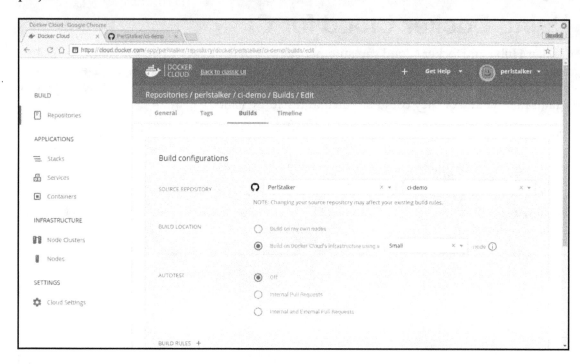

By default, a new build will be generated every time a commit is pushed to the `master` branch. Additional build rules can be created to fit the needs of the project. For example, whenever a new version tag is pushed to Git, Docker Cloud can build a new image that uses that version for the image label.

Testing the image

Once a repository has an image, it can be deployed as a service in the following steps:

1. Click on the **Launch Service** button from the **General** tab and a new page will load with all of the deployment options. That page allows one to set nearly any option that is available with `docker run`.

2. When all of the settings are ready, click on **Create & Deploy**. Docker Cloud will run the service on any nodes that have been configured:

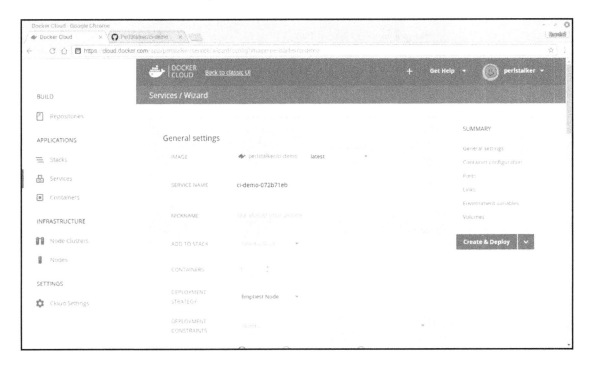

Once the service has started, the list of containers will be available in the **Containers** list or in the details of the service in the **Services** section.

3. To log in to the container's console, click on the container and go to the **Terminal** tab. The tests can be run from there:

Summary

This chapter showed how to use CI with Docker. It showed how to use GitLab to automatically build, test, release, and deploy new images. It also showed how to use Docker Cloud to automatically build images and run them for testing. In the next chapter, you will learn how to automate the infrastructure that the cluster runs on.

10
Why Stop at Containers? Automating Your Infrastructure

The last nine chapters have talked a lot about automating Docker. That is what this book is about, after all. It is important to remember that there is more to a Docker cluster than just Docker. There is the registry, shared storage, overlay networks, and the actual orchestration tool, be it Swarm, Kubernetes, Mesos, or something else. There is one last, very important piece to the puzzle. The servers that all of that run on. Whether those servers are hardware or part of a public cloud, they too need to be managed. After all, what good is it if the Docker orchestration tool can quickly scale an image out if it takes hours to deploy a new Docker host?

This chapter will look at strategies and tools that can be used to automate the server-side of a Docker cluster. It will start by examining the servers themselves, then move on to options for running those machines in the cluster. Finally, it will look at options for removing servers from the cluster.

The following topics will be covered:

- Using configuration management on the server
- Configuring a server on boot with Cloud-Init
- Using and building specialized server images
- Deploying new servers on AWS and Azure
- Using Terraform to orchestrate cloud servers
- Deploying a new cluster with Docker Cloud
- Removing servers from the cluster

Configuring Docker hosts

In many ways, Docker abstracts the server away from the application. It no longer matters which Linux distribution a server is running. A Docker application can be based on any distribution available. Multiple applications can run on the same server and use different base images. Despite that, without the server, nothing runs.

In Chapter 9, *Using Continuous Integration to Build, Test, and Deploy Containers*, we discussed the importance of having a consistent build process for Docker images because doing so provides consistency and reliability. The same is true for the servers those applications run on. If the servers are not consistent, it could cause problems for the containers running on them. This section will discuss different ways of ensuring that the server images are consistent.

Using configuration management

Configuration management has been around on servers in many forms for decades. Sometimes it was as simple as mounting /usr from a remote server or using rcp, scp, or rsync to keep configurations in sync. Later, more powerful tools, such as CFEngine, Puppet, Chef, and Ansible, came along that managed everything from configuration files and installed applications, to managing local users and running services.

Configuration management is an important and powerful tool for any orchestrated cluster. It can perform two important tasks for a server. First, it can set up a server from just the base operating system. It ensures that everything is installed, configured, and running. Second, it makes sure that everything that was installed, configured, and running remains so.

First things first. Puppet needs to be installed on the host:

 Note that this a manual step on an existing server.

```
$ sudo apt-get install puppet
```

Now that Puppet is installed, a manifest can be created to install Docker. The following sample installs Docker on an Ubuntu server and ensures that the `docker` service is running:

```
node default {
  exec { 'install docker' :
    command => "/usr/bin/wget -O - http://get.docker.com |
    /bin/bash",
    creates => '/etc/apt/sources.list.d/docker.list',
  }

  package { "docker-engine" :
    ensure => "installed",
    require => Exec['install docker']
  }
  service { "docker" :
    ensure => "running",
    require => Package['docker-engine']
  }
}
```

This manifest defines a default node. This means that this manifest will be applied to any node that does not match a more specific node definition. Puppet best practice is to only use modules in node definitions. This example breaks that practice in favor of brevity and simplicity.

The `exec` resource checks to see if `/etc/apt/sources.list.d/docker.list` exists, and if not, runs the install script from `get.docker.com`. The script will create `docker.list` and install Docker. This example uses the security nightmare of downloading the script and piping it directly to bash. In a production environment, the verified script should be added to the server as a puppet resource.

The `package` resource ensures that the `docker-engine` package is installed. If, for some reason, `docker-engine` is uninstalled, Puppet will re-install it on the next run. The `require` option tells Puppet that the `install docker` resource must have happened first.

Finally, the `service` resource ensures that the `docker` service is running. If the service is stopped, Puppet will attempt to restart it. This resource requires that the `docker-engine` package is installed before it tries to start the service.

 There is a very useful module from Puppetlabs to manage Docker, images, and containers on a host. For more details, refer to
`https://forge.puppet.com/puppetlabs/docker_platform`.

When the manifest is ready, it can be applied to the server with `puppet apply` if running masterless, or with puppet agent when using Puppet Server:

```
$ puppet apply docker-host.pp
Notice: Compiled catalog for ubuntu in environment production in 0.43
seconds
Notice: /Stage[main]/Main/Node[default]/Exec[install docker]/returns:
executed successfully
Notice: Finished catalog run in 31.86 seconds
```

 Puppet Server provides for easy distribution of manifests to servers in the cluster. Documentation on configuring Puppet Server may be found at `https://docs.puppet.com/puppetserver/latest/services_master_pupp etserver.html`.

All that this configuration does is install Docker. Adding it to the cluster is a different matter. A check should be written to see if the host is part of the cluster, and if not, run the appropriate commands to join the cluster. These scripts will vary depending on the orchestration tool used.

The `exec` resource in the following snippet runs `docker swarm join`, and if successful, touches the `/root/swarm-joined` file:

```
exec { 'join swarm' :
  command => "/usr/bin/docker swarm join --token SWMTKN-...    manager:2377
&& /usr/bin/touch /root/swarm-joined",
  creates => '/root/swarm-joined'
}
```

Every time `puppet apply` is run, it will check to see if `/root/swarm-joined` exists. If it does not, Puppet will rerun the command to join the swarm. This is an overly simplistic check since it does nothing to attempt to re-establish a connection to the swarm. However, if the node had joined successfully before, it will attempt to rejoin on its own.

Configuring a server on boot

Using configuration management to configure a host is great, but there is a problem with it. There was the manual step of installing Puppet and running `puppet apply` the first time. The fewer manual steps there are in an automated environment, the lesser chance there is of something getting missed or done differently.

There is a solution which works very well for servers running in a cloud environment called **Cloud-Init**. Cloud-Init was created specifically to deal with the problems of configuring servers started in AWS and similar services. The base image was fine to start with, but things such as user accounts and applications needed to be added or run when the server was started and people did not want to have to log in to every machine by hand to add them.

Cloud-Init has made several appearances in this book already. Chapter 1, *Getting Started with Docker Orchestration* showed how to use it to add login credentials to CoreOS, RancherOS, and Project Atomic hosts. It showed up again in Chapter 3, *Cluster Building Blocks – Registry, Overlay Networks, and Shared Storage* and Chapter 7, *Using Simpler Orchestration Tools – Fleet and Cattle* when enabling Flannel and Fleet on CoreOS. The cloud images for Ubuntu, RHEL, Fedora, and CentOS all have support for Cloud-Init.

The configuration file for Cloud-Init is a YAML file that starts with #cloud-config as the first line. It is usually added to a new server instance through a field named user-data. It can also be made available through a mounted disk such as a CD-ROM. Full documentation is available at https://cloudinit.readthedocs.io/en/latest/index.html.

Let's first assume that the image being started needs to have Docker installed and will be joining a Docker Swarm. The following example shows how to do both of these things. It first downloads and runs the Docker install script. Then Cloud-Init will run the command to join a Docker Swarm:

```
#cloud-config
runcmd:
  - "/usr/bin/wget -O - http://get.docker.com | /bin/bash",
  - ['/usr/bin/docker', 'swarm', 'join', '--token', 'SWMTKN-...',
'manager:2377']
```

The runcmd module takes a list of commands to run when the instance is first booted. Each command can be either a string or a list.

Cloud-Init can also set up and run Puppet. The following example will install Puppet and run it on boot:

```
puppet:
  install: true
  conf:
    server: "puppet.example.com"
    certname: "%i.%f"
```

The `conf` section contains key/value pairs that will be added to the `[puppetd]` section of `/etc/puppet/puppet.conf` on the client. The `server` option is the address of the Puppet server. The `certname` option sets the name of the certificate that the client will use to authenticate. The `%i` and `%f` variables are the instance ID and the fully qualified domain name, respectively.

Using a custom image

The problem with installing and configuring an application with configuration management or Cloud-Init is that it can lead to subtle differences in the versions of the installed software. It also takes extra time when the server first boots to install and configure everything. A faster and more consistent solution is to use an image which has been custom built for the task. CoreOS and Project Atomic are two distributions that are custom built to run Docker containers and very little else. It is also possible to build a custom image with all of the required software pre-installed.

Building a new image with Packer

HashiCorp has created a tool called Packer, which can be used to create custom images for use with OpenStack, AWS, Azure, GCE, and VMWare. It can also create images for Xen, Linux KVM, and can even deploy to hardware via cobbler.

A Packer configuration is a JSON file. There are three major sections, which are as follows:

- The `builders` section is a list that contains the list of image types to build.
- The `provisioners` section is a list of tasks to perform to provision an image. This includes running scripts, uploading files, and running configuration management.
- Finally, the `post-processors` section contains a list of tasks to do after the build is completed.

Those tasks can generate a manifest, run local commands, or upload an image to VMWare vSphere or Amazon S3.

Multiple images can be built from the same configuration file. Each image will have an entry in the `builders` list. This allows multiple images to be built in parallel using the same `provisioners`. For example, this could be used to build a new image to be deployed to Amazon, Azure, and locally to OpenStack.

 Full documentation for Packer is available at `https://www.packer.io/docs/`.

Preparing the Ubuntu Cloud Image

This example uses the `qemu` builder for easy testing on a local Linux box. The `qemu` builder works from a base image. By default, the new image is installed from an ISO installer, but it can also be clones from an existing disk image. This example uses the Ubuntu Cloud Image. This is the same basic image that is available on most cloud providers. The image is available at `https://cloud-images.ubuntu.com`.

The cloud image is a great starting point because it is a very minimal server installation. It has two problems that need to be fixed before it can be used with Packer. First, the `qemu` builder uses SSH to log in to the system for provisioning. Unfortunately, there are no accounts available to log in with. Second, the `qemu` builder can only log in with a username and password, but the SSH daemon is configured to deny password authentication. The following script fixes both of these problems. It must be run as root to allow it to mount the image and make the necessary changes:

```
#!/bin/bash

IMAGES=/packer/images
BASE=xenial-server-cloudimg-amd64-disk1.img
NEW=xenial-server-cloudimg-amd64-prep.img
MNT=/mnt

cd $IMAGES
cp $BASE $NEW

modprobe nbd max_part=16
qemu-nbd -c /dev/nbd0 $NEW
partprobe /dev/nbd0
mount /dev/nbd0p1 $MNT
sed -i 's/^PermitRootLogin .*$/PermitRootLogin yes/' $MNT/etc/ssh/sshd_config
sed -i 's/^PasswordAuthentication no/PasswordAuthentication yes/' $MNT/etc/ssh/sshd_config
```

```
chroot $MNT sh -c 'echo "root:s3cret-s@uce" | /usr/sbin/chpasswd'
umount $MNT
qemu-nbd -d /dev/nbd0
md5sum $NEW > $NEW.md5sum
```

The script copies the original image to a new file and mounts the new file. It then reconfigures sshd to allow password login in general and root logins specifically. Next, it uses chpassed within chroot to set a root password. Finally, it unmounts the image and creates a checksum file.

Instead of using the root user, a separate build user could be added to the image. To simplify the build process, the image should be configured to allow the build user to use sudo without a password. The user could then be removed at the end of the build process.

Building the image

Now that the image is prepared, it can be used to build a new image. Following is a Packer configuration that will build a new image that will install all available updates and install Docker:

```
{
  "builders" : [
  {
    "type" : "qemu",
    "iso_urls" : ["file:///packer/images/xenial-server-
      cloudimg-amd64-prep.img"
    ],
    "iso_checksum_url" : "file:///packer/images/xenial-
      server-cloudimg-amd64-prep.img.md5sum",
    "iso_checksum_type" : "md5",
    "disk_image" : true,
    "output_directory" : "/packer/images/xenial-cloudimg",
    "vm_name": "xenial-cloudimg-amd64-custom.img",
    "shutdown_command" : "shutdown -P now",
    "format" : "qcow2",
    "disk_size" : 20000,
    "headless" : true,
    "ssh_username": "root",
    "ssh_password": "s3cret-s@uce",
    "ssh_wait_timeout": "10m"
  }
  ],
  "provisioners" : [
  {
    "type" : "shell",
    "scripts" : [
```

```
        "/packer/scripts/install-updates.sh",
        "/packer/scripts/install-docker.sh"
      ]
    }
    ]
}
```

First is the `builders` section. The only entry is the qemu builder which is specified by the `type` setting. The `iso_*` settings specify the URLs of the images to use, a checksum file to verify the images, and the type of the checksum. In this case, there is only a single image file. Since the image is a disk image rather than an ISO, the `disk_image` setting must be set to true.

The `format` setting sets the output format to qcow2. The format can also be set to `raw`. The `disk_size` setting sets the size of the new disk image in MB. This sets the size of the disk but does not change the file system. Cloud-Init will resize the root filesystem when the VM is booted with the disk image. The output directory and the name of the generated image are set in the `output_directory` and `vm_name` options, respectively. The path set in `output_directory` may be absolute or relative to the location where Packer is run.

By default, the qemu builder will start a VM using the SDI console. This will only work if X11 is available. In most cases, the `headless` setting should be set to `true`. The console is available via VNC to watch the console during the provisioning process.

The `ssh_*` settings control how the qemu builder connects to the VM for provisioning. The `ssh_username` and `ssh_password` settings set the credentials needed to log in to the VM. In this case, it is configured to use the root user and the password set when the image was prepared. The qemu builder will continually try to connect to SSH after the VM starts, but will give up after the amount of time specified in `ssh_wait_timeout`. Ensure that the timeout provides enough time for the VM to boot.

The `provisioners` section is a list of provisioners that are to be used to provision the image. This example has a single shell provisioner, which runs the scripts specified in the scripts section on the VM. The `install-updates.sh` script simply runs `apt-get update && apt-get dist-upgrade -y`. The second script, `install-docker.sh`, is the install script from `get.docker.com`.

When the configuration is ready, the image can be built by running `packer build` `<config>`, where `<config>` is the name of the configuration file. A sample is given here. Most of the output has been removed for brevity:

```
$ packer build xenial-cloudimg.json
qemu output will be in this color.

==> qemu: Downloading or copying ISO
    qemu: Downloading or copying: file:///packer/images/xenial-server-
cloudimg-amd64-prep.img
==> qemu: Copying hard drive...
==> qemu: Resizing hard drive...
==> qemu: Found port for communicator (SSH, WinRM, etc): 3475.
==> qemu: Looking for available port between 5900 and 6000 on 127.0.0.1
==> qemu: Starting VM, booting disk image
    qemu: The VM will be run headless, without a GUI. If
you want to
    qemu: view the screen of the VM, connect via VNC without a password to
    qemu: 127.0.0.1:5983
==> qemu: Waiting 10s for boot...
==> qemu: Connecting to VM via VNC
==> qemu: Typing the boot command over VNC...
==> qemu: Waiting for SSH to become available...
==> qemu: Connected to SSH!
==> qemu: Provisioning with shell script: /packer/scripts/install-
updates.sh
==> qemu: Provisioning with shell script: /packer/scripts/install-docker.sh
==> qemu: Gracefully halting virtual machine...
==> qemu: Converting hard drive...
Build 'qemu' finished.

==> Builds finished. The artifacts of successful builds are:
--> qemu: VM files in directory: /packer/images/xenial-cloudimg
```

 Ensure the user running Packer has permission to use KVM, when using the qemu builder. Qemu may throw permission-denied errors if the user does not have the access needed. On Ubuntu, the user needs to be in the kvm group.

The run will take a few minutes and, assuming everything runs properly, the new image will be placed in the directory set in the `output_directory`. Packer will not run if the output directory exists unless the `-force` option is set to avoid accidental deletion of build images.

Using Puppet with Packer

Provisioning a new image with scripts works if the needed changes are relatively simple. More complicated changes require more complicated scripts. Configuration management tools are ideally suited to the task and can be used to provision the new image. Ansible, Chef, Puppet, and Salt are all supported.

An added benefit to using a configuration management tool to provision an image is that the same configuration can be used to ensure that it stays properly configured while the server is running. The exact process to do that will vary depending on the tool being used.

The following Packer snippet uses Puppet in the masterless mode to configure the image. The same Puppet manifest that was used in the *Using configuration management* section is used here as well. A command to join the Docker cluster should not be included. The command to join the cluster can be run after a new instance is started in the cluster:

```
"provisioners" : [
  {
    "type" : "shell",
    "scripts" : [
      "/packer/scripts/install-updates.sh",
      "/packer/scripts/install-puppet.sh"
    ]
  },
  {
    "type" : "puppet-masterless",
    "manifest_file" : "/packer/puppet/docker-host.pp"
  }
]
```

The first difference is that the `install-docker.sh` script was replaced by `install-puppet.sh` which runs `apt-get install -y puppet`. Second is the new `provisioner` block with a `type` of `puppet-masterless`. The `manifest_file` option specifies the manifest that will be used to configure the image; a directory may also be used. In that case, all of the manifests will be applied to the node.

Treating infrastructure like code

Let's pause for a moment and consider what was just done. The server has been completely defined in one or more files with a scriptable build process. We have just turned our servers into code.

The server images can be built through a CI process. Rather than performing updates on the running servers, new images can be built that incorporate the updates. The images can be fully tested through a test suite before being deployed. They can be fully vetted in a test environment before being deployed into production. Even the deployment process can be controlled through the CI process, just like the Docker images.

The other benefit of this approach is that it is very easy to roll back updates. If a problem is discovered, new servers can be started on the previous, working image to restore services quickly. The broken image can be tested and debugged offline or in a different environment.

This is, basically, the same approach to running versioned containers. The important thing from a troubleshooting perspective is that important data, such as logs, are not stored on the server. Instead, they should be stored on network storage or shipped to services such as Elasticsearch and Kibana.

Post-build configuration

Using a custom image does not eliminate the need for boot-time and ongoing configuration management. Boot-time configuration can be minimized to simple things like the hostname or joining a cluster. When running in multiregion or multicloud environments, Cloud-Init sets information specific to the region.

Configuration management of a running system is still important. It can ensure that the configurations that were put in place when the server was built, remain in place. It can also make simple changes such as updating administrators' SSH keys without needing to fully rebuild the image.

Automating host deployment

There are many ways to automate the deployment of Docker hosts. The specifics, as always, depend on the orchestration system. For example, adding new hosts to a Docker Swarm cluster running on Amazon EC2 is as easy as running something like the following:

```
$ docker-machine create --driver amazonec2
$ docker swarm join --token ABC... manager
```

For Azure or GCE, it would be the same. Simply replace the driver and pass the appropriate driver specific flags to `docker-machine`.

This section will look at a couple of different tools that can be used to manage the hosts for a Docker cluster. The first is Terraform which works with just about everything. Next is Docker's own cloud management tool, Docker Cloud. Finally, it will introduce two tools which are in public beta, Docker for AWS and Docker for Azure.

 If you plan on running on AWS, GCE, or Azure, consider using the container hosting services that each of them offers. With each service, the tasks of creating and managing hosts is taken care of by the service. Administrators only need to concern themselves with the containers.

Deploying hosts with Terraform

Terraform is a multicloud deployment tool. It uses a configuration file to define what the cluster should look like. It then builds a plan for creating or updating the cluster based on the configuration. The plan gives the administrator a chance to review what is going to be done before it happens. If the plan looks good, Terraform will execute the plan to bring the cluster into compliance with the configuration.

Terraform is completely cloud agnostic. It works with AWS, GCE, Microsoft Azure, OpenStack, and others. It can be used in combination with cobbler to manage hosts running on local hardware. It even has limited support for Docker. Even better, it can be used to configure multiple clouds at the same time.

Creating a Terraform configuration

Let's look at an example Terraform configuration. This example creates two new instances on Amazon EC2. The file can be named anything but must end in .tf. Full documentation for Terraform may be found at https://www.terraform.io/docs/index.html.

```
provider "aws" {
  access_key = "ACCESS_KEY"
  secret_key = "SECRET_KEY"
  region = "us-west-2"
}

resource "aws_instance" "docker-hosts" {
  count = 2
  ami = "ami-a9d276c9"
  instance_type = "t2.micro"
  user_data = "${file("cloud-init.yml")}"
  key_name = "aws-key"
  vpc_security_group_ids = [ "sg-ID" ]
```

```
    tags {
      Name = "dock${count.index}"
    }
  }
```

Each `provider` block specifies a cloud service. In this case, the provider is `aws`. The `access_key` and `secret_key` options are the appropriate keys to manage the EC2 service. The `region` option specifies the region to where these instances are going to be started. A `provider` block can be specified for each region that instances will be started in.

The `resource` block defines a resource that will be started on a provider. Terraform matches resources to the appropriate `provider` type. A resources with a type of `aws_instances`, as in this case, will be started on an `aws` provider.

The `count` option specifies the number of identical resources to start. The default is one. This can be changed later to scale the cluster up or down.

The `ami` option sets the AMI to use for this instance. This can be a public AMI such as the Ubuntu Xenial cloud image, as in this example. Private AMIs can also be used. For example, Packer can build a new image and make it available as an AMI. The `instance_type` is the type of instance to start.

> The specific AMI will depend on the version of image and the region it will run in. A complete list of APIs for Ubuntu cloud images is at `https://cloud-images.ubuntu.com/locator/ec2/`.

A Cloud-Init file can be specified for each resource with the `user_data` option. The easiest way to do it is to specify a file using the `file()` function. The path is relative to the location that Terraform is run from. The configuration will be encoded and added to the instance when it is created.

The `key_name` specifies the SSH key to add to the default user. The key must already exist in EC2. A list of VPC security groups may be set with the `vpc_security_group_ids` option. The security groups must exist for this example to work. Make sure that the security group allows SSH access or you may find yourself locked out of the instance.

Terraform can be used to create the VPC, security groups, and anything else that might be needed. Full documentation is available at `https://www.terraform.io/docs/providers/aws/index.html`.

Finally, the `tags` option provides a way to set tags on the instance. This example sets the `Name` tag. The `${count.index}` variable is the current count if multiple instances are created from the same resource. In this case, the two instances are named `dock0` and `dock1`.

Running Terraform

Creating or updating a cluster with Terraform happens in two steps. The first step is to generate a plan, while not strictly necessary, the plan shows exactly what Terraform is going to do; that way there are no surprises. To see the plan, run `terraform plan` in the directory with your configuration. It will read the configuration from the `.tf` files in the directory and create a plan:

```
$ terraform plan
Refreshing Terraform state in-memory prior to plan...
The refreshed state will be used to calculate this plan, but will not be
persisted to local or remote state storage.
The Terraform execution plan has been generated and is shown below.
Resources are shown in alphabetical order for quick scanning. Green
resources will be created (or destroyed and then created if an existing
resource exists), yellow resources are being changed in-place, and red
resources
will be destroyed. Cyan entries are data sources to be read.
Note: You didn't specify an "-out" parameter to save this plan, so when
"apply" is called, Terraform can't guarantee this is what will execute.
+ aws_instance.docker-hosts.0
    ami:                                "ami-a9d276c9"
    associate_public_ip_address:        "<computed>"
    availability_zone:                  "<computed>"
    ebs_block_device.#:                 "<computed>"
    ephemeral_block_device.#:           "<computed>"
    instance_state:                     "<computed>"
    instance_type:                      "t2.micro"
    key_name:                           "aws-key"
    network_interface_id:               "<computed>"
    placement_group:                    "<computed>"
    private_dns:                        "<computed>"
    private_ip:                         "<computed>"
    public_dns:                         "<computed>"
    public_ip:                          "<computed>"
    root_block_device.#:                "<computed>"
```

```
        security_groups.#:                "<computed>"
        source_dest_check:                "true"
        subnet_id:                        "<computed>"
        tags.%:                           "1"
        tags.Name:                        "dock0"
        tenancy:                          "<computed>"
        user_data:
            "23845b687111f6870657ecb38214e6a8f18b231e"
        vpc_security_group_ids.#:         "1"
        vpc_security_group_ids.839449168: "sg-..."
+ aws_instance.docker-hosts.1
        ami:                              "ami-a9d276c9"
        associate_public_ip_address:      "<computed>"
        availability_zone:                "<computed>"
        ebs_block_device.#:               "<computed>"
        ephemeral_block_device.#:         "<computed>"
        instance_state:                   "<computed>"
        instance_type:                    "t2.micro"
        key_name:                         "aws-key"
        network_interface_id:             "<computed>"
        placement_group:                  "<computed>"
        private_dns:                      "<computed>"
        private_ip:                       "<computed>"
        public_dns:                       "<computed>"
        public_ip:                        "<computed>"
        root_block_device.#:              "<computed>"
        security_groups.#:                "<computed>"
        source_dest_check:                "true"
        subnet_id:                        "<computed>"
        tags.%:                           "1"
        tags.Name:                        "dock1"
        tenancy:                          "<computed>"
        user_data:
            "23845b687111f6870657ecb38214e6a8f18b231e"
        vpc_security_group_ids.#:         "1"
        vpc_security_group_ids.839449168: "sg-..."
Plan: 2 to add, 0 to change, 0 to destroy.
```

If the plan looks good, it can be put into action by running `terraform apply`. The following output was trimmed for brevity:

```
$ terraform apply
aws_instance.docker-hosts.1: Creating...
ami:                              "" => "ami-a9d276c9"
...
aws_instance.docker-hosts.0: Creating...
ami:                              "" => "ami-a9d276c9"
...
```

```
aws_instance.docker-hosts.1: Still creating... (10s elapsed)
aws_instance.docker-hosts.0: Still creating... (10s elapsed)
aws_instance.docker-hosts.1: Still creating... (20s elapsed)
aws_instance.docker-hosts.0: Still creating... (20s elapsed)
aws_instance.docker-hosts.0: Creation complete
aws_instance.docker-hosts.1: Creation complete
Apply complete! Resources: 2 added, 0 changed, 0 destroyed.
The state of your infrastructure has been saved to the path below. This
state is required to modify and destroy your infrastructure, so keep it
safe. To inspect the complete state use the `terraform show` command.
State path: terraform.tfstate
```

The generated `terraform.tfstate` file is important. It provides a map from the resources defined in the configuration to what is actually running. Anyone operating on the same Terraform cluster must use the same `terraform.tfstate` file. The state file is small enough that it can be stored in version control, but that can cause merge conflicts. Instead, Terraform has a option to store the state remotely. Several backends are supported including S3, Azure, and etcd. Full documentation, including the list of backends, is available at `https://www.terraform.io/docs/state/remote/index.html`.

To update the cluster, simply change the configuration and run `terraform plan` and `terraform apply` again. The requested change will be made throughout the cluster. Be advised that some changes will require Terraform to remove and recreate running instances. It is possible that enough of the instances will be stopped as to affect services.

Showing the cluster state

It can be useful to see what state the cluster is in. To see the state, run `terraform show`. The output is potentially long depending on how large the cluster is. The following example shows the type of information that is available. Of special note are the private and public IP addresses:

```
$ terraform show
aws_instance.docker-hosts.0:
    id = i-0095dceada25205bf
    ami = ami-a9d276c9
    associate_public_ip_address = true
    availability_zone = us-west-2c
    disable_api_termination = false
    ebs_block_device.# = 0
    ebs_optimized = false
    ephemeral_block_device.# = 0
    iam_instance_profile =
    instance_state = running
    instance_type = t2.micro
```

```
key_name = aws-key
monitoring = false
network_interface_id = eni-44e0df15
private_dns = ip-172-31-12-31.us-west-
2.compute.internal
private_ip = 172.31.12.31
public_dns = ec2-35-164-109-235.us-west-
2.compute.amazonaws.com
public_ip = 35.164.109.235
root_block_device.# = 1
root_block_device.0.delete_on_termination = true
root_block_device.0.iops = 100
root_block_device.0.volume_size = 8
root_block_device.0.volume_type = gp2
security_groups.# = 0
source_dest_check = true
subnet_id = subnet-7160dc29
tags.% = 1
tags.Name = dock0
tenancy = default
user_data = 23845b687111f6870657ecb38214e6a8f18b231e
vpc_security_group_ids.# = 1
vpc_security_group_ids.839449168 = sg-...
aws_instance.docker-hosts.1:
id = i-08eb6ebb75b788823
...
```

Deploying hosts with Docker Cloud

Docker Cloud is an excellent tool to manage Docker Swarms on various cloud services. It makes it easy to create new clusters and scale them up or down to meet the needs of the services running on the cluster.

To create a new cluster, click on **Node Clusters** and then on **Create**. A window will pop up and ask for information such as the cluster name, cloud provider, disk size, and the initial number of nodes. After everything is configured, click on **Launch node cluster**. The new nodes will be started and, after a few minutes, be ready to run containers:

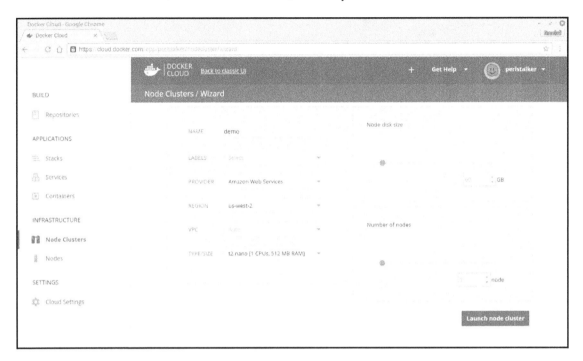

Adding a new node is very easy. Click on **Node Clusters** and select the cluster to add nodes to. At the top right of the page, there is a slider which can be used to scale up the number of nodes. Adjust the slider and click on the **Scale** link. Additional nodes will be added and will be ready to run containers:

Introducing Docker for AWS and Docker for Azure

Docker for AWS is a process that uses CloudFormation to automatically build a Docker Swarm on AWS. The process creates a new VPC for the Swarm including subnets and security groups. Two Auto Scaling groups are also created; one for the managers and one for the workers. The number of each can be adjusted by changing the number instances in the respective Auto Scaling groups. New instances will automatically join the swarm.

Docker for Azure provides a similar service for clusters running on Azure. It automatically creates all of the services required to run a Docker Swarm. It ties into the scaling features of Azure to make it easy to scale up the number of masters and workers.

More information is available at the following locations:

- Docker for AWS: `https://beta.docker.com/docs/aws/`
- Docker for Azure: `https://beta.docker.com/docs/azure/`

Scaling down nodes

One of the benefits of cloud computing is the ability to scale down the number of hosts when they are no longer needed. For example, a web store may increase the number of hosts during the Christmas shopping season and then scale them down in January. How that happens will, again, depend on the orchestration solution chosen and the platform it is running on.

Most orchestration systems have a command that will shut down containers on a specific node and reschedule them elsewhere in the cluster. This gives the orchestration tool a chance to cleanly move services around the cluster before a node is removed. Services such as Docker Cloud and GKE take care of that automatically.

The command to change the node's availability could be added to the shut down scripts. However, care must be made to ensure that all of the containers have stopped before the system is shutdown. In most cases, another command will need to be run to permanently remove a node from the cluster. Again, the specific command will vary depending on the orchestration tool being used.

Summary

This chapter explored different ways to automate the infrastructure that is used to run a Docker cluster. It looked at using configuration management while a node is running, configuring a node at boot with Cloud-Init, and building custom images with Packer. We also covered using Terraform and Docker Cloud to manage a cluster. Finally, some tips were shared for deprovisioning nodes when they are no longer needed.

Where you go next is up to you. This book has provided an introduction to Docker Orchestration using several tools. Successfully running a Docker cluster requires a number of different services including registries, overlay networks, shared storage, the orchestration tool itself, log and resource monitoring, and continuous integration. The specific tools and work flows will vary from cluster to cluster. This book was only able to scratch the surface of what is possible. Hopefully, you will be able to take what you have learned here and use it to build a scalable, reliable service for your organization using Docker.

Index

www.ingramcontent.com/pod-product-compliance
Lightning Source LLC
Chambersburg PA
CBHW060524060326
40690CB00017B/3380